Roberto Braccini

European Vocabulary of Music

Italian – English – German – French

SCHOTT

A CIP catalogue record for this book is available from the British library

For il tasto vivo

SEM 8289
ISBN 978-3-254-08289-3

This title is a revised and enhanced edition of “Praktisches Wörterbuch der Musik” by Roberto Braccini
www.schott-music.com
www.schott-buch.de

Typeset by Text & Grafik Service Martin, Birstein
Printed in Germany by CPI – Clausen & Bosse, Leck
BSS 55762

I sincerely wish to thank the following highly competent people
who had the kindness to help me.

Desidero ringraziare di cuore le seguenti persone,
più che competenti, le quali hanno avuto la gentilezza di aiutarmi.

Es ist mir ein Bedürfnis, mich bei den nachfolgend genannten
kompetenten Persönlichkeiten zu bedanken,
die die Freundlichkeit hatten, mich bei meiner Arbeit zu unterstützen.

Je désire sincèrement remercier les personnes suivantes,
plus que compétentes, qui ont eu la gentilesse de m'aider.

Ellen Frau, San Francisco
Eva Schoenenberger-Groebner, Wien
Maître Michel Vigneau, Paris

Contents

Preface

This four-language dictionary of music is intended for musicians, teachers, students and amateurs who wish to understand and use specialist foreign terms. The book is not academic in scope; it is based on practical experience, derived from the examination of directions given on a large number of orchestral scores, piano pieces and transcriptions, and instrumental parts. In order to complement and clarify this vocabulary, specialist dictionaries and reference books have been consulted. Contemporary musical terms taken, for example, from the fields of jazz, pop and electronic music, have also been included.

How to use this dictionary

The entries are arranged alphabetically within the individual sections – except for English resp. American, German and French specialist terms – on the basis of initial headwords given in Italian. The correct stress is indicated by a short line under the appropriate vowel; English, German and French translations follow. Each headword is given an entry number which applies to all four languages; the headwords are then listed alphabetically in the index, along with their assigned numbers and an initial indicating the respective language. This index allows for:

1. the translation of a foreign word into English
2. the translation of an English word into another language
3. the translation of a foreign word from one language into another.

For each of the above, proceed as follows:

If, for example, you find the word "sempre" in a score – assuming that its meaning is unknown to you – look it up in the index. There you will find an "I" (for Italian) and the entry number. Now locate the number in the first part of the book, where you will find English, German and French translations of the word.

Detailed technical terms (from p. 210) have not been included in the index but have to be looked up there and then according to the alphabetical order (of their first word).

Abbreviations:

I	Italian	F	French	*m*	masculine
E	English	L	Latin	*f*	feminine
D	German	Am.	American	*n*	neuter
				pl	plural

Indice

Prefazione

Lo scopo di questo libro, che non deve essere inteso come una enciclopedia, è di poter aiutare qualsiasi persona interessata alla musica a trovare la traduzione d'una determinata parola nelle seguenti lingue: italiano, inglese, tedesco e francese. E stato concepito sfogliando innumerevoli composizioni. Alcune parole antiquate, oppure scritte con errori sono rimaste volutamente tali. Inoltre, un gran numero di dizionari specializzati sono stati consultati per completarne il suo vocabolario. Forme musicali recenti come la musica pop, il jazz e la musica elettronica sono ugualmente incluse.

Instruzioni per l'uso di questo libro

Tutti i capitoli sono raggruppati alfabeticamente. I termini italiani sono sempre menzionati per primi ad eccezione di quelli concernenti la terminologia inglese ed americana, la terminologia francese e quella tedesca. Seguono le traduzioni in inglese, tedesco e francese. Ogni rigo ha il suo numero, identico per le quattro lingue. Una linetta sotto una sillaba italiana indica dove cade l'accento. Tutte queste parole si ritrovano nell'indice alfabetico finale. Accanto ad ognuna di esse si trova l'iniziale della lingua alla quale appartiene (per es. E per l'inglese) ed il suo numero. Questo capitolo vi offre la possibilità di:

1. Tradurre una parola straniera in italiano.
2. Tradurre una parola italiana in una lingua straniera.
3. Tradurre una parola straniera in un'altra lingua straniera.

Nei tre casi, il modo di procedere sarà lo stesso. Esempio:

In una partitura, s'incontra la parola „immer" e si desidera sapere il significato in italiano. Nell'indice alfabetico, accanto a „immer" ci sarà la lettera D (tedesco) ed un numero. Basterà cercare questo numero in uno dei capitoli precedenti. Avendolo trovato, si vedrà alla sua destra „sempre" ed il termine corrispondente in inglese, tedesco e francese.

Le frasi specifiche dei differenti idiomi non sono riprodotte nell'indice finale. Il lettore dovrà cercarle (da pag. 210) per ordine alfabetico nella lingua desiderata.

Abbreviazioni:

I	Italiano	F	Francese	*m*	maschile
E	Inglese	L	Latino	*f*	femminile
D	Tedesco	Am.	Americano	*n*	neutro
				pl	plurale

Inhalt

Vorwort

Das vorliegende Fachwörterbuch der Musik in vier Sprachen wendet sich an Musiker, Lehrer, Studenten und Laien, die die Übertragung fremdsprachiger Fachwörter suchen und verwenden möchten. Das Buch erhebt keinen wissenschaftlichen Anspruch. Es ist aus der Praxis heraus entstanden, ausgehend von der Sammlung von Anweisungen in unzähligen Partituren, Klavierauszügen und Notenstimmen. Zur Vervollständigung und Abrundung des Wortschatzes wurden Fachlexika und Fachwörterbücher ausgewertet. Zeitnahe Sachgebiete, wie zum Beispiel Jazz-, Pop- und elektronische Musik, sind eingeschlossen.

Hinweise zur Benutzung dieses Buches

Die in den einzelnen Kapiteln alphabetisch zusammengestellten Stichwörter gehen – mit Ausnahme der Kapitel „Englische und amerikanische Fachausdrücke“ , „Deutsche Fachausdrücke“ und „Französische Fachausdrücke“ – von der italienischen Sprache aus, wobei die korrekte Silbenbetonung durch Unterstreichung des betreffenden Vokals angezeigt wird. Die englische, deutsche und französische Übertragung schließen sich an. Jedes Stichwort ist mit fortlaufenden Zahlen versehen, die für alle Sprachen gelten. In einem Register erscheinen alle Stichwörter in alphabetischer Reihenfolge mit den ihnen zugeordneten Zahlen, denen die Abkürzung der zugehörigen Sprache beigefügt ist. Mit Hilfe dieses Registers kann man

1. ein fremdsprachiges Wort ins Deutsche,
2. ein deutsches Wort in eine Fremdsprache und
3. ein fremdsprachiges Wort in eine andere Fremdsprache übersetzen.

In allen Fällen geht man wie folgt vor:

Man trifft in einer Partitur beispielsweise auf das Wort „sempre“. Vorausgesetzt, das Wort ist einem nicht bekannt, sucht man „sempre“ im Register. Dort steht neben „sempre“ ein I (für Italienisch) und eine Zahl. Nun erblättert man diese Zahl im vorderen Teil des Buches und findet dort die deutsche, englische und französische Bedeutung.

Sehr ausführlich formulierte Fachausdrücke (ab S. 210) wurden nicht ins Register aufgenommen, sondern müssen an Ort und Stelle entsprechend der alphabetischen Reihenfolge (ihres 1. Wortes) aufgesucht werden.

Abkürzungen:

I	Italienisch	F	Französisch	*m*	Maskulinum
E	Englisch	L	Latein	*f*	Femininum
D	Deutsch	Am.	Amerikanisch	*n*	Neutrum
				Pl	Plural

Contenu

Préface

Le but de ce livre est d'aider toute personne intéressée à la musique, à trouver la traduction d'un mot déterminé dans les langues suivantes: italien, anglais, allemand et français. Ce livre ne doit pas être considéré comme une encyclopédie. C'est en parcourant d'innombrables partitions musicales qu'il a été conçu. Un grand nombre de dictionnaires musicaux spécialisés ont été consultés pour en compléter son vocabulaire. Les formes musicales récentes comme la musique pop, le jazz et la musique électronique y sont également incluses.

Instructions pour l'usage de ce livre

Tous les chapitres sont groupés alphabétiquement. Les termes italiens sont mentionnés en premier à l'exception de ceux concernant la terminologie anglaise et américaine, la terminologie française et celle allemande. Suivent les traductions en anglais, allemand et français. Chaque ligne a son propre numéro qui est le même pour les quatre langues. Un petit trait sous un mot italien signifie qu'il faut accentuer cette voyelle. On retrouve tous ces mots dans l'index alphabétique. A côté de chaque mot se trouve l'initiale de la langue en question (par exemple E pour l'anglais). Ce chapitre vous donne la possibilité de:

1. traduire un mot étranger en français
2. traduire un mot français dans une langue étrangère
3. traduire un mot étranger dans une autre langue étrangère

Dans les trois cas, on procédera de la même façon. Exemple:

Dans une partition, il y a le terme „sempre" et on désire savoir ce qu'il signifie en français. On le cherche dans l'index alphabétique. A côté de „sempre" on trouvera la lettre I (italien) ainsi qu'un numéro. On cherchera celui-ci dans un des chapitres précédents. On verra alors „sempre" et le terme correspondant en anglais, allemand et français.

Les termes techniques décrits en détail (à partir de p. 210) n'ont pas été inclus dans l'index mais doivent être cherchés par ordre alphabétique dans la langue désirée.

Abréviations:

I	Italien	F	Français	*m*	masculin
E	Anglais	L	Latin	*f*	féminin
D	Allemand	Am.	Américain	*n*	neutre
				pl	pluriel

	Strumenti a corda	**Stringed instruments**
1	arciliuto *m*	archlute
2	arpa *f* / arpa a pedali *f*	harp / pedal harp
3	arpa a doppio movimento *f*	double action harp
4	autoarpa *f*	autoharp
5	balalaica *f*	balalaika
6	banjo *m*	banjo
7	cetra *f*	cittern
8	cetra da tavolo *f*	zither
9	cimbalom *m*	cimbalom
10	chitarra *f*	guitar
11	chitarra battente *f* / chitarra jazz *f*	jazz guitar
12	chitarra hawaiana *f*	Hawaiian guitar
13	colascione *m*	colascione
14	contrabbasso *m*	double bass
15	contrabbasso a pizzico *m*	slap bass
16	crotta *f*	crowd
17	ghironda *f*	hurdy-gurdy
18	Hardingfele *m*	Harding / Hardanger fiddle
19	lira *f*	lyre
20	liuto *m*	lute
21	mandolino *m*	mandolin
22	pochette *f*	kit
23	salterio *m*	psaltery
24	salterio tedesco *m*	dulcimer
25	sitar *f*	sitar
26	tiorba *f*	theorbo
27	viella *f*	fiddle
28	viola *f*	viola
29	viola da gamba *f*	viola da gamba
30	violino *m*	violin
31	violino di ferro *m*	nail violin
32	violoncello *m*	violoncello

Saiteninstrumente	**Instruments à cordes**	
Erzlaute *f*	archiluth *m*	1
Harfe *f* / Pedalharfe *f*	harpe *f* / harpe à pédales simples *f*	2
Doppelpedalharfe *f*	harpe à double mouvement *f*	3
Akkordzither *f*	cithare d'amateur *f*	4
Balalaika *f*	balalaika *f*	5
Banjo *n*	banjo *m*	6
Cister *f*	cistre *m*	7
Zither *f*	cithare *f*	8
Zimbal *n* / Cymbal *n*	cymbalum *m*	9
Gitarre *f*	guitare *f*	10
Schlaggitarre *f* / Jazzgitarre *f*	guitare de jazz *f*	11
Hawaii-Gitarre *f*	guitare hawaïenne *f*	12
Colascione *m*	colachon *m*	13
Kontrabass *m*	contrebasse *f*	14
Schlagbass *m*	contrebasse jouée sans archet *f*	15
Chrotta *f*	chrotta *f*	16
Drehleier *f* / Radleier *f* / Leier *f*	vielle à roue *f*	17
Hardanger Fiedel *f*	violon de Hardanger *m*	18
Lyra *f*	lyre *f*	19
Laute *f*	luth *m*	20
Mandoline *f*	mandoline *f*	21
Taschengeige *f*	pochette *f*	22
Psalterium *n*	psaltérion *m*	23
Hackbrett *n*	tympanon *m*	24
Sitar *f*	sitar *m*	25
Theorbe *f*	théorbe *m*	26
Fiedel *f* / Fidel *f*	vièle *f* / vielle *f* / violon rustique *m*	27
Viola *f* / Bratsche *f*	alto *m*	28
Gambe *f*	viole de gambe *f*	29
Violine *f* / Geige *f*	violon *m*	30
Nagelgeige *f*	violon de fer *m*	31
Violoncello *n*	violoncelle *m*	32

	Parti componenti ed accessori	**Component parts and accessories**
33	anima *f*	sound post
34	archetto *m* / arco *m*	bow
35	astuccio *m* / custodia *f*	case
36	bischero *m* / pirolo *m* / voluta *f*	tuning peg / tuning pin
37	bottone *m*	endpin
38	cantino *m*	treble
39	capotasto *m*	capotasto / top nut
40	cassa armonica *f* / cassa di risonanza *f*	resonant body / sound-box
41	catena *f*	bass-bar / tuning bar
42	cavigliere *m*	peg box
43	colofonia *f*	rosin / resin
44	corda *f*	string
45	corda del sol *f* / quarta corda *f*	bass string
46	corda di budello *f*	gut string
47	corda d'acciaio *f*	steel string
48	corda di metallo *f*	metal string
49	corda di bordone *f*	drone string
50	corda di risonanza *f*	aliquot string
51	corda melodica *f*	treblestring / fretted string
52	corda simpatica *f*	sympathetic string
53	cordiera *f*	tailpiece / string holder
54	coro *m*	course
55	crini dell'arco *m pl*	hair of the bow
56	curva della meccanica *f*	neck / harmonic curve
57	effe *f*	sound-hole
58	fascia *f*	side / rib
59	filetto *m*	purfling
60	fondo *m*	back
61	manico *m*	neck
62	mentoniera *f*	chin-rest
63	parapenne *m*	plectrum guard
64	plettro *m*	jack / plectrum
65	ponticello *m*	bridge
66	punta *f* / nasello *m*	tip / peak / point
67	puntale *m*	tailpin / spike
68	riccio *m* / chiocciola *f*	scroll

Bestandteile und Zubehör	**Parties composantes et accessoires**	
Stimmstock *m*	âme *f*	33
Bogen *m*	archet *m*	34
Kasten *m*	étui *m* / housse *f*	35
Wirbel *m*	cheville *f*	36
Knopf *m*	bouton *m*	37
Sangsaite *f* / Singsaite *f*	chanterelle *f*	38
Kapodaster *m* / Saitenfessel *f* / Obersattel *m*	capodaste *m* / barre *f*	39
Resonanzkörper *m* / Resonanzboden *m* / Schallkasten *m*	caisse de résonance *f*	40
Bassbalken *m* / Stimmbalken *m*	barre *f*	41
Wirbelkasten *m*	chevillier *m*	42
Kolophonium *n*	colophane *f*	43
Saite *f*	corde *f*	44
G-Saite *f*	quatrième corde *f*	45
Darmsaite *f*	corde de boyau *f*	46
Stahlsaite *f*	corde d'acier *f*	47
Metallsaite *f*	corde métallique *f*	48
Bordunsaite *f*	corde hors manche *f*	49
Aliquotsaite *f*	corde de résonance *f*	50
Melodiesaite *f*	corde mélodique *f*	51
Resonanzsaite *f*	corde sympathique *f*	52
Saitenhalter *m*	cordier *m*	53
Saitenchor *m*	jeu *m* / chœur *m*	54
Bogenhaare *n Pl*	crins de l'archet *m pl*	55
Mechanikbogen *m*	console *f*	56
F-Loch *n*	ouïe *f*	57
Zarge *f*	éclisse *f*	58
Einlage *f* / Ader *f*	filet *m*	59
Boden *m*	fond *m*	60
Hals *m*	manche *m*	61
Kinnhalter *m*	mentonnière *f*	62
Schlagbrett *n*	plaque de protection *f*	63
Spielblättchen *n* / Plektrum *n*	plectre *m*	64
Steg *m*	chevalet *m*	65
Spitze *f*	pointe *f*	66
Stachel *m*	pied *m*	67
Schnecke *f*	volute *f* / coquille *f*	68

69	rosa *f*	rose
70	ruota a sfregamento *f*	friction wheel
71	sella *f*	saddle
72	spalliera *f*	shoulder rest
73	tallone *m*	heel / frog
74	tastato	fretted
75	tastiera *f*	fingerboard / fretboard
76	tasto *m*	fret
77	tavola armonica *f*	table / belly
78	uncino *m*	fork
79	volta superiore *f* / sagoma superiore *f*	upper bout
80	volta inferiore *f* / sagoma inferiore *f*	lower bout
81	zoccolo *m*	pedestal

	Modi di suonare	**Playing techniques**
82	alla corda	on the string
83	alla punta d'arco / colla punta d'arco, -di arco/-dell'arco	at the point / tip of the bow
84	al tallone *m*	at the heel / at the frog
85	arcata *f* / colpo d'arco *m*	bowing / stroke of the bow
86	arcata in giù *f*	down-bow
87	arcata in su *f*	up-bow
88	archeggiamento	whipped
89	balzato	bouncing / springing (bowing)
90	balzellato	bouncing / springing
91	barré	barré
92	bisbigliando (arpa)	tremolo (harp)
93	cambiamento di posizione *m*	shift
94	coll'arco *m*	with the bow
95	col legno *m* / picchettato	with the wood
96	con sordina / con sordino	muted
97	corda vuota *f*	empty string / open string
98	disperdere	to die out
99	doppia corda *f*	double stop
100	emissione *f*	speech / reponse

Rosette *f*	rose *f*	69
Streichrad *n*	roue de frottement *f*	70
Sattel *m*	sillet *m*	71
Schulterstütze *f*	coussin *m*	72
Frosch *m*	talon *m* / hausse *f*	73
mit Bünden versehen	avec sillets	74
Griffbrett *n*	touche *f*	75
Bund *m*	sillet *m*	76
Decke *f*	table d'harmonie *f*	77
Gabel *f*	fourchette *f*	78
Oberbügel *m*	courbe supérieure *f*	79
Unterbügel *m*	courbe inférieure *f*	80
Fuß *m* (Harfe)	cuvette *f* / socle *m*	81

Spielarten — Façons de jouer

auf der Saite / an der Saite	à la corde	82
an der Bogenspitze *f*	avec la pointe de l'archet / de/à la pointe	83
am Frosch *m*	au talon *m* / à la hausse *f*	84
Bogenführung *f* / Bogenstrich *m* / Strichart *f*	coup d'archet *m*	85
Abstrich *m*	tiré *m*	86
Aufstrich *m* / Anstrich *m*	poussé *m*	87
gepeitscht	fouetté	88
Springbogen *m* / fliegendes Staccato	bondi / staccato volant	89
gehüpft	sautillé	90
barré (Quergriff bei Gitarre / Laute)	barré	91
tremolo (Harfe)	trémolo (harpe)	92
Lagenwechsel *m*	changement de position *m*	93
mit dem Bogen	avec l'archet *m*	94
mit der Bogenstange *f*	avec le bois *m*	95
mit Dämpfer	avec sourdine / étouffé	96
leere Saite *f*	corde à vide *f*	97
ausschwingen	cesser de vibrer	98
Doppelgriff *m*	double corde *f*	99
Ansprache *f*	émission *f*	100

101	gettato	thrown
102	ondeggiando	undulating
103	piccato / picchiettato	lightly detached
104	pizzicato	plucked
105	presso la tavola	near the sounding board
106	rimbalzando	rebounding
107	saltato	jumped
108	saltellato / balzellato	bouncing / springing
109	scordatura *f*	scordatura
110	senza sordina	without mute
111	separato / staccato	detached
112	spiccato / saltato	detached staccato (bowing)
113	strappato	torn / raked
114	strisciando	touching slightly
115	sulla tastiera / flautando	on the fingerboard
116	sul ponticello	close to the bridge

Strumenti a fiato — Wind instruments

117	armonica a bocca *f*	mouth organ
118	bombarda *f*	bombarde
119	bombardino *m*	euphonium / baritone
120	bombardone *m*	bombardon
121	cennamella *f* / ciaramella *f*	shawm
122	clarinetto *m*	clarinet
123	clarinetto piccolo *m*	soprano clarinet
124	clarinetto basso *m*	bass clarinet
125	clarinetto contrabbasso *m*	double bass clarinet
126	clarinetto contralto *m*	alto clarinet
127	contrafagotto *m*	double bassoon / contrabassoon
128	cornetta *f*	cornet
129	cornetta a pistoni *f*	valve cornet
130	cornetto *m*	cornett
131	corno *m*	French horn / horn
132	corno da caccia *m*	hunting horn
133	corno delle Alpi *m*	Alphorn / Alpenhorn
134	corno di bassetto *m*	bassethorn
135	corno di postiglione *m* / cornetta di postiglione *f*	post horn

geworfen	jeté	101
wogend	ondoyant	102
gestochen	piqué	103
gezupft / gezwickt	pizzicato / pincé	104
nahe am Korpus anzupfen	près de la table	105
abprallendes Stakkato	ricochet	106
gesprungen	sauté	107
gehüpft (Bogenstrich)	sautillé	108
Skordatur *f*	scordatura *f*	109
ohne Dämpfer	sans sourdine	110
abgesetzt / getrennt	détaché	111
deutlich getrennt	très détaché / très net	112
gerissen	arraché	113
streifend	en frôlant	114
nahe am Griffbrett	sur la touche	115
am Steg	près du chevalet	116

Blasinstrumente — Instruments à vent

Mundharmonika *f*	harmonica *f*	117
Bomhard *m* / Pommer *m*	bombarde *f*	118
Baritonhorn *n*	euphonium *m*	119
Basstuba *f* / Bombardon *n*	bombardon *m*	120
Schalmei *f* / Hirtenpfeife *f*	pipeau *m* / chalumeau *m*	121
Klarinette *f*	clarinette *f*	122
kleine Klarinette *f*	petite clarinette *f*	123
Bassklarinette *f*	clarinette basse *f*	124
Kontrabassklarinette *f*	clarinette contrebasse *f*	125
Altklarinette *f*	clarinette alto *f*	126
Kontrafagott *n*	contrebasson *m*	127
Kornett *n*	cornet *m*	128
Piston *m* / Ventilkornett *n*	cornet à pistons *m*	129
Zink *m*	cornet à bouquin *m*	130
Horn *n* / Waldhorn *n*	cor *m*	131
Jagdhorn *n* / Signalhorn *n*	cor de chasse *m* / bugle *m*	132
Alphorn *n*	cor des Alpes *m*	133
Bassetthorn *n*	cor de basset *m*	134
Posthorn *n*	cor de postillion *m* / cornet de poste *m*	135

136	corno inglese *m*	cor anglais (E) / English horn (Am.)
137	corno di toro *m*	cow horn
138	cromorno *m*	crumhorn
139	dulciana *f*	dulcian
140	elicon *m*	helicon
141	fagotto *m*	bassoon
142	fischietto *m*	whistle / fife / pipe
143	flauto *m*	flute
144	flauto a becco basso *m*	bass recorder
145	flauto a becco contralto *m*	alto recorder (Am.) / treble recorder (E)
146	flauto a becco sopranino *m*	sopranino recorder
147	flauto a becco soprano *m*	soprano recorder (Am.) / descant recorder (E)
148	flauto a becco tenore *m*	tenor recorder
149	flauto a tiro *m* / zufolo a pistone *m*	swanee whistle / piston flute
150	flauto contralto *m*	alto flute / bass flute
151	flauto di Pan *m* / siringa *f*	panpipes
152	flauto dolce *m* / flauto diritto *m*	recorder
153	flauto traverso *m*	transverse flute / German flute
154	flicorno *m*	flugelhorn / saxhorn
155	Heckelphon *m*	heckelphone
156	oboe *m*	oboe
157	oboe d'amore *m*	oboe d'amore
158	ocarina *f*	ocarina
159	oficleide *m*	ophicleide
160	ottavino *m* / flauto piccolo *m*	piccolo
161	piffero *m* / fiffero *m*	fife
162	piva *f* / cornamusa *f*	bagpipe
163	rankett *m* / rocchetta *f*	racket / rankett
164	sarrusofono *m*	sarrusophone
165	sassofono *m*	saxophone
166	sassofono baritono *m*	baritone saxophone
167	sassofono basso *m*	bass saxophone
168	sassofono contralto *m*	alto saxophone
169	sassofono soprano *m*	soprano saxophone
170	sassofono tenore *m*	tenor saxophone
171	serpentone *m*	serpent
172	sordone *m*	sordun

Englischhorn *n*	cor anglais *m*	136
Stierhorn *n*	cor de vache *m*	137
Krummhorn *n*	cromorne *m*	138
Dulzian *m*	douçaine *f*	139
Helikon *n*	hélicon *m*	140
Fagott *n*	basson *m*	141
Pfeife *f*	sifflet *m*	142
Flöte *f*	flûte *f*	143
Bassblockflöte *f*	flûte à bec basse *f*	144
Altblockflöte *f*	flûte alto / flûte à bec alto *f*	145
Sopraninoblockflöte *f*	flûte à bec sopranino *f*	146
Sopranblockflöte *f*	flûte à bec soprano *f*	147
Tenorblockflöte *f*	flûte à bec ténor *f*	148
Lotusflöte *f* / Stempelflöte *f*	flûte lotine *f* / flûte à coulisse *f*	149
Altflöte *f*	flûte alto *f* / flûte basse *f*	150
Panflöte *f*	flûte de Pan *f* / syrinx *m*	151
Blockflöte *f*	flûte douce *f* / flûte droite *f*	152
Querflöte *f*	flûte traversière *f*	153
Bügelhorn *n* / Flügelhorn *n*	flicorne *m* / bugle à pistons *m*	154
Heckelphon *n*	heckelphone *m*	155
Oboe *f*	hautbois *m*	156
Oboe d'amore *f* / Liebesoboe *f*	hautbois d'amour *m*	157
Okarina *f*	ocarina *m*	158
Ophikleide *f*	ophicléide *m*	159
Pikkolo *n* / kleine Flöte *f*	petite flûte *f* / piccolo *f*	160
Querpfeife *f*	fifre *m*	161
Dudelsack *m* / Sackpfeife *f*	cornemuse *f*	162
Rankett *n* / Stockfagott *n* / Wurstfagott *n*	racket *m* / cervelas *m*	163
Sarrusophon *n*	sarrusophone *m*	164
Saxophon *n*	saxophone *m*	165
Baritonsaxophon *n*	saxophone baryton *m*	166
Basssaxophon *n*	saxophone basse *m*	167
Altsaxophon *n*	saxophone alto *m*	168
Sopransaxophon *n*	saxophone soprano *m*	169
Tenorsaxophon *n*	saxophone ténor *m*	170
Serpent *m* / Schlangenbass *m*	serpent *m*	171
Sordun *m*	sordun *m*	172

173	sousafono *m*	sousaphone
174	tromba *f*	trumpet
175	tromba bassa *f*	bass trumpet
176	tromba da jazz *f*	jazz trumpet
177	tromba naturale *f*	natural trumpet
178	tromba a pistoni *f*	valve trumpet
179	tromba a tirarsi *f* / tromba a tiro *f*	slide trumpet
180	trombone *m*	trombone
181	trombone a cilindri *m*	valve trombone
182	trombone contrabbasso *m*	contrabass trombone / double-bass trombone
183	trombone da jazz *m*	jazz trombone
184	trombone a tiro *m*	slide trombone
185	tuba *f*	tuba
186	tuba bassa *f*	bass tuba
187	tuba contrabbasso *f*	double-bass saxhorn
188	tuba wagneriana *f*	Wagner tuba
189	zampogna *f*	bagpipe
190	zufolo *m*	whistle / tin whistle

	Parti componenti ed accessori	**Component parts and accessories**
191	ancia *f*	reed
192	ancia battente *f*	striking reed / beating reed
193	ancia doppia *f*	double reed
194	anello *m*	ring key
195	anello del pollice *m*	thumb-hold
196	apertura *f*	aperture
197	barilotto *m*	barrel socket
198	becco *m*	mouthpiece
199	bocchino *m*	mouthpiece
200	campana *f*	bell
201	camera d'aria *f*	windway / air-passage

Sousaphon *n*	sousaphone *m*	173
Trompete *f*	trompette *f*	174
Basstrompete *f*	trompette basse *f*	175
Jazztrompete *f*	trompette de jazz *f*	176
Naturtrompete *f*	trompette naturelle *f*	177
Ventiltrompete *f*	trompette à pistons *f*	178
Zugtrompete *f*	trompette à coulisse *f*	179
Posaune *f*	trombone *m*	180
Ventilposaune *f*	trombone à pistons *m*	181
Kontrabassposaune f	trombone contrebasse *m*	182
Jazzposaune *f*	trombone de jazz *m*	183
Zugposaune *f*	trombone à coulisse *m*	184
Tuba *f*	tuba *m*	185
Basstuba *f*	tuba basse *m* / contrebasse à pistons *f*	186
Kontrabasstuba *f*	contrebasse à pistons *f* / saxhorn contrebasse *m*	187
Wagner-Tuba *f* / Waldhorn-Tuba *f*	tuba Wagner *m* / tuba ténor *m*	188
Sackpfeife *f*	biniou *m*	189
Hirtenpfeife *f*	chalumeau *m* / pipeau *m*	190

Bestandteile und Zubehör	**Parties composantes et accessoires**	
Rohrblatt *n*	anche *f* / épiglotte *f*	191
aufschlagendes Rohrblatt *n* / Gegenschlagzunge *f*	anche battante f	192
Doppelrohrblatt *n* / Doppelzunge *f*	anche double *f*	193
Brille *f*	anneau *m*	194
Daumenring *m*	anneau du pouce *m*	195
Mundspalt *m* / Aufschnitt *m*	lumière *f* / ouverture *f* / biseau *m*	196
Birne *f* / Wulst *m*	baril *m* / barillet *m*	197
Schnabel *m*	bec *m*	198
Mundstück *n*	embouchure *f*	199
Schallbecher m / Stürze *f*	pavillon *m* / bonnet *m*	200
Kernspalt *m*	canal pour l'air *m*	201

202	capsula *f* / copri-ancia *m*	windcap
203	chiave *f*	key
204	chiave dell'acqua *f*	water key
205	cilindro rotativo *m*	rotary valve
206	cuscinetto *m*	plate / cup
207	foro *m*	finger-hole / tone hole
208	imboccatura *f*	mouth-hole / embouchure
209	linguetta *f*	tongue
210	macchina *f*	valve unit
211	meccanismo delle chiavi *m*	key work
212	padiglione *m*	bell
213	padiglione piriforme *m*	pear-shaped bell
214	pezzo di mezzo *m*	middle joint
215	pezzo inferiore *m*	lower joint
216	pistone *m*	piston / valve
217	pompa mobile a coulisse *f* / pompa a tiro *f*	slide
218	portamusica *f*	music lyre
219	ritorto *m*	crook
220	rotella *f*	shank
221	sacco *m*	double joint / butt
222	sordina a cappello *f*	hat mute
223	sordina a doppio cono *f*	double mute
224	sordina di cartone *f*	cardboard mute
225	sordina di metallo *f*	metal mute
226	sordina diritta *f*	straight mute
227	sordina hush-hush *f*	hush mute
228	sordina wawa *f*	wow-wow mute
229	tazza *f*	cup
230	testata con becco *f*	head joint with beak
231	tiro *m*	slide casing / case
232	traversino *m*	cross-stay
233	tubetto *m*	tube / staple
234	tubo piccolo *m* / aletta *f*	wing / tenor joint
235	vite *f*	screw

Deutsch	Français	Nr.
Windkapsel *f*	bocal *m* / capsule *f*	202
Klappe *f*	clé *f*	203
Wasserklappe *f*	clé d'eau *f*	204
Drehventil *n* / Zylinderventil *n*	cylindre à rotation *m*	205
Deckel *m*	plateau *m*	206
Griffloch *n* / Fingerloch *n*	trou *m*	207
Mundloch *n* / Ansatz *m*	embouchure *f*	208
Zunge *f*	anche *f*	209
Ventilmaschine *f*	mécanisme du piston *m*	210
Klappenmechanik *f*	mécanisme des clefs *m*	211
Aufsatz *m* / Schallbecher *m* / Schallstück *n*	pavillon *m*	212
Liebesfuß *m*	pavillon piriforme *m*	213
Mittelstück *n*	second corps *m*	214
Fußstück *n* / Unterstück *n*	patte *f* / troisième corps *m*	215
Ventil *n* / Pumpventil *n*	piston *m* / cylindre *m*	216
Zug *m*	coulisse *f*	217
Notenhalter *m*	pupitre portatif *m*	218
Stimmbogen *m* / Aufsatzbogen *m*	corps de rechange *m*	219
Walze *f*	rouleau *m*	220
Stiefel *m* / Bogen *m* / Doppelloch *n*	culasse *f*	221
Hutdämpfer *m*	sourdine à calotte *f*	222
Doppelkegeldämpfer *m*	sourdine à double cône *f*	223
Kartondämpfer *m*	sourdine en carton *f*	224
Metalldämpfer *m*	sourdine en métal *f*	225
Spitzdämpfer *m*	sourdine droite *f*	226
Huschdämpfer *m*	sourdine à calotte *f*	227
Wau-wau-Dämpfer *m*	sourdine wa-wa *f*	228
Kessel *m*	bassin *m*	229
Kopfstück mit Schnabel *n*	corps supérieur *m* / tête avec bec *f*	230
Scheide *f*	coulisse *f*	231
Quersteg *m*	barrette *f*	232
Hülse *f* / Stift *m*	corps *m*	233
Flügelröhre *f* / Oberstück *n*	petit corps *m* / petite branche *f*	234
Schraube *f*	vis *f*	235

Modi di suonare — Playing techniques

236	attacco *m*	attack
237	campane in alto / padiglioni in alto	bell up / bell in the air / raise the bell
238	chiuso / tappato	stopped
239	colpo di lingua *m*	attack with the tongue
240	colpo di lingua semplice *m*	single tonguing
241	doppio colpo di lingua *m*	double tonguing
242	forchetta *f*	fork fingering / cross-fingering
243	frullato	flutter-tonguing
244	imboccatura *f*	embouchure / lip
245	metalizzare il suono / ottavizzare / quinteggiare	brassy overblowing
246	mettere la sordina	to mute
247	posizione normale	bell down
248	togliere la sordina	mute off / to take off the mute
249	triplo colpo di lingua *m*	triple-tonguing

Strumenti a percussione — Percussion instruments

250	almgloken *f*	almglocken
251	armonica / armonica a vetro *f*	glass harmonica
252	asse per lavare *f*	washboard
253	batteria *f*	drums
254	block cinese *m* / testa di morto *f* / wood block *m*	temple block / Chinese block / wood block
255	bongo *m*	bongo
256	cabaza *f*	cabasa
257	campana *f*	bell
258	campanaccio *m*	cowbell
259	campane doriche *f pl*	Dorian bells
260	campane tubolari *f pl*	tubular bells
261	campanelli *m pl*	glockenspiel
262	campanello *m* / campanella *f*	handbell
263	campanelli della messa *m pl*	sanctus bells
264	campanelli a tastiera *m pl*	keyed glockenspiel

Spielarten **Façons de jouer**

Deutsch	Français	Nr.
Anstoß *m*	attaque *f*	236
Stürze hoch / Schalltrichter hoch	pavillon en l'air	237
gestopft / gedeckt	bouché / étouffé	238
Zungenstoß *m* / Zungenschlag *m*	coup de langue *m*	239
einfacher Zungenstoß *m*	coup de langue simple *m*	240
Doppelzunge *f*	double articulation *f*	241
Gabelgriff *m*	doigté fourché *m*	242
Flatterzunge *f*	trémolo dental *m*	243
Embouchure *f* / Ansatz *m*	embouchure *f*	244
schmettern / überblasen	cuivrer / quintage / action d'octavier	245
Dämpfer auf / dämpfen	mettre la sourdine	246
natürliche Position	position naturelle	247
Dämpfer weg / Dämpfer ab	ôter la sourdine / enlever la sourdine	248
Tripelzunge *f*	triple articulation *f* / triple coup de langue *m*	249

Schlaginstrumente — Instruments à percussion

Deutsch	Français	Nr.
Almglocken *f Pl*	almglocken *f*	250
Glasharmonika *f*	harmonica de verre *f*	251
Waschbrett *n*	washboard *m* / planche à laver *f*	252
Schlagzeug *n*	batterie *f*	253
Tempelblock *m* / Woodblock *m* / Holzblock *m*	templeblock *m* / wood bloc *m* / bloc de bois m	254
Bongo *n* / Bongotrommel *f*	tambour bongo *m*	255
Cabaza *f*	calebasse *f*	256
Glocke *f*	cloche *f*	257
Kuhglocke *f*	cloche de vache *f*	258
dorische Glocken *f Pl*	cloches doriennes *f pl*	259
Röhrenglocken *f Pl*	cloches tubulaires *f pl*	260
Glockenspiel *n* / Stabglockenspiel *n*	jeu de timbres *m*	261
Handglocke *f*	clochette *f*	262
Messglöckchen *n* / Messklingeln *m Pl*	clochettes pour la messe *f pl*	263
Klaviaturglockenspiel *n*	timbres à clavier *m pl*	264

265	carillon *m*	carillon
266	carillon a tastiera *m*	carillon
267	cassa *f*	drum
268	cassa rullante *f* / cassa chiara *f*	tenor drum
269	castagnette *f pl* / nacchere *f pl*	castanets
270	castagnette con manico *f pl*	handle castanets
271	castagnette di metallo *f pl*	metal castanets
272	castagnette spagnole *f pl*	hand castanets
273	caccavella *f* / tamburo a frizione *m*	friction drum / string drum
274	catene *f pl*	chains
275	charleston *m*	hi-hat pedal
276	chocallo *m* / tubo sonoro *m*	chocolo / chocalho
277	cimbali *m pl*	antique cymbals
278	cimbalini *m pl*	finger-cymbals / crotales
279	claves *f pl* / bacchette *f pl* / legnetti da percuotere *m pl*	claves
280	conga *m* / rumba *m*	conga
281	corno da nebbia *m*	fog horn
282	cuculo *m*	cuckoo
283	cuica *f*	cuica
284	eolifono *m*	wind machine
285	flexaton *m*	flexatone
286	frusta *f*	whip
287	gong *m*	gong
288	gong cinesi *m pl*	tuned gong-carillon
289	grancassa *f*	bass drum / big drum
290	guiro *m*	guiro / scraper
291	incudine *f*	anvil
292	lastra *f*	steel plate
293	legno frullante *m* / tavoletta sibilante *f*	thunder stick / bull roarer
294	litofono *m*	litophone / stone discs
295	macchina per il tuono *f*	thunder machine

Turmglockenspiel *n* / Glockenspiel *n*	carillon *m*	265
Klaviaturglockenspiel *n*	carillon à clavier *m*	266
Trommel *f*	caisse *f*	267
Rührtrommel *f* / Rolltrommel *f* / Wirbeltrommel *f* / Tenortrommel *f*	caisse roulante *f*	268
Kastagnetten *f Pl*	castagnettes *f pl*	269
Stielkastagnetten *f Pl*	castagnettes à manches *f pl*	270
Metallkastagnetten *f Pl* / Gabelbecken *f Pl*	castagnettes de métal *f pl*	271
Tanzkastagnetten *f* Pl	castagnettes espagnoles *f pl*	272
Reibtrommel *f* / Brummtopf *m*	tambour à friction *m*	273
Ketten *f Pl*	chaînes *f pl*	274
Charlestonmaschine *f*	pédale hi-hat *f*	275
Chocolo *m* / Tubo *m*	chocolo *m*	276
antike Cymbeln *f Pl*	cymbales antiques *f pl*	277
Fingercymbeln *f Pl* / Crotales *f pl*	cymbales digitales *f pl* / crotales *f pl*	278
Holzstäbe *m Pl* / Klangstäbe *m Pl* / Klanghölzer *n Pl* / Rumbastäbe *m Pl* / Schlagstäbe *m Pl*	claves *f pl* / baguettes de percussion *f pl* / baguettes entrechoquées *f pl*	279
Conga *f*	conga *m*	280
Nebelhorn *n*	sirène de brume *f*	281
Kuckuckspfeife *f*	coucou *m*	282
Cuica *f*	cuica *f*	283
Windmaschine *f*	machine à vent *f*	284
Flexaton *n*	flexaton *m*	285
Peitsche *f* / Klappholz *n*	fouet *m*	286
Gong *m*	gong *m*	287
Gongspiel *n* (chromatisch)	jeu de gongs *m pl*	288
große Trommel *f*	grosse caisse *f*	289
Guiro m / Kürbisrassel *f*	guiro *m*	290
Amboss *m*	enclume *f*	291
Stahlplatte *f*	feuille d'acier *f*	292
Schwirrholz *n*	planchette ronflante *f*	293
Litophon *n* / Steinspiel *n*	litophone *m*	294
Donnermaschine *f*	machine pour le tonnerre *f*	295

296	maracas *f pl*	maracas
297	marimba *f*	marimba(phone)
298	metal block *m*	metal block
299	metalofono *m*	metalophone
300	mezza luna f / cappello cinese *m*	bell tree
301	mirliton *m*	kazoo / eunuch flute
302	naccherone *m*	nakers
303	piatti *m pl* / cinelle *f pl*	cymbals
304	piatti chiodati *m pl*	rivet cymbals / sizzle cymbals
305	piatti cinesi *m pl*	Chinese cymbals
306	piatti turchi *m pl*	Turkish cymbals
307	piatto charleston *m*	charleston cymbal
308	piatto sospeso *m*	suspended cymbal
309	raganella *f*	rattle
310	raspa *f*	raspe / scraper
311	reco-reco *m*	bamboo scraper
312	richiamo per uccelli *m*	bird pipe
313	sansa *f* / mbira *f*	sansa
314	sapo cubano *m*	sapo
315	scacciapensieri *m*	jew's harp
316	sega *f*	musical saw
317	shaker *m*	shaker
318	sirena *f*	siren
319	sistro *m*	sistrum
320	sonagliera *f*	sleigh bells
321	sonaglio *m*	rattle / clapper
322	spazzolino metallico *m*	wire / rhythm brush
323	tamburello m / tamburo a cornice *m*	frame drum
324	tamburello basco *m* / tamburo basso *m*	tambourine / timbrel
325	tamburino provenzale *m*	tabor
326	tamburino *m*	tambourine
327	tamburo *m*	drum
328	tamburo a mano *m*	hand drum
329	tamburo di legno *m*	wood drum
330	tamburo di legno a fessura *m*	slit drum

Kürbisrassel *f* / Rumba-kugeln *f Pl*	maracas *m pl*	296
Marimbaphon *n*	marimba *m*	297
Metallblock *m*	metal block *m*	298
Metallophon *n*	métalophone *m*	299
Schellenbaum *m*	pavillon *m* / chapeau chinois *m*	300
Mirliton *m* / Flatsche *f* / Zwiebelflöte *f*	mirliton *m*	301
Nacara *f* (sarazenische Hand-pauke)	nacaire *m*	302
Becken *n Pl*	cymbales *f pl*	303
Nietenbecken *n Pl*	cymbales sur tiges *f pl*	304
chinesische Becken *n Pl*	cymbales chinoises *f pl*	305
türkische Becken *n Pl*	cymbales turques *f pl*	306
Charleston-Becken *n*	cymbale charleston *f*	307
hängendes Becken *n*	cymbale suspendue *f*	308
Ratsche *f* / Knarre *f* / Schnarre *f*	crécelle *f*	309
Raspel *f*	râpeur *m*	310
Bambusraspel *f*	reco-reco *m* / râpeur en bambou *m*	311
Vogelpfeife *f*	appeau *m*	312
Sansa *f* / Zanza *f*	sansa *f*	313
Sapo *m*	sapo *m*	314
Maultrommel *f* / Brummeisen *n*	guimbarde *f*	315
singende Säge *f*	scie musicale *f*	316
Schüttelrohr *n*	batteur *m*	317
Sirene *f*	sirène *f*	318
Sistrum *n*	sistre *m*	319
Schellengeläute *n*	sonnailles *f pl*	320
Schelle *f* / Rassel *f*	crécelle *f* / hochet *m*	321
Jazzbesen *m*	brosse *f* / balai de jazz *m*	322
Rahmentrommel *f* / Hand-trommel *f*	tambour de cadre *m* / tambourin à main *m*	323
Schellentrommel *f* / Tamburin *n*	tambour de basque *m* / tambourin basque *m*	324
Provenzalische Trommel *f* / Tamburin *n*	tambour de provence *m* / tambourin provençal *m*	325
Tamburin *n*	tambourin *m*	326
Trommel *f*	tambour *m*	327
Handtrommel *f*	tambour *m*	328
Holztrommel *f*	tambour en bois *m*	329
Schlitztrommel *f*	tambour de bois *m*	330

331	tamburo di latta *m* / tamburo di ferro *m*	steel drum
332	tamburo militare *m* / cassa chiara *f*	snare drum / sidedrum
333	tavola da frizione *f*	friction board
334	tavoletta *f*	bones
335	tam-tam *m*	tam-tam
336	timpani *m pl*	timpani *pl* / kettledrums *pl*
337	timpano a macchina *m*	machine drum
338	timpano cromatico *m*	chromatic timpano
339	timpano pedale *m*	pedal drum
340	tom-tom *m* / tamburo muto *m*	tom-tom
341	triangolo *m*	triangle
342	tubo sonoro di bambù *m*	bamboo brasilene
343	vibrafono *m*	vibraphone
344	xilofono *m*	xylophone
345	xilofono a tastiera *m*	keyed xylophone
346	xilomarimba *f*	xylomarimba

Parti componenti ed accessori — Component parts and accessories

347	bacchetta *f*	stick / beater / striker
348	bacchetta da tamburo *f*	drum stick
349	bacchetta di cuoio *f*	leather stick
350	bacchetta di feltro *f*	felt stick
351	bacchetta di legno *f*	wooden stick
352	bacchetta di spugna *f*	sponge-headed stick
353	bacchetta imbottita *f*	padded stick
354	bacchetta per piatti *f*	cymbal stick
355	bacchetta per timpani *f*	timpani stick
356	battaglio *m* / battente *m*	clapper
357	battitoia *f*	drumhead / skin
358	bordoniera *f*	snare
359	caldaia *f*	shell
360	cerchio *m*	counter-hoop
361	fascia *f*	shell / body
362	mazza *f* / mazzuolo *m*	mallet
363	mazza del tambur maggiore *f*	drum major's baton

Steel-Drum *f* / Benzinfass *n*	steel-drum *m*	331
Militärtrommel *f* / kleine Trommel *f*	tambour militaire *m* / caisse claire *f*	332
Reibbrett *n*	planche de friction *f*	333
Brettchenklapper *f*	tablette *f*	334
Tam-tam *n*	tam-tam *m*	335
Pauken *f Pl*	timbales *f pl*	336
Maschinenpauke *f*	timbale mécanique *f*	337
chromatische Pauke *f*	timbale chromatique *f*	338
Pedalpauke *f*	timbale chromatique mécanique *f*	339
Tom-tom *n*	tom-tom *m*	340
Triangel *n*	triangle *m*	341
Bambusschüttelrohr *n*	bambou brésilien *m*	342
Vibraphon *n*	vibraphone *m*	343
Xylophon *n*	xylophone *m*	344
Klaviaturxylophon *n*	xylophone à clavier *m*	345
Xylomarimba *n*	xylomarimba *f*	346

Bestandteile und Zubehör	**Parties composantes et accessoires**	
Schlägel *m*	baguette *f*	347
Trommelschlägel *m*	baguette de tambour *f*	348
Lederschlägel *m*	baguette de cuir *f*	349
Filzschlägel *m*	baguette de feutre *f*	350
Holzschlägel *m*	baguette de bois *f*	351
Schwammschlägel *m*	baguette d'éponge *f*	352
wattierter Schlägel *m*	baguette rembourrée *f*	353
Beckenschlägel *m*	baguette de cymbales *f*	354
Paukenschlägel *m*	baguette de timbales *f*	355
Klöppel *m*	battant *m*	356
Schlagfell *n*	peau supérieure *f* / peau de batterie *f*	357
Schnarrsaite *f* / Trommelsaite *f*	timbre *m*	358
Kessel *m*	fût *m*	359
Trommelreifen *m*	cadre *m*	360
Zarge *f*	fût *m*	361
Schlägel *m*	mailloche *f*	362
Tambourstab *m*	canne de tambour major *f*	363

364	martello *m*	hammer
365	membrana *f*	drumhead / vellum
366	orlo *f*	rim / edge
367	pedale della gran cassa *m*	bass drum pedal
368	pelle *f* / membrana *f*	skin / vellum
369	risuonatore *m*	resonator
370	spazzole *f pl*	wire brushes / steel brushes
371	tiracorda *f*	strainer
372	verga *f*	twig brush

Modi di suonare — Playing techniques

373	al centro	stroked in the middle
374	colpo *m* / battito *m*	beat
375	colpo del battaglio *m*	bell stroke
376	colpo di tamburo *m*	drumbeat
377	con due bacchette	with two sticks
378	con la mano	with the hand
379	coperto / velato	muffled
380	percuotere	to strike
381	raschiare	to scrape
382	rullo di tamburo *m*	drum roll
383	rullo del timpano *m*	drum roll
384	scoperto	uncovered
385	scuotere	to shake
386	sfregare	to rub
387	sul bordo *m* / sull'orlo *m*	at the edge / on the rim
388	tendere	to tighten
389	velare / coprire	to choke / to damp / to muffle

Strumenti a tastiera — Keyboard instruments

390	armonio *m*	harmonium / reed organ
391	bandoneon *m*	bandoneon
392	celesta *f*	celesta
393	clavicembalo *m* / gravicembalo *m*	harpsichord
394	clavicordo *m*	clavichord

Hammer *m*	marteau *m*	364
Fell *n* / Paukenfell *n* / Trommelfell *n*	peau *f*	365
Rand *m*	bord *m*	366
Fußmaschine *f*	pédale de la grosse caisse *f*	367
Fell *n*	peau *f*	368
Resonator *m*	résonateur *m*	369
Besen *m Pl*	balais *m pl*	370
Saitenschraube *f*	pontet *m*	371
Rute *f*	verge *f*	372

Spielarten — Façons de jouer

in der Mitte geschlagen	au centre frappé	373
Schlag *m*	battement *m* / coup *m*	374
Glockenschlag *m*	coup de cloche *m*	375
Trommelschlag *m*	coup de tambour *m*	376
mit zwei Schlägeln	avec deux baguettes	377
mit der Hand	avec la main	378
bedeckt	couvert / sourd	379
schlagen	frapper	380
schrapen	râper	381
Trommelwirbel *m*	roulement de tambour *m*	382
Paukenwirbel *m*	roulement de timbales *m*	383
unbedeckt	découvert	384
schütteln	secouer	385
reiben	frotter	386
am Rand *m*	sur le bord *m*	387
spannen / schränken	tendre	388
dämpfen / abdämpfen	étouffer	389

Tasteninstrumente — Instruments à clavier

Harmonium *n*	harmonium *m*	390
Bandoneon *n*	bandonéon *m*	391
Celesta *f*	célesta *m*	392
Cembalo *n*	clavecin *m*	393
Klavichord *n*	clavicorde *m*	394

395	fisarmonica *f*	accordion
396	fisarmonica a bottoni *f* / fisarmonica bitonica *f*	button accordion
397	fisarmonica con tastiera di pianoforte *f*	piano accordion
398	organo *m*	organ
399	organo portativo *m*	portative organ
400	pianoforte *m*	piano
401	pianoforte a coda *m*	grand piano
402	pianoforte preparato *m*	prepared piano
403	pianoforte a un quarto di coda *m*	baby grand
404	pianoforte verticale *m*	upright piano
405	spinetta *f*	spinet
406	virginale *m*	virginal

	Parti componenti ed accessori	**Component parts and accessories**
407	accoppiamento *m*	coupler
408	anima *f*	block
409	bilancia *f*	tongue
410	bottone *m*	press stud
411	bottoni dei registri *m pl*	draw-stops
412	canale *m*	groove / channel
413	canna *f*	pipe
414	canna ad ancia *f*	reed pipe
415	canna labiale *f*	labial pipe / flute pipe
416	cassa *f*	body / case
417	cassa espressiva *f*	swell-box
418	cilindro *m*	player roll
419	consolle *f*	console
420	coperchio *m*	roller / lid / fall
421	corde incrociate *f pl*	cross-strung / overstrung scale
422	cuscinetto *m*	cushion
423	doppio scappamento *m*	doublehopper / escapement
424	feltro *m*	felt
425	fori *m*	bore
426	grand'organo *m*	full organ / great organ

Handharmonika *f* / Akkordeon *m*	accordéon *m*	395
Knopfgriff-Akkordeon *m*	accordéon à boutons	396
Pianoakkordeon *n* / Schiffer-klavier *n*	accordéon à clavier *m*	397
Orgel *f*	orgue *m*	398
Portativ *n*	orgue portatif *m*	399
Klavier *n*	piano *m* / pianoforte *m*	400
Flügel *m*	piano à queue *m*	401
präpariertes Klavier *n*	piano préparé *m*	402
Stutzflügel *m*	crapaud *m*	403
Klavier *n* / Pianino *m*	piano droit *m*	404
Spinett *n*	épinette *f*	405
Virginal *n*	virginal *m*	406

Bestandteile und Zubehör	**Parties composantes et accessoires**	
Koppel *f*	accouplement *m*	407
Kern *m*	biseau *m*	408
Zunge *f*	languette *f*	409
Knopf *m*	bouton *m*	410
Registerzüge *m Pl* / Züge *m Pl*	boutons de registres *m pl*	411
Windladenraum *m*	gravure *f*	412
Pfeife *f*	tuyau *m*	413
Zungenpfeife *f*	tuyau à anche *m*	414
Labialpfeife *f*	tuyau à bouche *m*	415
Gehäuse	buffet *m* / caisse *f*	416
Schwellkasten *m*	boîte expressive *f*	417
Walze *f*	cylindre *m* / rouleau *m*	418
Spieltisch *m*	console *f*	419
Deckel *m* / Welle *f* / Klappe *f*	couvercle *m* / rouleau *m*	420
kreuzsaitig	cordes croisées *f pl*	421
Polster *n*	garniture *f*	422
doppelte Auslösung *f*	coussinet *m* / double échappement *m*	423
Filz *m*	feutre *m*	424
Bohrung *f*	perce *f*	425
Hauptwerk *n*	grand orgue *m*	426

427	manetta *f*	hard lever
428	mantice *m*	bellows
429	manuale *m*	manual
430	martello *m* / martelletto *m*	hammer
431	meccanica *f*	action
432	pedale *m*	pedal
433	pedale destro *m* / pedale di risonanza *m*	right pedal / sustaining pedal
434	pedale sinistro *m* / pedale del piano *m*	left pedal / damping pedal / soft pedal
435	pedale tonale *m*	sostenuto pedal
436	pedaliera *f*	pedal keyboard
437	perno *m*	centre pin
438	plettro *m*	plectrum / quill / jack
439	registro *m*	stop / register
440	salterello *m*	jack
441	scappamento *m*	escapement lever / hopper
442	segreta *f*	wind chest
443	sgabello *m* / panchina *f*	piano stool
444	smorzo *m*	damper
445	somiere *m*	windchest / sound-board
446	tangente *f*	tangent
447	tastiera *f*	keyboard
448	tasto *m*	key
449	tavola armonica *f*	sound board
450	telaio *m*	frame
451	trasmissione *f*	action
452	tremolo *m*	tremulant
453	tirante *m*	tracker
454	valvola *f*	pallet / valve

Modi di suonare — Playing techniques

455	a due manuali	double manual
456	a quattro mani	for four hands
457	arpeggiato	arpeggiated
458	a un manuale	single manual
459	con sordina	with damper

Manubrium *n*	registre *m*	427
Balg *m*	soufflet *m*	428
Manual *n*	manuel *m*	429
Hammer *m*	marteau *m*	430
Mechanik *f*	mécanique *f*	431
Pedal *n* / Pedalwerk *n*	pédale *f*	432
rechtes Pedal *n* / Fortepedal *n*	pédale droite *f* / pédale forte *f*	433
linkes Pedal *n* / Verschiebungs- pedal *n* / Dämpfer *m*	pédale gauche *f* / sourdine *f*	434
Tonhaltepedal *n*	pédale de prolongation *f*	435
Pedalklaviatur *f*	pédalier *m*	436
Achse *f*	axe *m*	437
Plektrum *n* / Kiel *m*	plectre *m* / bec *m*	438
Register *n*	registre *m* / jeux d'orgue *m pl*	439
Docke *f* / Springer *m*	sautereau *m*	440
Auslöser *m*	échappement *m*	441
Windkasten *m*	laye *f*	442
Klavierstuhl *m*	tabouret de piano *m* / banquette *f*	443
Dämpfer *m*	étouffoir *m* / sourdine *f*	444
Windlade *f*	sommier *m*	445
Tangente *f*	tangente *f*	446
Klaviatur *f*	clavier *m*	447
Taste *f*	touche *f*	448
Klangboden *m* / Resonanz- boden *m*	table d'harmonie *f*	449
Rahmen *m*	cadre *m*	450
Traktur *f*	traction *f*	451
Tremulant *m*	tremblant *m*	452
Abstrakte *f* / Zug *m*	vergette *f* / tirant *m*	453
Ventil *n*	soupape *f*	454

Spielarten — Façons de jouer

zweimanualig	à deux claviers manuels	455
vierhändig	à quatre mains	456
arpeggiert	arpégé	457
einmanualig	à un (seul) clavier manuel	458
mit Dämpfer	avec sourdine / en sourdine	459

460	disposizione *f*	specification
461	due corde	two strings
462	mani incrociate / volteggiando	crossing hands
463	martellato	hammered
464	organo pieno *m*	full organ
465	passaggio del pollice *m*	passing the thumb under
466	perlato	pearly
467	peso del braccio *m*	armweight
468	peso del corpo *m*	bodyweight
469	registrazione *f*	registration
470	sostituzione delle dita *f*	change of finger
471	tocco *m* / attacco *m*	touch / action
472	togliere il pedale sinistro	take the damper away
473	tre corde	three strings
474	una corda	one string

Strumenti musicali meccanici — Mechanical musical instruments

475	carillon *m* / scatola musicale *f*	musical box / snuff box
476	orchestrion *m*	orchestrion
477	organetto automatico *m* / orologio a soneria *m*	musical clock
478	organo di Barberia *m* / organetto *m*	barrel-organ / street organ
479	orologio a carillon *m* / cariglione *m*	musical clock / musical box
480	pianola *f*	player piano

Strumenti elettrici/elettronici, registrazione e riproduzione — Electric/electronic musical instruments, recording of music and playback units

481	altoparlante *m*	loudspeaker
482	ampiezza *f*	amplitude
483	amplificatore *m*	amplifier
484	attrezzature ritmiche *f pl*	rhythm units

Disposition *f*	disposition *f*	460
zwei Saiten	deux cordes	461
Hände kreuzend / übergreifen	mains croisées	462
gehämmert	martelé	463
volles Werk *n*	plein jeu *m*	464
Daumenuntersatz *m*	passage du pouce *m*	465
perlend	jeu perlé / perlé	466
Armgewicht *n*	poids du bras *m*	467
Körpergewicht *n*	poids du corps *m*	468
Registrierung *f*	registration *f*	469
Fingerwechsel *m*	substitution des doigts *f*	470
Anschlag *m*	toucher *m* / attaque *f*	471
mit aufgehobener Dämpfung	enlever la pédale gauche	472
drei Saiten	trois cordes	473
eine Saite	une corde	474

Mechanische Musikinstrumente — Instruments musicaux mécaniques

Spieldose *f*	boîte à musique *f* / tabatière à musique *f*	475
Orchestrion *m*	orchestrion *m*	476
Flötenuhr *f* / Flötenwerk *n*	pendule à carillon *f*	477
Drehorgel *f* / Leierkasten *m*	orgue de Barbarie *m*	478
Spieluhr *f*	pendule à carillon *f* / pendule à musique *f*	479
Pianola *n*	piano mécanique *m*	480

Elektrische/elektronische Musikinstrumente, Musikaufnahme- und Wiedergabegeräte — Instruments électriques/ électroniques, enregistrement et reproduction

Lautsprecher *m*	hautparleur *m*	481
Amplitude *f*	amplitude *f*	482
Verstärker *m*	amplificateur *m*	483
Rhythmusmaschine *f*	machine à rythme *f*	484

485	banda di frequenza *f*	frequency band
486	batteria elettronica *f*	electronic drums
487	battimento *m*	beat
488	canale *m*	channel
489	cancellare / annullare	to erase
490	chitarra elettrica *f*	electric guitar
491	colonna sonora *f*	soundtrack
492	comando del suono *m*	sound control
493	compressore *m*	compressor
494	correttore di tonalità *m* / regolatore del suono *m*	tone control
495	cuffia *f*	headphone
496	decibel *m*	decibel
497	dente di sega *m*	saw tooth
498	diaframma *m*	cartridge / pick-up
499	digitale	digital
500	disco *m*	record
501	distorsione *f*	distortion
502	eco *m*	echo
503	effetto sonoro *m*	tonal effect / sound effect
504	elaboratore *m*	computer
505	elaboratore musicale *m*	music computer
506	elettroacustica *f*	electroacoustics
507	elettrofono *m* / strumento elettrofono *m*	electrophone / electrophonic instrument
508	elettronica musicale *f*	musical electronics
509	entrata *f*	input
510	equalizzatore *m*	equalizer
511	filtro *m*	filter
512	filtro passabanda *m*	bandpass filter
513	frequenza *f*	frequency
514	generatore *m*	generator
515	generatore di suoni sinusoidali *m*	sine-wave generator
516	giradischi *m*	record player
517	grammofono *m*	gramophone (Engl.) / phonograph (Am.)
518	impulso *m*	impulse
519	larghezza di banda *f*	bandwidth
520	limitatore *m*	limiter

Frequenzband *n*	bande de fréquences *f*	485
elektronisches Schlagzeug *n*	instrument de percussion électronique *m*	486
Schwebung *f*	battement *m*	487
Kanal *m*	chaîne *f*	488
löschen	effacer / annuler	489
Elektrogitarre *f* / E-Gitarre *f*	guitare électrique *f*	490
Tonspur *f*	colonne sonore *f*	491
Klangsteuerung *f*	commande du son *f*	492
Kompressor *m*	compresseur *m*	493
Klangregler *m*	régleur de tonalité *m*	494
Kopfhörer *m*	casque d'écoute *m*	495
Dezibel *n*	décibel *m*	496
Sägezahn *m*	dent de scie *f*	497
Schalldose *f*	diaphragme *m*	498
digital	numérique	499
Schallplatte *f*	disque *m*	500
Verzerrung *f*	distorsion *f*	501
Echo *n* / Nachhall *m*	écho *m*	502
Klangeffekt *m*	effet sonore *m*	503
Computer *m* / Rechner *m*	calculateur *m*	504
Musikcomputer *m*	ordinateur musical *m*	505
Elektroakustik *f*	électro-acoustique *f*	506
Elektrophon *n*	électrophone *m*	507
Musikelektronik *f*	électronique musicale *f*	508
Eingang *m*	entrée *f*	509
Entzerrer *m*	égalisateur *m*	510
Filter *m/n*	filtre *m*	511
Bandpassfilter *m*	filtre passe-bande *m*	512
Frequenz *f*	fréquence *f*	513
Generator *m*	générateur *m*	514
Sinustongenerator *m*	générateur de sons sinussoidaux *m*	515
Plattenspieler *m*	tourne-disques *m*	516
Grammophon *n*	gramophone *m*	517
Impuls *m*	impulsion *f*	518
Bandbreite *f*	largeur de bande *f*	519
Begrenzer *m*	limiteur *m*	520

521	lineare	linear
522	livello *m*	level
523	lunghezza d'onda *f*	wave-length
524	mellotron *m*	mellotron
525	memorizzazione *f*	storage
526	memorizzazione del suono *f*	sound storage
527	mescolatore di suono *m* / tavolo di missaggio *m*	sound mixer / mixing board
528	microfono *m*	microphone
529	microfono a condensatore *m*	condenser microphone
530	microfono a contatto *m*	contact microphone
531	microfono elettrodinamico *m*	electrodynamic microphone
532	microfono elettromagnetico *m*	electromagnetic microphone
533	microsolco *m*	long-playing record / LP
534	miscelare	to mix
535	mistura *f*	tone mixture / sound mixture
536	musica informatica *f*	computer music
537	nastro magnetico *m*	magnetic tape
538	onda *f*	wave
539	organo elettronico *m*	electronic organ
540	organo Hammond *m*	Hammond organ
541	oscillatore *m*	oscillator
542	oscillazione *f*	oscillation / beat
543	parametro *m*	parameter
544	playback *m*	playback
545	potenziometro *m*	potentiometer
546	produzione del suono *f*	sound production
547	puntina *f*	needle
548	quadrifonia *f*	quadrophony
549	quadro di distribuzione *m*	switchboard
550	reazione *f*	feed back
551	regia *f*	studio (transmitting station)
552	registratore *m*	tape-recorder
553	registratori a cassetta *m pl*	cassette recorder
554	registrazione *f*	recording
555	registrazione a più piste *f*	multitrack recording
556	registrazione dal vero *f*	live recording

linear	linéaire	521
Pegel *m*	niveau *m*	522
Wellenlänge *f*	longueur d'onde *f*	523
Mellotron *n*	mélotron *m*	524
Speicherung *f*	mémorisation *f*	525
Klangspeicherung *f*	mémorisation du son *f*	526
Tonmischpult *n* / Mischpult *n*	mélangeur de son *m*	527
Mikrophon *n*	microphone *m*	528
Kondensatormikrophon *n*	microphone à condensateur *m*	529
Kontaktmikrophon *n*	microphone à contact *m*	530
elektrodynamisches Mikrophon *n*	microphone électrodynamique *m*	531
elektromagnetisches Mikrophon *n*	microphone électromagnétique *m*	532
Langspielplatte *f* / LP *f*	microsillon *m*	533
abmischen	mélanger / mixer	534
Tongemisch *n* / Klanggemisch *n*	mixage *m*	535
Computermusik *f*	musique par ordinateur *f*	536
Tonband *n* / Magnetband *n*	bande magnétique *f*	537
Welle *f*	onde *f*	538
elektronische Orgel *f*	orgue électronique *m*	539
Hammondorgel *f*	orgue Hammond *m*	540
Oszillator *m* / Schwingungserzeuger *m*	oscillateur *m*	541
Schwingung *f* / Schwebung *f*	oscillation *f* / battement *m*	542
Parameter *m*	paramètre *m*	543
Playback *n*	playback *m* / réenregistrement *m*	544
Potentiometer *n*	potentiomètre *m*	545
Klangerzeugung *f*	production du son *f*	546
Nadel *f* (Grammophon)	aiguille *f* (phono)	547
Quadrophonie *f*	quadrophonie *f*	548
Schalttafel *f*	tableau de distribution *m*	549
Rückkoppelung *f*	réaction *f*	550
Aufnahmestudio *n*	studio *m* / atelier *m*	551
Magnetbandgerät *n* / Tonbandgerät *n*	magnétophone *m*	552
Kassettenrekorder *m*	cassettophone *m*	553
Aufzeichnung *f* / Aufnahme *f*	enregistrement *m*	554
Mehrspurverfahren *n*	enregistrement à pistes multiples *m*	555
Mitschnitt *m* / Live-Aufnahme *f*	enregistrement original *m*	556

557	registrazione di dimostrazione *f*	demo tape
558	registrazione radiofonica *f*	radio recording
559	registrazione televisiva *f*	television recording
560	rettangolo *m*	rectangle
561	riduttore di rumore *m*	noise reduction / noise supression
562	riproduzione *f*	reproduction
563	risonanza *f*	resonance
564	rivelatore *m*	pick-up
565	riverbo *m*	reverb
566	rumore *m*	noise
567	scatola dell'altoparlante *f*	speaker cabinet
568	scurire	to cover
569	sequencer *m*	sequencer
570	sfiorare	to scan
571	sincronizzazione *f*	synchronization
572	sintetizzatore *m*	synthesizer / moog
573	sintesi del suono *f*	tone synthesis
574	sound sampler *m* (memorizzazione del suono)	sound sampler
575	spettro *m*	spectrum
576	stereofonia *f*	stereophony / stereo
577	strumenti a tastiera elettronica *m pl*	keyboards / electronic keyboards
578	strumenti generatori di effetti *m pl*	special effects equipment
579	suono sinusoidale *m*	sine tone
580	suono trasduttore *m*	sound transducer
581	supporti a lettura ottica *m pl*	compact disc / CD
582	taglio *m*	cut
583	tecnica digitale *f*	digital techniques
584	telecomando *m*	remote control
585	testina magnetica *f*	magnetic head
586	trasformatore *m*	transformer
587	trasformazione del suono *f*	sound modulation / sound shaping
588	trasmissione radiofonica *f*	radio transmission
589	trasmissione televisiva *f*	television transmission
590	transistor *m*	transistor

Demo-Aufnahme *f* / Demo-Band *n*	enregistrement de démonstration *m*	557
Rundfunkaufnahme *f*	enregistrement radiophonique *m*	558
Fernsehaufnahme	enregistrement télévisé *m*	559
Rechteck *n*	rectangle *m*	560
Rauschunterdrückung *f*	suppression du bruit *f* / amortissement du bruit *m*	561
Wiedergabe *f*	reproduction *f*	562
Resonanz *f* / Nachklang *m*	résonance *f*	563
Tonabnehmer *m*	pick-up *m*	564
Hall *m*	révérbération	565
Rauschen *n* / Geräusch *n* / Lärm *m*	bruit *m*	566
Lautsprecherbox *f*	haut-parleur en coffret *m*	567
decken	couvrir	568
Sequencer *m*	sequencer *m*	569
abtasten	lire / explorer	570
Synchronisation *f*	synchronisation *f*	571
Synthesizer *m*	synthétiseur *m*	572
Klangsynthese *f*	synthèse électronique *f*	573
Sound Sampler *m* / Naturklangspeicher *m*	soundsampler / enregistrement du son *m*	574
Spektrum *n*	spectre *m*	575
Stereophonie *f* / Raumklang *m*	stéréophonie *f*	576
elektronische Tasteninstrumente *n Pl*	claviers éléctroniques *m pl*	577
Effektgerät *n*	appareils générateurs d'effets *m pl*	578
Sinuston *m*	son sinussoidale *m*	579
Schallwandler *m*	transducteur acoustique *m* / transducteur de son *m*	580
CD *f* (Abk. für Compact Disc)	disque compact *m*	581
Schnitt *m*	coupure *f*	582
Digitaltechnik *f*	technique numérique *f*	583
Fernbedienung *f*	télécommande *f*	584
Magnetkopf *m* / Tonkopf *m*	tête magnétique *f*	585
Wandler *m*	transformateur *m*	586
Klangumwandlung *f*	transformation du son *f*	587
Rundfunkübertragung *f*	diffusion radiophonique *f*	588
Fernsehübertragung *f*	diffusion télévisée *f*	589
Transistor *m*	transistor *m*	590

591	trasmissione dal vivo *f*	live broadcast / live transmission
592	triangolo *m*	triangle / triangle-wave (oscillation)
593	uscita *f*	output
594	variazione del suono *f*	sound moderation
595	velocità del nastro *f*	tape speed
596	vibrazione *f*	vibration / sound wave
597	voltaggio *m*	voltage
598	volume sonoro *m*	loudness / intensity

Cantanti e canto — Singers and singing

599	baritono *m*	baritone
600	basso *m*	bass
601	basso buffo *m*	basso buffo
602	contralto *m*	contralto / alto
603	contraltista *m* / falsettista *m*	countertenor
604	educazione della voce *f* / formazione della voce *f*	vocal training / voice training
605	esercizio vocale *m*	vocal exercise
606	estensione vocale *f* / tessitura *f*	range
607	filar la voce	to spin the voice
608	fioritura *f* / gorgia *f*	florid ornaments
609	gorgheggio *m*	warble
610	gutturale	guttural
611	inflessione *f*	inflection
612	innalzare la voce	to raise the voice
613	messa di (in) voce *f* / impostazione *f*	placing of the voice
614	mezza voce	with half voice
615	mezzosoprano *m*	mezzo soprano
616	muta *f* / cambio della voce *m*	mutation
617	nasale	nasal
618	partitura vocale *f*	vocal score
619	portamento	carrying the voice
620	prima donna *f*	leading soprano
621	pronuncia *f*	pronunciation
622	rauco / roco	hoarse / raucous
623	registro *m*	register
624	respiro *m*	breathing pause

Live-Sendung *f*	émission originale *f*	591
Dreieck *n* (besser: Dreieckschwingung)	triangle *m* / oscillation triangulaire *f*	592
Ausgang *m*	sortie *f*	593
Klangänderung *f*	modification du son *f*	594
Bandgeschwindigkeit *f*	vitesse de la bande *f*	595
Schwingung *f*	vibration *f*	596
Spannung *f*	voltage *m*	597
Schallstärke *f* / Lautstärke *f*	intensité du son *f* / volume *m*	598

Sänger und Gesang / Chanteurs et chant

Bariton *m*	baryton *m*	599
Bass *m*	basse *f*	600
Bass-Buffo *m*	basse bouffe *f*	601
Alt *m* / Altistin *f*	alto *m*	602
Kontratenor *m*	haute-contre *f*	603
Stimmbildung *f*	éducation de la voix *f*	604
Gesangsübung *f*	exercice vocal *m*	605
Stimmumfang *m*	registre *m* / tessiture *f*	606
den Ton ausspinnen	filer le son	607
Verzierung *f*	fioriture *f*	608
Gurgeltriller *m*	roulade *f*	609
kehlig	guttural	610
Tonfall *m* / Stimmfall *m*	inflexion *f*	611
die Stimme heben	lever la voix	612
Führung der Stimme *f* / Ansatz der Stimme *m*	pose de la voix *f*	613
mit halber Stimme	à mi-voix	614
Mezzosopran *m*	mezzo-soprano *m*	615
Mutation *f* / Stimmbruch *m*	mue *f*	616
nasal	nasal	617
Gesangspartitur *f*	partition vocale *f*	618
Tragen der Stimme *n*	porter la voix	619
erste Sängerin *f*	première chanteuse *f*	620
Aussprache *f*	prononciation *f*	621
heiser / rau	rauque / enroué / éraillé	622
Register *m* / Stimmlage *f*	registre *m*	623
Luftpause *f* / Atempause *f*	respiration *f* / soupir *m*	624

625	ribattuta di gola *f*	ribattuta
626	schiarirsi la voce	to clear one's voice
627	soprano *m*	soprano
628	soprano drammatico *m*	dramatic soprano / high dramatic soprano
629	soprano leggero *m*	coloratura soprano
630	soprano lirico *m*	lyric soprano
631	soprano lirico spinto *m*	young dramatic soprano
632	tenore *m*	tenor
633	tenore drammatico *m* / tenore eroico *m* / tenore di forza *m*	heroic tenor
634	tenore lirico *m*	lyrical tenor
635	a bassa voce / sommesso	to speak in a low voice / with a damped voice
636	a bocca chiusa	humming / with mouth closed
637	a mezza voce	with half voice

Modi di cantare e tecniche vocali / Voice types and singing techniques

638	afono	voiceless
639	appoggiare	to support
640	appoggio (sulla maschera) *m*	voice / breath support
641	arte del canto *f*	art of singing / vocal art
642	associazione corale *f* / società di canto *f*	choral society
643	atono	toneless
644	attacco dolce *m*	soft attack
645	attacco duro *m*	glottal attack
646	attacco sul fiato *m*	aspirated attack
647	a voce piena / spiegata	with full voice
648	bel canto *m*	beautiful singing
649	bisbigliare / sussurrare	to whisper
650	calare	to sing flat
651	canoro	for singing
652	cantare a prima vista	to sight-sing
653	cantare giusto	to sing in tune
654	canticchiare	to hum
655	canto parlato *m*	speech song

Zurückschlag *m* (Verzierung)	ribattuta *f*	625
sich räuspern	s'éclaircir la voix	626
Sopran *m* / Sopranistin *f*	soprano *m*	627
dramatischer Sopran *m* / hochdramatischer Sopran *m*	soprano dramatique *m*	628
Koloratursopran *m*	soprano léger *m*	629
lyrischer Sopran *m*	soprano lyrique *m*	630
jugendlich-dramatischer Sopran *m*	soprano dramatique lyrique d'agilité *m*	631
Tenor *m*	ténor *m*	632
Heldentenor *m*	ténor dramatique *m* / ténor héroïque *m*	633
lyrischer Tenor *m*	ténor lyrique *m*	634
mit leiser Stimme / mit gedämpfter Stimme	à voix basse	635
summen / mit geschlossenem Mund	à bouche fermée	636
mit halber Stimme	à mi-voix	637

Gesangsarten und -technik / Façons de chanter et technique vocale

stimmlos	aphone	638
stützen	appuyer	639
Atemstütze *f*	appui du souffle *m*	640
Gesangskunst *f*	art vocal *m* / art du chant *m*	641
Gesangverein *m*	société chorale *f*	642
tonlos	atone	643
weicher Einsatz *m*	entrée douce *f*	644
harter Einsatz *m* / Glottisschlag *m*	attaque dure *f* / coup de glotte *m*	645
gehauchter Einsatz *m*	attaque murmurée *f*	646
mit voller Stimme	à pleine voix	647
schöner Gesang *m*	beau chant *m*	648
flüstern / lispeln	chuchoter / susurrer	649
zu tief singen	chanter trop bas	650
für Gesang	pour le chant	651
vom Blatt singen	chanter à vue	652
rein singen	chanter juste	653
trällern	chantonner	654
Sprechgesang *m*	chant parlé *m*	655

656	castrato *m* / evirato *m*	castrato
657	catena di trilli *f*	chain of trills
658	cerone *m*	grease point
659	classi vocali *f pl*	voice type
660	coro *m*	choir / chorus
661	coro della radio *m*	radio choir / radio chorus
662	coro di chiesa *m*	church choir
663	coro di fanciulli *m*	boys' choir / children's choir
664	coro d'opera *m*	opera chorus
665	coro femminile *m*	women's choir / women's chorus
666	coro maschile *m*	men's choir / men's chorus
667	coro misto *m*	mixed chorus / choir
668	coro parlato *m*	choral speaking
669	coloratura *f*	coloratura
670	corde vocali *f pl*	vocal cords
671	crescere	to sing sharp
672	crudele	cruel
673	declamazione *f*	declamation
674	direttore del coro *m*	choral conductor / choirmaster
675	dizione *f*	diction
676	falsetto *f*	falsetto
677	fato *m* / destino *m*	destiny
678	libretto *m*	libretto
679	lirica *f*	lyric
680	morire	to die
681	pietà *f*	pity / mercy
682	ridente / rioso	laughing
683	sbadigliare	to yawn
684	schiarirsi la gola	to clear one's throat
685	simulare / fingere	to feign / to sham
686	singhiozzando	sobbing
687	sorridendo	smiling
688	sospiro *m*	sigh
689	sostenere	to support
690	soubrette *f*	soubrette
691	spinto	pushed
692	stonare	to sing out of tune
693	tecnica della respirazione *f*	breath control

Kastrat *m*	castrat *m*	656
Trillerkette *f*	série de trilles *f*	657
(Theater-)Schminke *f*	fard *m* (pour la scène)	658
Stimmgattung *f*	catégories de voix *f pl*	659
Chor *m*	chœur *m*	660
Rundfunkchor *m*	chœur de radio *m*	661
Kirchenchor *m*	chœur d'église *m*	662
Knabenchor *m* / Kinderchor *m*	chœur de garçons *m* / chœur d'enfants *m*	663
Opernchor *m*	chœur d'opéra *m*	664
Frauenchor *m*	chœur de femmes *m*	665
Männerchor *m*	chœur d'hommes *m*	666
gemischter Chor *m*	chœur mixte *m*	667
Sprechchor *m*	chœur parlé *m*	668
Koloratur *f*	colorature *f*	669
Stimmbänder *n Pl*	cordes vocales *f pl*	670
zu hoch singen	chanter trop haut	671
grausam	cruel	672
Deklamation *f*	déclamation *f*	673
Chordirigent *m*	chef de chœur *m*	674
Diktion *f* / Vortrag *m*	diction *f*	675
Falsett *n* / Fistelstimme *f*	fausset *f*	676
Schicksal *n*	destin *m* / sort *m*	677
Operntextbuch *n* / Textbuch *n*	livret d'opéra *m* / livret *m*	678
Lyrik *f*	lyrique *f*	679
sterben	mourir	680
Erbarmen *n* / Mitleid *n*	pitié *f*	681
lachend	en riant / rieur	682
gähnen	bâiller	683
(sich) räuspern	s'éclaircir la voix	684
heucheln / vorgeben	simuler / feindre	685
schluchzend	en sanglotant	686
lächelnd	en souriant	687
Seufzer *m*	soupir *m*	688
stützen	soutenir	689
Soubrette *f*	soubrette *f*	690
gestoßen	poussé	691
detonieren / falsch singen	détonner	692
Atemtechnik *f* / Atembehandlung *f*	contrôle du souffle *m*	693

694	tecnica vocale *f*	vocal techniques
695	tossire	to cough
696	tremolando	tremolando
697	tremolare	to wobble
698	tremolo *m*	tremolo
699	usignolo *m*	nightingale
700	velato / fioco	veiled / husky
701	vendetta *f*	vengeance
702	vincere	to win
703	vocale	vocal
704	vocalizzo *m*	vocalise
705	voce *f*	voice
706	voce aspra *f*	harsh voice
707	voce chiara *f*	clear voice
708	voce cupa *f*	deep voice
709	voce di gola *f*	throat voice
710	voce di petto *f*	chest voice
711	voce di testa *f*	head voice
712	voce femminile *f*	female voice
713	voce granita *f*	solid voice
714	voce infantile *f*	child's voice
715	voce maschile *f*	male voice
716	voci miste *f pl*	mixed voices
717	zufolando / fischiettando	whistling

Gesangstechnik *f* / Stimmtechnik *f*	technique vocale *f*	694
husten	tousser	695
bebend / tremolierend	en tremblottant / en chevrottant	696
tremolieren / wackeln	chevroter	697
Tremolo *n*	trémolo *m*	698
Nachtigall *f*	rossignol *m*	699
verschleiert	voilé	700
Rache *f*	vengeance *f*	701
siegen	vaincre / gagner	702
vokal / sanglich	vocal	703
Vokalise *f*	vocalise *f*	704
Stimme *f*	voix *f*	705
barsche Stimme *f*	voix âpre *f*	706
helle/klare Stimme *f*	voix claire *f*	707
dunkle Stimme *f*	voix grave *f*	708
Kehlstimme *f*	voix de gorge *f*	709
Bruststimme *f*	voix de poitrine *f*	710
Kopfstimme *f*	voix de tête *f*	711
Frauenstimme *f*	voix féminine *f*	712
volle, kräftige Stimme *f*	voix pleine *f*	713
Kinderstimme *f*	voix enfantine *f*	714
Männerstimme *f*	voix masculine *f*	715
gemischte Stimmen *f Pl*	voix mixtes *f pl*	716
pfeifend	en sifflotant	717

Il linguaggio delle partiture | The language of the scores

Velocità | Velocity

Le parole con * possono significare al tempo stesso più presto e più forte oppure più lento e più piano.

The words marked by * can indicate faster and louder as well as slower and softer.

No.	Italiano	English
718	a beneplacito	as you like
719	a piacere / a volontà	at one's pleasure
720	a tempo / in tempo / a battuta / a misura / in misura	in time
721	adagietto / adagino	somewhat faster and lighter than adagio
722	adagio	slow
723	adagissimo / lentissimo	extremely slow
724	ad libitum (L)	at one's pleasure
725	affrettato	hurried
726	allegretto	not as fast as allegro
727	allegrissimo / allegro assai	very fast / very lively
728	allegro	lively / cheerful
729	andante	walking pace
730	andantino	somewhat quicker or slower than andante
731	animato	animated
732	celeramente / celere	swiftly / swift
733	circolando	circulating
734	con celerità	with celerity
735	con fretta / in fretta	with haste / in haste
736	con lentezza	with slowness
737	con molta libertà	with much freedom
738	con moto / con movimento	with movement
739	con precipitazione	with precipitation
740	con qualche licenza	somewhat freely
741	con rapidità / con prestezza	with rapidity / with speed
742	con rigore	with rigour
743	con speditezza / con prontezza	with quickness
744	con velocità	with velocity
745	corrente / correndo	running
746	esitando / esitante	hesitating
747	frettoloso	in a hurry / hasty

Die Sprache der Partituren / Le langage des partitions

Tempo / Vitesse

Tempo	Vitesse	
Die mit * gekennzeichneten Wörter können gleichzeitig schneller und lauter oder langsamer und leiser bedeuten.	Les mots marqués avec * peuvent signifier en même temps plus vite et plus fort ou plus lent et plus doucement.	
nach Belieben	à votre gré	718
nach Belieben	librement	719
im Takt / im Zeitmaß	en mesure / au mouvement / bien en mesure	720
ziemlich langsam / kürzer und schneller als Adagio	plus court et plus rapide que adagio	721
langsam	lent / adage	722
sehr langsam	très lent / extrêmement lent	723
nach Belieben	à volonté	724
eilig / übereilt	hâté	725
weniger bewegt als Allegro	moins rapide que allegro	726
sehr lebhaft / sehr schnell	très rapide / très vif	727
lebhaft / heiter	allègre	728
gehend / mäßig bewegt	en allant	729
schneller oder langsamer als Andante	plus lent ou plus rapide que andante	730
belebt	animé	731
rasch	rapidement / rapide	732
kreisend	en circulant	733
schnell	avec célérité	734
eilig / hastig	avec hâte	735
mit Langsamkeit	avec lenteur	736
mit großer Freiheit	avec beaucoup de liberté	737
bewegt	avec mouvement / avec allant	738
überstürzt	avec précipitation	739
mit einiger Freiheit	avec quelques licences	740
mit Schnelligkeit	avec rapidité	741
mit Strenge / streng im Takt	avec rigueur	742
mit Geläufigkeit	avec promptitude	743
mit Geschwindigkeit	avec vélocité	744
laufend / rennend	courant / en courant	745
zögernd / stockend	en hésitant / hésitant	746
hastig / hektisch	pressé	747

748	grave	very slow
749	incalzante	pressing on
750	larghetto	somewhat quicker and lighter than largo
751	largo	broad
752	largo assai	very slow
753	lentamente	slowly
754	lento / tardo	slow
755	libero	free
756	l'istesso tempo / lo stesso tempo / medesimo tempo	the same speed / the same pace
757	moderatamente	moderately
758	moderato	moderate
759	mosso	with movement
760	non presto	not fast
761	precipitato / precipitoso	precipitate / tumbling
762	prestissimo	extremely fast
763	presto	fast
764	prontamente / pronto	promptly
765	rapidamente / prestamente	rapidly
766	rapido	rapid
767	riprendendo / rimettendo	picking up again speed / picking up again volume
768	rubato / rubando	"robbed" / with some freedom
769	senza fretta	without haste
770	senza misura	without measure
771	senza strascicare / senza trascicare	without dragging
772	sollecito	prompt
773	sostenuto	sustained
774	spedito	quick
775	svelto	speedy
776	tempo anteriore	former speed / previous tempo
777	tempo giusto	appropriate speed
778	tempo primo / tempo ordinario	original speed
779	tornando al tempo	returning to the original speed
780	tostamente / tosto	fleetly / fleet
781	velocemente / veloce	quickly / quick

Deutsch	Français	Nr.
sehr langsam	très lent	748
drängend	talonnant	749
kürzer und schneller als Largo	plus court et plus rapide que largo	750
breit	large	751
sehr langsam	extrêmement lent	752
langsam	lentement	753
langsam	lent	754
frei	libre	755
im gleichen Tempo / dasselbe Zeitmaß	le même mouvement / au même mouvement	756
in mäßiger Weise	modérément	757
gemäßigt / mäßig	modéré	758
bewegt	mû	759
nicht schnell	pas vite	760
überstürzt / überhetzt	précipité / bousculé	761
sehr schnell	très vite	762
schnell / mit großer Geschwindigkeit	vite	763
prompt	promptement / prompt	764
schnell / in schneller Weise	rapidement	765
schnell / zügig	rapide	766
wieder aufnehmend / zurücksetzend	en reprenant / en remettant	767
„geraubt" / ein wenig frei	volé / dérobé / en dérobant	768
ohne Eile	sans se presser	769
ohne bestimmtes Zeitmaß	sans mesure	770
ohne zu schleppen	sans traîner	771
schleunig	empressé	772
verhalten / getragen	soutenu	773
geläufig	expédié	774
geschwind	svelte	775
voriges Zeitmaß	au tempo précédent / au mouvement antérieur	776
richtiges Zeitmaß / angemessenes Zeitmaß	temps juste	777
erstes Zeitmaß / Anfangstempo	temps premier / mouvement initial	778
zum Zeitmaß zurückkehrend	en revenant au mouvement	779
hurtig	vite	780
rasch	rapidement / rapide	781

782	vivace	vivacious
783	vivacissimo	most vivacious
784	vivamente	lively

SINONIMI — SYNONYMS

Più presto — Faster

785	accelerando / sollecitando	getting faster / urging
786	accelerato	accelerated
787	affrettando / frettando	hastening / hurrying
788	andando / procedendo	going on / to proceed
789	animando*	becoming more animated
790	avanti / avanzando	forward / moving forward
791	avvivando*	enlivening
792	camminando	walking
793	doppio movimento	double the speed
794	incalzando*	in a hectic pace
795	movendo / muovendo	moving
796	più tosto	swifter
797	più veloce	quicker
798	precipitando	precipitately / rushing
799	pressando / pressante	pressing
800	ravvivando*	reviving
801	ravvivato*	revived
802	rianimando*	reanimating
803	riscaldando*	warming up
804	ristringendo	restricting / drawing together again
805	sempre più animato	always more animated
806	serrato	tightly
807	spedendo	promptly
808	spingendo	pushing / pressing forward
809	stretto / ristretto	drawn together / tight
810	stringendo / serrando	drawing together / tightening
811	urgente	urgent

lebhaft	vivace	782
sehr lebhaft	très vif	783
auf lebhafte Weise	vivement	784

SYNONYME / SYNONIMES

Schneller / Plus vite

beschleunigend	en accélerant	785
beschleunigt	accéléré	786
eilend	en pressant	787
vorwärts gehend / fortschreitend	en allant / en procédant	788
belebend / lebhafter werdend	en animant	789
vorwärts / vorantreibend	en avant / en avançant	790
neu belebend	en ranimant	791
gehend / vorangehend / vorwärts gehend	en marchant	792
doppelt so schnell	en doublant le mouvement	793
drängend	en talonnant	794
bewegend	mouvant	795
eiliger	plus vite	796
mit höherem Tempo	plus rapide	797
sich überstürzend / gehetzt	en précipitant	798
bedrängend	en pressant / pressez	799
wiederbelebend	en ravivant	800
wieder belebt	ravivé	801
wieder lebhafter	en ranimant	802
erwärmend	en réchauffant	803
enger werdend	en resserrant	804
immer belebter	de plus en plus animé	805
gedrängt	serré	806
beeilend	en se hâtant	807
stoßend / treibend	en poussant	808
eng	serré / étroit	809
zusammendrängend / allmählich schneller werdend	en serrant	810
dringend	urgent	811

Più lento — Slower

	Più lento	Slower
812	allargando / slargando	broadening
813	allentando / slentando	loosening
814	allungando / dilungando	stretching out
815	calmando*	calming
816	calmandosi*	calming down
817	estendendo / espandendosi	extending
818	estenuandosi*	getting exhausted
819	frenando / raffrenando	braking
820	indugiando	delaying
821	largando	widening
822	mancando*	lacking
823	moderando	moderating
824	morendo*	dying away
825	prolungando	prolonging
826	rallentando / lentando	getting slower / slowing down
827	rallentato	slower
828	rilasciando / rilassando	releasing
829	ritardando / tardando	retarding
830	ritardato	delayed
831	ritenuto / trattenuto	held back
832	spirando / espirando*	fading away / dying out
833	stentando / penando	toiling / struggling
834	stiracchiando	tugging
835	stirando	stretching
836	strascinando / trascinando / trascicando / trainando	dragging
837	svanendo*	vanishing
838	tirando	drawing / pulling
839	trattenendo / rattenendo / ritenendo	holding back
840	tratto	dragged

Dinamica e articulazione — Dynamics and articulation

	Dinamica e articulazione	Dynamics and articulation
841	accentuato	accentuated
842	appoggiando	leaning
843	appoggiato / poggiato	leaned

Langsamer | Plus lent

Deutsch	Français	Nr.
breiter werdend	en élargissant	812
lockernd	en relâchant	813
verlängernd	en allongeant	814
beruhigend	en calmant	815
sich besänftigend	en se calmant	816
ausdehnend	en s'étandant	817
sich erschöpfend	en s'exténuant	818
bremsend	en freinant	819
zögernd	en s'attardant	820
verbreiternd	en élargissant	821
entschwindend / ausklingen lassend	en défaillant	822
mäßigend	en modérant	823
sterbend / ersterbend	en mourant	824
verlängernd	en prolongeant	825
langsamer werdend	en ralentissant	826
verlangsamt	ralenti	827
nachlassend	en relâchant	828
verzögernd	en retardant	829
verzögert	retardé	830
zurückgehalten	retenu	831
hinsterbend / ausatmend	en expirant	832
angestrengt	en peinant	833
zerrend	en tiraillant	834
dehnend	en s'étendant	835
schleppend / verschleppend	en traînant	836
entschwindend	en s'estompant / en s'effaçant	837
ziehend	en tirant	838
zurückhaltend	en retenant	839
geschleppt	traîné	840

Dynamik und Artikulation | Dynamique et articulation

Deutsch	Français	Nr.
betont	accentué / ponctué	841
stützend / betonend	en appuyant	842
gestützt	appuyé	843

844	articolando	articulating
845	articolato	articulated
846	ben ritmato	well rhythmed
847	con tutta la forza	with full force
848	estinto / spento	extinguished
849	forte	strong / loud
850	fortissimo	very loud
851	forzando	forcing
852	forzato	forced
853	glissando	sliding
854	legato / ligado	bound / tied
855	lontano	far away
856	marcando	marking
857	marcato	marked
858	martellando	hammering
859	mezzoforte	half loud
860	mezzopiano	half soft
861	molto accentuato	very accentuated
862	percosso	struck
863	pianissimo	extremely soft
864	piano	soft / low
865	più forte possibile	as loud as possible
866	più piano possibile	as soft as possible
867	portando	carrying over
868	portato	carried over
869	quasi niente	almost nothing
870	risaltato	emphasized
871	ritmico / ritmato	rhythmical / rhythmic
872	sferzando	whipping
873	sforzato / sforzando	forced / forcing
874	slegato / non legato	not slurred
875	smorzato	subdued
876	sottovoce	"under the voice" / in an undertone
877	staccato	detached
878	tremolando	trembling / tremolo
879	vibrato	vibrato / "vibrated"

artikulierend	en articulant	844
artikuliert	articulé	845
sehr rhythmisch	bien rythmé	846
mit voller Kraft / mit größter Kraft	de toutes ses forces	847
erlöscht / ausgelöscht	éteint	848
kräftig / stark / laut	fort	849
sehr laut	très fort	850
forcierend / stark betonend	en contraignant	851
forciert / stark betont	contraint	852
gleitend	en glissant / glisser	853
gebunden	lié	854
fern / weit / entfernt	lointain	855
markierend	en marquant	856
markiert	marqué	857
hämmernd	en martelant	858
halblaut / mittelstark	mi-fort	859
halbleise / mittelleise	mi-doux	860
sehr betont	très accentué	861
geschlagen	percuté	862
sehr leise	très doucement	863
leise	doucement	864
so laut wie möglich	le plus fort possible	865
so leise wie möglich	le plus doucement possible	866
tragend	en portant	867
getragen	porté	868
fast nichts	presque rien	869
hervorgehoben	mis en relief	870
rhythmisch	rythmique / rythmé	871
peitschend	en cinglant	872
stark hervorgehoben	forcé / en forçant	873
ungebunden	non lié	874
gedämpft	amorti	875
„unter der Stimme“ / mit leiser Stimme	à voix basse	876
abgestoßen	détaché / piqué	877
tremolierend / bebend	trembloté / trémolo	878
vibriert / Bebung *f*	vibré	879

SINONIMI — SYNONYMS

Più forte — Louder

880	accrescendo	augmenting
881	alzando	rising
882	ampliando	amplifying
883	aumentando	increasing
884	calcando / premendo	compressing
885	crescendo	growing louder
886	rafforzando / rinforzando	strengthening
887	rinforzato	strengthened
888	risvegliando* / risvegliato	re-awakening
889	spiegando	unfolding
890	svegliando*	wakening

Più piano — Softer

891	abbassando	lowering
892	acchetandosi* / acquietandosi	becoming calmer
893	addolcendo	softening
894	affievolendo / indebolendo	weakening
895	allontanandosi / allontanando	receding / moving away
896	assottigliando	dwindling
897	attenuando	lessing
898	calando* / calante	waning / lowering
899	cedendo*	yielding
900	decrescendo	decreasing
901	diluendo	thinning out / weakening
902	diminuendo / sminuendo	diminishing
903	estinguendosi / estinguendo	extinguishing
904	evaporandosi	evaporating
905	perdendosi*	decreasing to nothing
906	placando / mitigando	appeasing
907	raddolcendo / raddolcente	sweetening
908	scemando / deficiendo	getting less
909	smorzando	subduing

SYNONYME / SYNONIMES

Lauter / Plus fort

vermehrend / zunehmend	en accroissant	880
erhebend	en élevant	881
erweiternd	en agrandissant	882
steigernd / vermehrend / zunehmend	en augmentant	883
betonend / drängend	en comprimant	884
anwachsend / anschwellend	en croissant	885
verstärkend	en renforçant	886
verstärkt	renforcé	887
wieder erweckend	en réveillant / réveillé	888
entfaltend	en déployant	889
erweckend	en réveillant	890

Leiser / Plus doucement

absinkend	en abaissant	891
sich beruhigend	en s'apaisant	892
sanft werdend / abmildernd	en adoucissant	893
abschwächend / schwächer werdend	en affaiblissant	894
sich entfernend / entfernend	en s'éloignant	895
verringernd	en amenuisant	896
dämpfend	en attenuant	897
absinkend	en faisant descendre / en descendant	898
nachgebend	en cédant	899
abnehmend	en décroissant	900
auflösend / verdünnend	en diluant	901
vermindernd	en diminuant	902
verlöschend	en s'éteignant	903
verdunstend	en s'évaporant	904
sich verlierend / verebbend	en se perdant	905
besänftigend	en apaisant	906
sanfter werdend	en adoucissant	907
abnehmend	en amoindrissant	908
dämpfend / abschwächend	en amortissant	909

910	spegnendo*	extinguishing
911	stinto / spento	extinguished
912	temperando	moderating
913	togliendo*	taking away

	Carattere ed espressione	**Character and expression**
914	a ballata	in a ballad style
915	abbandonandosi	abandoning oneself
916	abbandonatamente / abbandono (con)	with abandonment
917	a capriccio	capricious
918	accarezzando / accarezzevolmente / accarezzevole / carezzevole	caressing / cuddle
919	accoramento (con) / afflizione (con)	with grief
920	accoratamente / accorato	sorrowful / grieved
921	accuratamente / accurato	carefully / careful
922	accuratezza (con) / cura (con)	with care
923	adiratamente	wrathful
924	adirato / stizzito	angry
925	adorazione (con)	adoringly (with adoration)
926	adornando / ornando	adorning
927	adornato / ornato	adorned
928	aereo / arioso	airy
929	affabile / cortesemente	affable / courteous
930	affannato	breathless
931	affanno (con) / angustia (con) / affannosamente / affannoso	with anxiety / anxious
932	affettato / manierato	affected
933	affetto (con)	with affection
934	affettuosamente	affectionately
935	affettuoso	lovingly
936	agevole	at ease
937	agevolezza (con) / facilità (con)	with ease
938	aggiustamente	very measured
939	agiatamente	comfortable
940	agile / agilmente	agile / nimble
941	agilità (con)	with agility

auslöschend	en éteignant	910
erloschen / erlöscht	éteint	911
mäßigend	en modérant	912
wegnehmend	en ôtant	913

Charakter und Ausdruck — Caractère et expression

wie eine Ballade	comme une ballade	914
sich hingebend	en s'abandonnant	915
mit Hingabe	avec abandon	916
launenhaft / kapriziös	capricieusement	917
liebkosend	en caressant / câlin	918
mit Betrübnis / trübselig	attristé	919
betrübt	chagriné	920
sorgfältig	soigneusement / soigné	921
mit Sorgfalt	avec soin	922
zornig / aufgebracht	coléreusement	923
erzürnt	en colère	924
mit Anbetung	avec adoration	925
zierend / schmückend	en ornant	926
verziert	orné	927
luftig	aéré	928
leutselig / mit Höflichkeit	affable / courtois	929
atemlos	essouflé	930
bangend	tourmenté / anxieusement	931
geziert / affektiert	affecté / maniéré	932
mit Zuneigung / liebevoll	avec affection	933
in herzlicher Weise	affectueusement	934
gemütsbewegend	affectueux	935
bequem	aisé	936
mit Leichtigkeit	avec aisance	937
genau im Takt	très en mesure	938
gemächlich / gemütlich	aisément	939
behände	agile / agilement	940
mit Behändigkeit	avec agilité	941

942	agitato / concitato / agitazione (con) / concitazione (con)	agitated / with agitation
943	agreste / campestre	rural
944	all'antica	in old style
945	alla contadina	like a peasant dance
946	alla maniera di / a la maniera	in the manner of
947	alla marcia	like a march
948	alla militare / militarmente	militarily
949	alla tedesca	in the style of German dance
950	alla turca	in Turkish style
951	alla zingara	in gipsy style
952	alla zoppa / zoppo	limping / lame
953	allarmato	alarmed
954	allegramente	briskly
955	allegrezza (con) / allegria (con)	cheerfully
956	all'ungherese / all'ongarese	in Hungarian style
957	altero / superbo	haughty
958	amabilità (con) / garbo (con)	with amiability
959	amabile / garbato	amiable
960	amaramente	bitterly
961	amareggiato	embittered
962	amarezza (con)	with bitterness
963	amaro	bitter
964	amore (con)	with love
965	amorevole / amoroso	tenderly
966	amorevolmente / amorosamente	lovingly
967	ampiezza (con)	with breadth
968	ampio / vasto	vast / spreading
969	ampolloso	inflated / bombastic
970	anelante / ansante	gasping / panting
971	angelico	angelic
972	angoscia (con)	with anguish
973	angoscioso / angosciosamente	anguished
974	anima (con)	with soul / with feeling
975	animo (con) / coraggio (con)	with courage
976	animoso / coraggioso	brave / courageous
977	ansia (con) / ansietà (con)	with anxiety
978	ansiosamente	anxiously
979	ansioso / trepidante	anxious
980	apatico	apathetic

erregt / unruhig	agité / avec agitation	942
ländlich	champêtre	943
im alten Stil	dans le style ancien	944
wie ein Bauerntanz / bäurisch	comme une danse paysanne	945
nach Art der/des/von	à la manière de	946
wie ein Marsch	dans le caractère d'une marche	947
militärisch	militairement	948
nach deutscher Tanzart	à l'allemande	949
nach türkischer Art (im Stil der Janitscharen-Musik)	à la turque	950
nach Art der Zigeuner	à la tzigane	951
hinkend	boiteux	952
beunruhigt	alarmé	953
fröhlich / flott	allégrement	954
mit Fröhlichkeit	avec allégresse	955
nach ungarischer Art	à la hongroise	956
hochmütig	hautain	957
mit Liebenswürdigkeit	avec amabilité	958
liebenswürdig	aimable	959
in bitterer Weise	amèrement	960
verbittert / erbittert	aigri	961
mit Bitterkeit	avec amertume	962
bitter	amer	963
mit Liebe	avec amour	964
liebevoll	doux / tendre	965
in liebevoller Weise	tendrement	966
mit Weite / mit Ausdehnung	avec ampleur	967
weit / ausgedehnt / ausladend	ample / vaste	968
schwülstig	enflé / ampoulé	969
keuchend	haletant	970
engelhaft	angélique	971
mit Seelenqual	avec angoisse	972
angstvoll	angoissant	973
mit Seele / gemütvoll	avec âme	974
mit Mut	avec courage	975
beherzt / mutig	hardi / courageux	976
mit Bangen	avec anxiété	977
bangend	anxieusement	978
bange	anxieux	979
apathisch	apathique	980

981	appassionatamente / sviscerato / appassionato / passionato	passionately / passionate
982	appenato	distressed
983	arcigno / scontroso	surly
984	ardente / rovente / fiammante	ardent
985	ardentemente	ardently
986	arditamente	boldly
987	arditezza (con)	with boldness
988	ardito / temerario	daring
989	ardore (con) / lena (con)	with ardour
990	armoniosamente / armonioso	harmoniously / harmonious
991	arrabbiato / rabbioso	angry
992	arroganza (con) / superbia (con)	with arrogance
993	artificiale / artificioso	artificial
994	arzillo	cheerily
995	asprezza (con)	with harshness
996	aspro	harsh
997	audace / franco	audacious
998	audacemente	audaciously
999	audacia (con)	with audacity
1000	autoritario	authoritarian
1001	balbettando / tartagliando	stammering
1002	baldanza (con) / baldanzoso	with boldness / bold
1003	barbaro	barbarous
1004	barcollando / vacillando	staggering / tottering
1005	beato	blissful
1006	beffardo / derisione (con)	mocking
1007	bellicoso / aggressivo / grintoso	bellicose / aggressive
1008	bilanciato / equilibrato	balanced / well balanced
1009	bizzarro / eccentrico	bizarre / eccentric
1010	bramosia (con)	with hankering
1011	bramoso / avido / famelico	greedy / craving
1012	bravura (con)	with skill
1013	brillante / lucente / luccicante	brilliant / shining / shimmering
1014	brio (con)	full of live
1015	brioso	full of pep / snappy
1016	brontolando / borbottando	grumbling
1017	brusco / bruscamente	brusque

leidenschaftlich	passionnément / passionné	981
bekümmert	peiné	982
mürrisch	hargneux / revêche	983
glühend / feurig	ardent / brûlant	984
brennend / heiß	ardemment	985
in kühner Weise	hardiment	986
mit Kühnheit / mit Verwegenheit	avec hardiesse	987
kühn / tollkühn	hardi / téméraire	988
voller Glut	avec ardeur	989
wohlklingend	harmonieusement / harmonieux	990
wütend / aufgebracht	enragé / rageur	991
anmaßend / mit Hochmut	avec arrogance	992
künstlich / gekünstelt	artificiel	993
munter / quietschfidel	guilleret	994
mit Schärfe	avec âpreté	995
harsch	âpre	996
kühn / verwegen	audacieux	997
in kühner Weise	audacieusement	998
mit Kühnheit	avec audace	999
autoritär	autoritaire	1000
stammelnd	en balbutiant	1001
mit Keckheit	avec assurance / crânement	1002
barbarisch	barbare	1003
wankend / schwankend	en chancelant / en vacillant	1004
glückselig	bienheureux	1005
spöttisch / höhnisch	railleur	1006
angreifend / aggressiv	belliqueux / agressif	1007
ausgewogen	balancé / équilibré	1008
sonderbar / wunderlich	bizarre / excentrique	1009
mit Begierde	avec convoitise	1010
begierig / gierig	désireux / avide	1011
mit Bravour	avec bravoure	1012
glänzend / schimmernd	brillant / luisant / miroitant	1013
voll Lebhaftigkeit / schwungvoll	avec verve / enlevé	1014
pfiffig / voll Leben / spritzig	plein d'allant / entraînant	1015
brummend	grognon	1016
brüsk / barsch	brusque / brusquement	1017

1018	brutale	brutal
1019	burlando / motteggiando	joking
1020	burlescamente / burlesco	mockingly
1021	caldamente	warmly
1022	caldo	warm
1023	calma (con) / calmamente	calmly
1024	calmo / quieto	calm / quiet
1025	calore (con)	with warmth
1026	calorosamente / caloroso	heartily
1027	candido / candidamente	candid / candidly
1028	candore (con)	with candour
1029	cantabile	in a singing style
1030	cantando	singing
1031	canzonando / deridendo	making fun / mocking
1032	caparbio / testardo	stubborn
1033	capricciosamente / capriccioso	capricious / whimsically
1034	carattere (con) / grinta (con)	with character
1035	caricato	charged
1036	carino / leggiadro	nice / lovely / charming
1037	casto / illibato	chaste
1038	cavalleresco	chivalrous
1039	celeste / celestiale	heavenly
1040	chiamando / invocando	calling / invocating
1041	chiaramente	clearly / distinctly
1042	chiarezza (con)	with clarity
1043	chiaro / limpido / nitido	clear / limpid
1044	cinetico / motore	kinetic / motor
1045	civettando	coquettish
1046	civetteria (con) / civettuolo	coquettishly
1047	collera (con) / incollerito	with anger / with wrath
1048	colorato	coloured
1049	comico / buffo	comical
1050	commosso	moved
1051	commovente	moving / touching
1052	comodamente	comfortably
1053	comodo / commodo	feeling comfortable / cosy
1054	concentrato	concentrated
1055	consolante / confortante	consoling
1056	con somma bravura	with the highest virtuosity
1057	contemplativo	contemplative

brutal / roh	brutal	1018
scherzend / spaßhaft	moquant	1019
scherzhaft / possenhaft	de façon burlesque	1020
in warmherziger Weise	chaleureusement	1021
warm	chaud	1022
mit Ruhe	avec calme	1023
ruhig	calme / calmement	1024
mit Wärme / seelenvoll	avec chaleur	1025
herzlich / warmherzig	chaleureusement / chaleureux	1026
treuherzig	candide / candidement	1027
einfältig	avec candeur	1028
gesanglich / gesangvoll	chantant	1029
singend	en chantant	1030
spottend / auslachend	moqueusement / avec dérision	1031
trotzig / eigensinnig / störrisch	têtu / entêté	1032
in launenhafter Weise / launisch	capricieusement / capricieux	1033
mit Charakter	avec caractère	1034
überladen	chargé	1035
reizend	mignon / charmant	1036
keusch / tugendhaft	chaste	1037
ritterlich	chevaleresque	1038
himmlisch	céleste	1039
rufend / anrufend	en appelant / en invoquant	1040
in klarer Weise	clairement	1041
mit Klarheit / mit Deutlichkeit	avec clarté	1042
klar / hell	clair / limpide	1043
motorisch	cinétique / moteur	1044
kokettierend / kokett	en coquettant / coquet	1045
mit Koketterie	avec coquetterie	1046
mit Zorn / mit Entrüstung	avec colère	1047
farbig	coloré / plein de couleur	1048
komisch / ulkig	comique / drôle	1049
gerührt / bewegt	ému	1050
rührend	émouvant / touchant	1051
in bequemer Weise / behaglich	commodément	1052
sich wohl fühlend / bequem	à l'aise	1053
konzentriert	concentré	1054
tröstend	consolant / reconfortant	1055
mit höchster Virtuosität	avec la plus haute virtuosité	1056
beschaulich	contemplatif	1057

1058	convinzione (con)	with conviction
1059	convulso	convulsive
1060	coscienzoso	conscientious
1061	costante / stabile	steady / stable
1062	cristallino	crystalline
1063	cristiano	christian
1064	cullando	rocking
1065	cuore (con)	with heart
1066	cupo / fosco	gloomy / dusky
1067	curioso	curious
1068	danzante / ballabile	in a dance style
1069	debile / debole / fievole	weak / faint
1070	debolezza (con)	with weakness
1071	debolmente	weakly
1072	decisione (con)	decisively
1073	deciso / risoluto	decided / resolute
1074	declamando	declaiming
1075	declamato	declaimed
1076	degno	worthy / dignified
1077	deliberatamente	deliberately
1078	delicatamente	delicately
1079	delicatezza (con)	with delicacy
1080	delicato	delicate / dainty
1081	delirando / vaneggiando	raving
1082	delirante / deliroso	delirious
1083	delirio (con)	with frenzy
1084	delizia (con) / diletto (con)	with delight
1085	deliziosamente	delightfully
1086	demoniaco	demonic
1087	denso / compatto	dense / compact
1088	descrittivo	descriptive
1089	desiderio (con) / vagheggiando	with desire
1090	desolato / sconsolato	desolate / disconsolate
1091	desto / sveglio	awake
1092	destrezza (con) / abilità (con)	with dexterity
1093	determinato	determined
1094	determinazione (con)	with determination
1095	devoto / divoto	devout
1096	dignità (con)	with dignity
1097	diligenza (con)	with diligence

mit Überzeugung	avec conviction / pénétré	1058
zuckend	convulsé	1059
gewissenhaft	concencieux	1060
beständig / stetig	constant / stable	1061
kristallklar	cristallin	1062
christlich	chrétien	1063
wiegend	en berçant	1064
mit Herz	avec cœur	1065
düster / dumpf	sombre / morne	1066
neugierig	curieux	1067
tanzend / tänzerisch	dansant	1068
schwächlich / schwach	faible	1069
mit Schwäche	avec faiblesse	1070
in schwacher Weise	faiblement	1071
mit Entschlossenheit	avec décision	1072
entschlossen / entschieden	décidé	1073
deklamierend	en déclamant	1074
deklamiert	déclamé	1075
würdig / würdevoll	digne / plein de dignité	1076
in entschlossener Weise	délibérément	1077
in zarter Weise	délicatement	1078
mit Zartheit	avec délicatesse	1079
zartfühlend	délicat / mignon	1080
irreredend	en délirant	1081
geistesverwirrt	délirant	1082
im Delirium / in Raserei	avec délire	1083
mit Wonne / mit Ergötzen	avec délice	1084
in entzückender Weise	délicieusement	1085
dämonisch	démoniaque	1086
dicht	dense / compact	1087
beschreibend	descriptif	1088
erwünscht / ersehnt	avec désir	1089
trostlos	désolé	1090
wach / aufgeweckt	éveillé	1091
mit Geschicklichkeit / mit Fertigkeit	avec adresse / avec dextérité	1092
bestimmt	déterminé	1093
mit Bestimmtheit	avec détermination	1094
andächtig	dévot	1095
mit Würde	avec dignité	1096
mit Fleiß	avec diligence	1097

1098	dinamico	dynamic
1099	discrezione (con)	with discretion
1100	disinvolto	unconstrained
1101	disinvoltura (con)	with unconstraint
1102	disordinato / confuso	untidy
1103	disperatamente	desperately
1104	disperato	desperate
1105	disperazione (con)	with despair
1106	disprezzo (con)	with scorn
1107	distante / in lontananza	distant / far away
1108	distinto / distintamente	distinct / distinctly
1109	divagando	wandering
1110	divertimento (con) / piacere (con)	with amusement / with pleasure
1111	doglia (con) / patimento (con)	with pain
1112	dolce	sweet / soft
1113	dolcemente	gently
1114	dolcezza (con)	with softness
1115	dolcissimo	very soft
1116	dolendo / soffrendo	suffering
1117	dolente / doglioso	in pain
1118	dolore (con) / duolo (con)	with pain
1119	doloroso / addolorato	painful / grieved
1120	dondolando	swinging
1121	drammatico	dramatic
1122	durezza (con)	with hardness
1123	duro	hard
1124	ebbrezza (con) / inebriante	with rapture
1125	eccitato / eccitante	excited / exciting
1126	elegantemente	elegantly
1127	eleganza (con)	with elegance
1128	elegiaco	elegiac
1129	elevamento (con) / elevatezza (con) / elevato	with loftiness / elevated
1130	emozione (con)	with emotion
1131	energia (con)	with energy
1132	energico	energetic / forceful
1133	enfasi (con)	with emphasis
1134	enfatico	emphatic

dynamisch	dynamique	1098
mit Diskretion	avec discrétion	1099
unbefangen	désinvolte / d'aplomb	1100
mit Unbefangenheit	avec désinvolture	1101
unordentlich	désordonné	1102
verzweiflungsvoll	désespérément	1103
verzweifelt	désespéré	1104
mit Verzweiflung	avec désespoir	1105
mit Verachtung	avec mépris	1106
entfernt	distant / éloigné	1107
deutlich / in deutlicher Weise	distinct / distinctement	1108
abschweifend	en divaguant	1109
mit Vergnügen	avec amusement / avec plaisir	1110
mit Schmerz	avec douleur	1111
sanft / weich	doux	1112
in sanfter Weise	doucement	1113
mit Sanftheit / mit Sanftmut	avec douceur	1114
sehr sanft	très doux	1115
leidend	en souffrant	1116
schmerzend / peinvoll	douloureusement	1117
mit Schmerz	avec douleur	1118
schmerzlich / schmerzhaft	douloureux	1119
schaukelnd	en balançant	1120
dramatisch	dramatique	1121
mit Härte	avec dureté	1122
hart	dur	1123
berauschend / wie im Rausch	avec ivresse	1124
aufgeregt / aufregend / spannend	excité / exitant	1125
in eleganter Weise	élégamment	1126
mit Eleganz	avec élégance	1127
elegisch	élégiaque	1128
mit Erhabenheit / erhaben	avec élévation / élevé	1129
mit Erregung / mit Gemütsbewegung	avec émotion	1130
mit Energie / mit Nachdruck	avec énergie	1131
energisch / nachdrücklich / markig	énergique	1132
mit Emphase	avec emphase	1133
emphatisch	emphatique	1134

1135	enigmatico	puzzling
1136	entusiasmo (con) / trasporto (con)	with enthusiasm
1137	epico	epic
1138	eroico / glorioso	heroic / glorious
1139	erotico	erotic
1140	esagerato	exaggerated
1141	esaltante	exalting
1142	esaltato	exalted
1143	esaltazione (con)	with exaltation
1144	esasperato	exasperated
1145	esattezza (con)	with exactitude
1146	esatto / giusto	exact / right
1147	esile / sottile / tenue / fioco	slender
1148	espansione (con)	with expansion
1149	espressione (con)	with expression
1150	espressivo	expressive
1151	estasi (con)	with ecstasy
1152	estatico	ecstatic
1153	estro (con)	with brightness
1154	estroso / ghiribizzoso	whimsical
1155	esultante / giubilante	exultant / jubilant
1156	esultanza (con) / esultazione (con)	with exultation
1157	etereo	ethereal
1158	facezia (con) / celia (con)	with jest
1159	facilmente	easily
1160	falso / traditore / perfido	false / treacherous
1161	fanatico	fanatic
1162	fantasia (con)	with fantasy
1163	fantasioso	fanciful
1164	fantastico	fantastic
1165	farsesco	farcical
1166	fascino (con)	with charm
1167	fastoso	sumptuous / costly
1168	fatica (con) / faticoso	with effort / tiring
1169	febbrile	feverish
1170	fermamente	firmly
1171	fermezza (con)	with firmness
1172	fermo	firm

rätselhaft	énigmatique	1135
mit Begeisterung / mit Überschwang	avec enthousiasme / avec transport	1136
episch	épique	1137
heroisch / glorreich	héroïque / glorieux	1138
erotisch	érotique	1139
übertrieben	exagéré	1140
schwärmerisch	exaltant	1141
überschwänglich / überspannt	exalté	1142
mit Überschwänglichkeit	avec exaltation	1143
aufgebracht	exaspéré	1144
mit Genauigkeit	avec exactitude	1145
genau / richtig	exact / juste	1146
schmächtig	grêle / mince / fluet / effilé	1147
mit Ausdehnung	avec expansion	1148
mit Ausdruck	avec expression	1149
ausdrucksvoll	expressif	1150
mit Verzückung / mit Ekstase	avec extase	1151
ekstatisch	extatique	1152
einer Eingebung folgend	avec inspiration	1153
schrullig / wunderlich	fantasque	1154
frohlockend	en exultant	1155
mit Jubel / mit Frohlocken	en jubilant	1156
ätherisch	éthéré	1157
mit Spaß	avec facétie	1158
in leichter Weise	facilement	1159
verräterisch / falsch / heimtückisch	faux / traître / perfide	1160
fanatisch	fanatique	1161
mit Phantasie	avec fantaisie	1162
schwärmerisch	fantasque	1163
phantastisch	fantastique	1164
possenhaft	farceur	1165
mit Zauber	avec charme	1166
prächtig / prachtvoll	fastueux / somptueux	1167
mit Mühe / mühsam	avec peine / avec fatigue	1168
fieberhaft	fébrile	1169
entschieden	fermement	1170
mit Festigkeit	avec fermeté	1171
standhaft	ferme	1172

1173	feroce	ferocious / fierce
1174	ferocia (con)	with ferocity
1175	fervido	fervid
1176	fervore (con)	with fervour
1177	festeggiante	rejoicing
1178	festivo / festoso	festive
1179	fiducia (con) / fede (con)	with confidence / with trust
1180	fieramente	proudly
1181	fierezza (con)	with pride
1182	filando	spinning
1183	fine / fino	fine
1184	finezza (con)	with fineness
1185	fioreggiando / fiorettando	embellishing / decorating
1186	flebile	plaintive
1187	flessibilità (con)	with flexibility
1188	fluidezza (con) / fluidità	with fluency
1189	fluido / fluente	fluent
1190	focoso / fuocoso	fiery
1191	folleggiando	frolicsome
1192	follemente / folle / insano	madly / mad / foolish
1193	forza (con)	with force
1194	fragile	fragile
1195	fragoroso / strepitoso	roaring
1196	francamente	frankly
1197	franchezza (con)	with frankness
1198	freddamente	coldly
1199	freddezza (con)	with coldness
1200	freddo	cold
1201	fremebondo / fremente	quivering
1202	fremito (con)	with thrill
1203	frenetico / frenesia (con)	frantic / frenzied
1204	freschezza (con)	with freshness
1205	fresco	fresh
1206	frivolo / futile	frivolous / trifling
1207	frizzante / spumeggiante	sparkling
1208	frusciando	rustling
1209	frustato	whipped
1210	fugace / sfuggevole	fleeting
1211	fulgido / splendido	resplendent / splendid
1212	fulminante / folgorante	fulminating

wild	féroce	1173
mit Wildheit	avec férocité	1174
inbrünstig	fervent	1175
mit Inbrunst	avec ferveur	1176
feiernd	joyeusement	1177
festlich	air de fête	1178
mit Vertrauen	avec confiance	1179
in stolzer Weise	fièrement	1180
mit Stolz	avec fierté / avec panache	1181
spinnend	en filant	1182
fein	fin	1183
mit Feinheit	avec finesse	1184
verzierend	en fleurissant	1185
kläglich / wehmütig	plaintif	1186
mit Flexibilität	avec flexibilité	1187
in fließender Weise	avec fluidité	1188
fließend	fluide	1189
feurig	fougeux	1190
in närrischer Weise	en folâtrant	1191
närrisch / wahnsinnig	follement / fou	1192
mit Kraft	avec force	1193
zerbrechlich	fragile	1194
tosend / polternd	retentissant / éclatant	1195
freimütig	franchement	1196
mit Freimut	avec franchise	1197
kühl	froidement	1198
mit Kälte	avec froideur	1199
kalt	froid	1200
bebend / schnaubend	frémissant	1201
mit Beben / mit Schaudern	avec frémissements	1202
tobend / mit Raserei	frénétique / avec frénésie	1203
mit Frische	avec fraîcheur	1204
frisch	frais	1205
leichtfertig / nichtig	frivole	1206
prickelnd / schäumend	pétillant	1207
raschelnd	en froufroutant	1208
gepeitscht	fouetté	1209
flüchtig	fugace / fuyant	1210
glänzend	resplendissant / splendide	1211
blitzend	fulminant / fulgurant	1212

1213	funebre / funereo	mournful / funereal
1214	fuoco (con)	with fire
1215	furbescamente / furbo	cunning / artful
1216	furente / furioso / furibondo	furious
1217	furia (con) / furore (con)	with fury
1218	fuso / omogeneo	melted / homogeneous
1219	gagliardo	vigorous
1220	gaiamente	gaily
1221	gaiezza (con)	with gaiety
1222	gaio	gay
1223	galante	gallant
1224	galanteria (con)	with gallantry
1225	galleggiante	floating
1226	gaudio (con) / godimento (con)	with happiness
1227	gelido	icy / freezing
1228	gemebondo / gemendo	moaning
1229	generoso	generous
1230	gentilezza (con) / compiacenza (con)	with kindness
1231	gentilmente / compiacente / compiacevole	kindly
1232	gigantesco / colossale	gigantic
1233	giocondo	playful / jolly
1234	giocoso	playful
1235	gioia (con) / letizia (con)	with joy
1236	gioioso	joyful
1237	gioviale	jovial
1238	giubilo (con) / giubilante	with jubilation / jubilant
1239	goffo / maldestro / impacciato	awkward / clumsy
1240	gracile	frail
1241	gradevole / gradito / aggradevole	agreeable
1242	grandezza (con)	with grandeur
1243	grandioso	grandiose
1244	gravità (con)	with gravity
1245	grazia (con) / vaghezza (con) / grazioso	with grace / graceful
1246	grossolano / rozzo	coarse
1247	grottesco	grotesque
1248	guerresco / guerriero	warlike
1249	gusto (con)	with taste

trauervoll	funèbre	1213
mit Feuer	avec feu	1214
schlau / schalkhaft	avec fourberie / rusé / malin	1215
rasend	furieux / furibond	1216
tobsüchtig	avec fureur / avec emportement	1217
verschmolzen / gleichartig	fondu / homogène	1218
stramm	gaillard	1219
in heiterer Weise	gaîment	1220
mit Heiterkeit	avec gaîté	1221
lustig	gai	1222
galant	galant / galamment	1223
mit Galanterie	avec galanterie	1224
schwimmend	flottant	1225
mit Genuss / mit Hochgenuss	avec bonheur	1226
eisig	glacial / glacé	1227
stöhnend	gémissant	1228
großmütig / großzügig	généreux	1229
mit Liebenswürdigkeit / mit Gefälligkeit	avec gentillesse	1230
gefällig	gentiment / complaisant	1231
riesig / riesenhaft	gigantesque	1232
fröhlich	gai	1233
spielerisch	enjoué	1234
mit Freude / mit Glückseligkeit	avec joie	1235
freudig	joyeux	1236
jovial	jovial	1237
jauchzend / jubelnd	jubilant	1238
plump / linkisch / tölpelhaft	pataud / maladroit	1239
schmächtig	frêle	1240
angenehm	agréable	1241
mit Größe	avec grandeur	1242
großartig	grandiose	1243
mit Ernsthaftigkeit	avec gravité	1244
anmutig / graziös	avec grâce / gracieux / gracieusement	1245
grob / derb	grossier	1246
grotesk	grotesque	1247
kriegerisch	guerrier	1248
mit Geschmack	avec goût	1249

1250	idilliaco	idyllic
1251	immaginazione (con)	with imagination
1252	impaziente	impatient
1253	impazienza (con)	with impatience
1254	imperioso	imperious
1255	impeto (con) / foga (con)	vehemently / with impulsion
1256	impetuoso / tumultuoso	impetuous / tumultuous
1257	implacabile	implacable
1258	implorante	imploring
1259	imponente	impressive
1260	improvvisando	improvising
1261	inafferando / incomprensibile	elusive
1262	incantato	charmed / enchanted
1263	incantevole / incanto (con)	charming / with enchantment
1264	incisivo	incisive
1265	indeciso	undecided
1266	indifferenza (con) / indifferente	with indifference / indifferent
1267	indignato	indignantly
1268	indistinto / indistinguibile	indistinctly
1269	indolenza (con) / indolente	with indolence / indolent
1270	indomito / indomabile / indocile	indomitable
1271	indulgente / clemente	lenient
1272	infantile	childish
1273	infernale / diabolico	infernal / diabolical
1274	infiammato / acceso	inflamed
1275	infocato	burning
1276	infuriato	enraged
1277	ingegnoso	ingenious
1278	ingenuo	ingenuous
1279	innocenza (con)	with innocence
1280	inquietante	disquieting
1281	inquieto / irrequieto	restless
1282	insensibile	insensible
1283	insensibilmente	insensitively
1284	insinuante / subdolo	ingratiating / stealthily
1285	insistenza (con)	with insistence
1286	insolenza (con) / insolente	with insolence
1287	in stile recitativo	recitative-like
1288	intensivo / intenso	intense

idyllisch	idyllique	1250
mit Vorstellungskraft	avec imagination	1251
ungeduldig	impatient	1252
mit Ungeduld	avec impatience	1253
gebieterisch	impérieux / impérieusement	1254
mit Ungestüm / mit Wucht	avec impétuosité / avec fougue	1255
ungestüm / wuchtig	impétueux / emporté / tumultueux	1256
unerbittlich	implacable	1257
erflehend	implorant	1258
eindrucksvoll	imposant	1259
improvisierend	en improvisant	1260
unfassbar / unverständlich	sans comprendre / insaisissable	1261
bezaubert	charmé	1262
zauberhaft / betörend	enchanteur / incantatoire	1263
einschneidend	incisif	1264
unentschlossen / unentschieden	indécis	1265
mit Gleichgültigkeit / gleichgültig	avec indifférence / indifférent	1266
entrüstet	indigné	1267
verschwommen / undeutlich	flou	1268
mit Trägheit / lässig	avec indolence / indolent	1269
zügellos / ungebändigt	indomptable	1270
nachsichtig / gütig	indulgent / clément	1271
kindlich	infantile / enfantin	1272
höllisch / teuflisch	infernal / diabolique	1273
entzündet	enflammé / allumé	1274
glühend / mit Liebesglut	embrasé	1275
rasend	furieux	1276
erfinderisch	ingénieux	1277
naiv / einfältig	ingénu / naïvement / naïf	1278
mit Unschuld	avec innocence	1279
beunruhigend	inquiétant	1280
beunruhigt / mit Unruhe	inquiet / avec inquiétude	1281
empfindungslos	insensible	1282
gefühllos / gemütlos	insensiblement	1283
einschmeichelnd	insinuant / sournois	1284
mit Beharrlichkeit	avec insistance	1285
mit Frechheit	avec insolence	1286
rezitativisch	en style récitatif	1287
intensiv	intensif / intense	1288

1289	intimo / interno	intimate / inward
1290	intrepido / impavido	intrepid
1291	invettivando / insultando	abusive
1292	iracondo / irascibile	irascible
1293	irato / iroso	irritated
1294	ironia (con)	with irony
1295	ironico	ironical
1296	irresoluto / titubante	irresolute
1297	irritante	irritating
1298	irritato	irritated
1299	lacero / squarciato	lacerated / torn
1300	lacrimoso / lagrimoso	tearful
1301	lamentoso / lagnoso	lamenting
1302	languendo / languidamente / languidezza (con)	languishing
1303	languido / illanguidendosi	languid
1304	largamente	broadly
1305	lasso / fiacco	tired / weary
1306	leggerezza (con) / leggermente	lightly / with lightness
1307	leggero / leggiero / lieve	light
1308	lesto / solerte	swift
1309	leziosamente / svenevole	affected
1310	liberamente / licenza (con)	freely
1311	lieto / ilare / giulivo	cheerful / joyous / glad
1312	liquido	liquid
1313	liricamente / lirico	in a lyrical way
1314	liscio / piatto	smooth / even
1315	lucido / lucidamente	lucid
1316	lugubre / tetro / sinistro	gloomy / sinister
1317	luminoso / lucente	bright
1318	lusingando / allettando	alluring
1319	lusingato	flattered
1320	lustro (con)	with lustre
1321	luttuosamente / funesto	mournful
1322	maestoso	majestic
1323	maestria (con)	with skill / mastery
1324	magico	magic
1325	malinconia (con)	with melancholy
1326	malinconico / melanconico	melancholic
1327	malizioso / maligno	malicious
1328	marziale	martial

innerst / innig / innerlich	intime / intérieur	1289
furchtlos	intrépide	1290
schmähend / beleidigend	invectivant / en insultant	1291
jähzornig	coléreux / irascible	1292
zornig	en colère	1293
mit Ironie	avec ironie	1294
ironisch	ironique	1295
unentschlossen / zaudernd	irrésolu / en titubant	1296
aufreizend	irritant	1297
gereizt	irrité	1298
zerrissen	déchiré	1299
tränenvoll	larmoyant	1300
klagend / wehklagend	plaintif / en gémissant	1301
schmachtend / mit Schmelz	languissamment / avec langueur	1302
schmachtend	languissant / languide	1303
ausgedehnt	largement	1304
ermattet / ermüdet	las / lassé	1305
mit Leichtigkeit	avec légèreté / légèrement	1306
leicht / duftig	léger	1307
flink	leste	1308
geziert	avec affectation	1309
in freier Weise / frei im Vortrag	dégagé / librement	1310
fröhlich / vergnügt	joyeux	1311
flüssig	liquide	1312
lyrisch	d'une façon lyrique	1313
glatt / schlicht	lisse / plat	1314
klar	lucide	1315
unheimlich / bedrohlich	lugubre / sinistre	1316
leuchtend / hell	lumineux	1317
schmeichelnd / verlockend	flatteur	1318
geschmeichelt	flatté	1319
mit Glanz	avec lustre	1320
trauernd	douloureusement / funeste	1321
majestätisch	majestueux	1322
mit Meisterschaft	avec maîtrise	1323
magisch	magique	1324
mit Schwermut	avec mélancolie	1325
schwermütig	mélancolique	1326
boshaft / verschmitzt	malicieux / espiègle	1327
kriegerisch	martial	1328

1329	maschio / virile	manly / virile
1330	meccanicamente	mechanically
1331	meditando / meditativo	meditating
1332	melodico	melodic
1333	melodioso	melodious
1334	mestamente	mournfully
1335	mesto / afflitto	afflicted
1336	minacciosamente / minaccioso	threatening / menacing
1337	misteriosamente / misterioso	mysterious
1338	mistico	mystic
1339	mobile / incostante	changeable / movable
1340	moderazione (con) / castigato	with moderation
1341	molle / floscio / mollezza (con)	flabby / with flabbiness
1342	monotono / tedioso	monotonous
1343	morbidezza (con)	limply
1344	mordace / mordente	biting
1345	mormorando / mormorato	murmuring
1346	narrante / narrando	narrating
1347	naturalezza (con)	naturally
1348	nebbioso	foggy / misty
1349	nebuloso	nebulous
1350	negligentemente	negligently
1351	nervosamente	nervously
1352	nettamente	clearly
1353	nobilmente	nobly
1354	nobiltà (con)	with nobility
1355	noncuranza (con)	carelessly
1356	nostalgico	nostalgic / longing
1357	nutrito	nourished
1358	nuziale	nuptial
1359	offeso	offended
1360	ondeggiante / ondulante	undulating / rolling
1361	opaco	opaque / dull
1362	oppresso	oppressed
1363	orgoglioso / fiero	proud
1364	orrendo / orrido / spaventoso	horrifying
1365	osservanza (con) / rispetto (con)	with respect
1366	ostinatezza (con) / ostinazione (con)	obstinately

männlich	viril	1329
mechanisch	mécaniquement	1330
sinnend / nachdenkend	en méditant / méditatif	1331
melodisch	mélodieux	1332
melodiös	mélodieusement	1333
auf betrübte Weise	tristement	1334
niedergeschlagen	affligé / triste / chagrin	1335
drohend	menaçant	1336
geheimnisvoll	mystérieusement / mystérieux	1337
mystisch	mystique	1338
beweglich / unbeständig / wankelmütig	mobile	1339
mit Mäßigung	avec modération	1340
schlaff	mou / flasque / avec mollesse	1341
eintönig / monoton	monotone	1342
weichlich	avec douceur	1343
bissig / spitzig	mordant	1344
murmelnd / gemurmelt / rauschend	en murmurant / en gazouillant	1345
erzählend	en narrant	1346
mit Natürlichkeit	naturellement	1347
neblig / vernebelt	brumeux	1348
nebelhaft / unklar	nébuleux	1349
nachlässig / sorglos	négligemment	1350
nervös / nervig	nerveusement	1351
in klarer Weise	nettement	1352
edel	noblement	1353
mit Adel	avec noblesse	1354
mit Sorglosigkeit	avec nonchalance	1355
nostalgisch	nostalgique	1356
voll / gesättigt	plein / nourri	1357
hochzeitlich	nuptial	1358
beleidigt	offensé	1359
wogend / wallend	en ondoyant / onduleux	1360
undurchsichtig / matt / trüb	opaque	1361
unterdrückt	opprimé / oppressé	1362
stolz	orgueilleux / fier	1363
fürchterlich / entsetzlich	horrible / affreux	1364
mit Hochachtung	avec respect	1365
mit Hartnäckigkeit	avec obstination	1366

	Il linguaggio delle partiture: Carattere ed espressione	The language of the scores: Character and expression
1367	ostinato / persistente	obstinate / persistent
1368	pacatamente	peaceably / peaceful
1369	pacato / pacifico	peaceable
1370	pace (con)	with peace
1371	paradisiaco	paradisiac
1372	parlando / dicendo	speaking / saying
1373	passione (con)	with passion
1374	pastorale / bucolico	pastoral
1375	pastoso	mellow
1376	patetico	pathetic
1377	paura (con)	with fear
1378	pauroso / paventato	fearful / timorous
1379	pazzamente / pazzescamente	madly / wantonly
1380	penetrante	penetrating / percing
1381	penoso	painful
1382	pensando	thinking
1383	pensieroso / pensoso	pensive
1384	pensosamente	thoughtful
1385	perseveranza (con) / costanza (con)	with perseverance / with steadfastness
1386	pesante	heavy
1387	pesato / ponderato	weighted
1388	piacevole / ameno / piacevolezza (con)	pleasant / pleasing
1389	piangendo / lacrimando	crying
1390	piangevole / piangente	weeping / weepy
1391	piccante / pungente	sharp / spiky / prikly
1392	pietoso / toccante	pitying / merciful
1393	pigro	lazy
1394	pio	pious
1395	pittoresco	picturesque
1396	placido / mite / mansueto	placid / mild / meek
1397	poetico	poetic
1398	pompa (con)	with pomp
1399	ponderoso	ponderous
1400	portamento (con)	with dignity / bearing
1401	posatamente / posato	calm / sedate / sedately
1402	possente / potente / poderoso	powerful
1403	precisione (con)	with precision
1404	preciso	precise
1405	pregando / invocando	praying / invoking

hartnäckig / eigensinnig	obstiné / persistant	1367
in ruhiger Weise	paisiblement	1368
ruhig / friedlich	paisible	1369
mit Frieden / mit Seelenfrieden	avec paix	1370
paradiesisch	paradisiaque	1371
sprechend / redend	en parlant / en disant	1372
mit Leidenschaft	avec passion	1373
nach Art der Hirten	pastoral	1374
geschmeidig	moelleux	1375
pathetisch	pathétique	1376
angstvoll	avec effroi	1377
ängstlich / furchtsam	peureux / craintif	1378
wahnsinnig / verrückt	follement	1379
durchdringend	pénétrant / perçant	1380
mühselig	pénible	1381
denkend	en réfléchissant	1382
gedankenvoll	pensif	1383
nachdenklich	gravement	1384
mit Ausdauer / mit Beständigkeit	avec persévérance / avec constance	1385
schwer / schwerfällig	pesant / lourd	1386
wohl erwogen / bedächtig	pesé / réfléchi	1387
angenehm / erfreulich	plaisant / avec agrément	1388
weinend	en pleurs	1389
weinerlich	larmoyant	1390
scharf / stechend	piquant / pointu	1391
mitleidig / barmherzig	charitable	1392
träge / behäbig / faul	paresseux	1393
fromm / ergeben	pieux	1394
malerisch	pittoresque	1395
friedlich / sanftmütig / gutmütig	débonnairement / placide	1396
dichterisch	poétique	1397
mit Feierlichkeit / mit Prunk	avec pompe	1398
gewichtig	pondéré	1399
mit Haltung	avec maintien	1400
gesetzt / bedächtig	posément / posé	1401
mächtig / gewaltig	puissant	1402
mit Präzision	avec précision	1403
präzis	précis	1404
betend / anrufend	en priant / en invoquant	1405

1406	profondo	profound / deep
1407	pronunciato / pronunziato	pronounced
1408	provocante	provocative
1409	prudente / cauto	prudent
1410	prudenza (con)	with prudence
1411	purezza (con) / purità (con)	with purity
1412	puritano	puritan
1413	puro / schietto / mero	pure
1414	quasi una fantasia	almost like a fantasy
1415	rabbia (con) / ira (con)	with rage / with wrath
1416	raccapriccio (con) / orrore (con)	with horror
1417	raccoglimento (con)	with devotion
1418	raccolto	thoughtful
1419	raccontando	narrating
1420	radioso / raggiante	radiant / beaming
1421	raffinatezza (con)	with refinement
1422	rallegrato / contento	pleased / delighted
1423	rassegnato	resigned
1424	rassegnazione (con)	with resignation
1425	recitando	reciting
1426	religioso	religious
1427	respirando / aspiratamente	breathing
1428	ribrezzo (con) / disgusto (con)	with disgust
1429	ricercatezza (con)	with refinement
1430	ricercato	exquisite / precious
1431	ricco	rich / wealthy
1432	ricordando / reminiscendo	reminiscing
1433	ridicolo / ridicolosamente	ridiculous
1434	rigidezza (con)	with rigidity
1435	rigido	rigid
1436	rigoglioso / florido	luxuriant / flourishing
1437	rigoroso	rigorous
1438	rilassato	relaxed
1439	rimbombante / rintronante	bombastic / roaring
1440	rimpianto (con)	with regret
1441	risentimento (con) / risentito	with resentment / resentful
1442	risolutezza (con) / risoluzione (con)	with resolution
1443	risonante / echeggiante	resonant / resoundig
1444	rispetto (con) / deferente	with respect / respectful

tief / tiefgründig	profond	1406
deutlich ausgesprochen	prononcé	1407
herausfordernd	provocant	1408
vorsichtig	prudent	1409
mit Vorsicht	avec prudence	1410
mit Reinheit	avec pureté	1411
puritanisch	puritain	1412
rein / echt	pur	1413
fast wie eine Fantasie	presque comme une fantaisie	1414
mit Wut	avec rage	1415
mit Schaudern	avec horreur	1416
mit Andacht	avec recueillement	1417
gesammelt / andächtig	recueilli	1418
erzählend	en racontant	1419
strahlend	radieux	1420
mit Raffinesse	avec raffinement	1421
erfreut	réjoui	1422
resigniert	résigné	1423
mit Ergebung	avec résignation	1424
rezitierend / vortragend	en récitant / en récit	1425
religiös	religieux	1426
atmend	en respirant	1427
mit Abscheu	avec dégoût	1428
mit Geziertheit	avec recherche / avec préciosité	1429
gesucht	recherché	1430
reich	riche	1431
sich erinnernd	en se souvenant	1432
lächerlich	ridicule	1433
mit Steifheit / mit Strenge	avec raideur	1434
steif / starr	raide / rigide	1435
üppig / blühend	exubérant / florissant	1436
streng	rigoureux	1437
entspannt / gelassen	détendu / décontracté	1438
dröhnend	retentissant / résonnant	1439
mit Bedauern	avec regret	1440
mit Groll	avec rancune / avec ressentiment	1441
mit Entschlossenheit	avec résolution	1442
schallend / widerhallend	résonnant	1443
mit Respekt / ehrerbietig	avec respect / avec déférence	1444

1445	riverente	reverent
1446	romantico	romantic
1447	rotondo / tondo	round
1448	rumoroso / rumorosamente	noisy / noisily
1449	rusticano / rustico / villanesco	rustic
1450	ruvido / rude / grezzo	rough
1451	saggiamente	wisely / sagely
1452	salmeggiando	psalmodic
1453	saltellando	hopping
1454	sarcastico	sarcastic
1455	scatenato	unrestrained
1456	scattante	darting
1457	scherno (con)	with mockery
1458	scherzando / scherzoso	jesting
1459	sciolto	free and easy
1460	scoppiante / crepitante	bursting / crackling
1461	scoramento (con) / avvilito	with discouragement
1462	scorrevole / scorrendo	flowing
1463	scrupoloso / minuzioso / meticoloso	scrupulous / meticulous / painstaking
1464	sdegno (con) / sdegnoso / disdegnoso	with disdain / disdainful
1465	secco	dry
1466	seducente	seductive
1467	selvaggio	wild
1468	semplice / scarno	simple
1469	semplicemente	simply
1470	semplicità (con)	with simplicity
1471	sensibilità (con)	with sensitivity
1472	sensibilmente	sensitively
1473	sensuale	sensual
1474	sentimentale	sentimental
1475	sentimento (con)	with feeling
1476	sentito	heart-felt
1477	senza colore / stinto	without colour
1478	senza sforzo	effortless
1479	serafico	seraphic
1480	serenità (con)	with serenity
1481	sereno	serene
1482	serietà (con)	with seriousness
1483	serio / grave / serioso	serious

ehrfurchtsvoll	révérenciel	1445
romantisch	romantique	1446
rund / voll	rond	1447
lärmend / geräuschvoll	bruyant / bruyamment	1448
ländlich	rustique	1449
grob / rau	rugueux / rude	1450
in besonnener Weise	sagement	1451
psalmodierend	en psalmodiant	1452
hüpfend	en sautillant	1453
sarkastisch	sarcastique	1454
entfesselt	déchaîné	1455
losschnellend	bondissant	1456
mit Hohn	avec moquerie	1457
scherzend / neckisch	en badinant / en plaisantant	1458
ungebunden	délié	1459
berstend	éclatant / crépitant	1460
mit Niedergeschlagenheit	avec accablement	1461
dahinfließend	coulant / coulamment	1462
peinlich genau / minuziös	scrupuleux / méticuleux	1463
verächtlich / mit Geringschätzung	avec dédain / dédaigneux	1464
trocken	sec	1465
verführerisch	séduisant	1466
wild	sauvage	1467
einfach	simple / dépouillé	1468
in einfacher Weise	simplement	1469
mit Einfachheit	avec simplicité	1470
mit Empfindsamkeit	avec sensibilité	1471
empfindlich	sensiblement	1472
sinnlich	sensuel	1473
sentimental	sentimental	1474
mit Empfindung / mit Gefühl	avec sentiment	1475
tief empfunden	ressenti	1476
farblos	sans couleur	1477
ohne Anstrengung	sans effort	1478
engelhaft	séraphique	1479
mit heiterer Gelassenheit	avec sérénité	1480
heiter	serein	1481
mit Ernsthaftigkeit	avec gravité	1482
ernst / würdevoll	sérieux / grave	1483

1484	severità (con)	with severity
1485	severo	severe
1486	sfacciato	cheeky
1487	sfarzo (con)	with splendor
1488	sfarzoso / pomposo	pompous
1489	sfavillante / scintillante	sparkling / scintilleting
1490	sfidando	defiant
1491	sfoggiando / ostentativo	showing off
1492	sfolgorante / splendente	resplendent
1493	sfrenato	unbridled / wantonly
1494	sfrontato / impertinente	impertinent / impudent
1495	sfumato / sfumando	shaded
1496	sgomento (con)	with dismay
1497	sibillino / enigmatico	mysterious
1498	sicurezza (con)	with selfconfidence
1499	silenzioso	silent
1500	sincero	sincere
1501	slancio (con)	with verve / with dash
1502	smania (con)	with restlessness
1503	smanioso	restless
1504	soave	suave
1505	sobrietà (con)	with sobriety
1506	sobrio / castigato	sober
1507	sognante / trasognato	dreaming
1508	solenne	solemn
1509	solennità (con)	with solemnity
1510	sommesso / sottomesso	submissive
1511	sonoro	sonorous
1512	sorvolando	flying above
1513	sospirando	sighing
1514	spassionato	dispassionate
1515	spazioso / ampio	spacious
1516	spensierato	without sorrow
1517	spettrale	ghastly / ghostly
1518	spianato	smooth / even
1519	spiccatamente	standing out
1520	spiegato	spread out
1521	spigliatezza (con)	with ease
1522	spigliato / disinvolto	free and easy / confident
1523	spirito (con)	with spirit

mit Strenge	avec sévérité	1484
streng	sévère	1485
frech / unverschämt	effronté	1486
mit Prunk	avec faste	1487
prunkvoll	fastueux / pompeux	1488
funkelnd / glitzernd	étincelant	1489
herausfordernd	avec défi	1490
prahlerisch	ostentatoire	1491
blendend	éblouissant	1492
zügellos / unbändig	effréné	1493
dreist / vorlaut	impertinent / impudent	1494
schattiert / verhaucht	estompé / en estompant	1495
bestürzt	avec désarroi	1496
geheimnisvoll / rätselhaft	sybillin	1497
mit Sicherheit	avec sûreté	1498
still	silencieux	1499
aufrichtig	sincère	1500
mit Schwung / mit Aufschwung	avec élan / envolé / avec essor	1501
mit Rastlosigkeit	avec frénésie	1502
rastlos	agité	1503
lieblich	suave	1504
mit Zurückhaltung	avec sobriété	1505
enthaltsam	sobre	1506
träumend / träumerisch / verträumt	en rêvant / rêveur	1507
feierlich	solennel	1508
mit Feierlichkeit	avec solennité	1509
unterwürfig	soumis	1510
klangvoll	sonore	1511
überfliegend	en survolant	1512
seufzend	en soupirant	1513
leidenschaftslos	sans passion	1514
geräumig	spacieux	1515
leichtsinnig / unbekümmert	sans soucis	1516
gespenstisch / geisterhaft	spectral	1517
geebnet / ungekünstelt	aplani	1518
in hervorstechender Weise	de façon saillante	1519
entfaltet	déployé	1520
mit Ungezwungenheit	avec aisance	1521
ungezwungen / keck	alerte / dégagé	1522
geistreich	avec esprit	1523

1524	spiritoso / spirituoso	spirited / witty
1525	spirituale	spiritual
1526	spontaneo	spontaneous
1527	squillante / argentino	ringing / piercing
1528	stanchezza (con) / stanco	with weariness / tired
1529	stentato / penosamente	arduous
1530	steso / disteso / esteso	stretched
1531	strano / strambo	odd / strange
1532	stravagante	extravagant
1533	straziante / lancinante	heart-breaking
1534	strepito (con)	with noise / with din
1535	stridente	screaching
1536	stridulo	shrill
1537	stupore (con) / meraviglia (con)	with amazement
1538	sublime	sublime
1539	sufficienza (con) / sussiego (con)	with conceit
1540	supplicando / implorando	pleadingly / imploring
1541	tempestosamente / tempestoso	tempestuous
1542	temporalesco / burrascoso	thundery / stormy
1543	tenace	tenacious
1544	tenebroso / scuro / oscuro	dark
1545	teneramente	tenderly
1546	tenerezza (con)	with tenderness
1547	tenero / morbido	tender / silky
1548	tepido / tiepido	tepid / lukewarm
1549	terribile / atroce	terrible / dreadful
1550	teso	tense
1551	tiepidamente	tepidly / lukewarmly
1552	tiepidezza (con) / distacco (con)	with tepidness / with detachment
1553	timidamente	timidly
1554	timidezza (con)	with timidity
1555	timore (con)	with dread
1556	timorosamente	timorously
1557	tintinnando	tinkling
1558	tonando / tuonando / tonante	thundering
1559	tormentato	tormented
1560	tormentoso	tormenting
1561	torvo / bieco / losco	grim / shifty
1562	tragico	tragic

geistreich / geistvoll / witzig	spirituel	1524
geistlich	spirituel	1525
spontan	spontané	1526
schallend / durchdringend	retentissant / comme une sonnerie	1527
mit Müdigkeit / müde	avec lassitude / fatigué	1528
mühevoll	laborieux / péniblement	1529
ausgedehnt / gedehnt	étendu	1530
seltsam	étrange	1531
extravagant	extravagant	1532
herzzerreißend / ergreifend	déchirant / poignant	1533
mit Lärm	avec fracas	1534
kreischend	strident	1535
schrill	perçant	1536
mit Staunen	avec stupeur	1537
erhaben	sublime	1538
mit Selbstgefälligkeit	avec suffisance	1539
flehend / anflehend	en suppliant / suppliant	1540
stürmisch	orageusement	1541
gewitterhaft	orageux / tempétueux	1542
hartnäckig / zäh	tenace	1543
finster / dunkel	ténébreux / obscur	1544
zärtlich	tendrement	1545
mit Zärtlichkeit	avec tendresse	1546
zart	tendre / soyeux	1547
lau	tiède	1548
schrecklich / entsetzlich	terrible / épouvantable	1549
straff / gespannt	tendu	1550
lau / leidenschaftslos	tièdement	1551
mit Leidenschaftslosigkeit / mit Lauheit	avec tièdeur / détaché	1552
schüchtern	timidement	1553
mit Schüchternheit	avec timidité	1554
mit Furcht	avec crainte	1555
furchtsam	craintivement	1556
klingelnd	en tintinnabulant	1557
donnernd / dröhnend	en tonnant / tonnant	1558
gequält	tourmenté	1559
qualvoll	torturant	1560
grimmig / verdächtig	torve / louche	1561
tragisch	tragique	1562

1563	tragicomico	tragi-comic
1564	tranquillità (con)	with calmness
1565	tranquillamente / tranquillo	quietly
1566	trasfigurato / trasmutato	transfigured
1567	trasparente / diafano	transparent
1568	tramando	conspiring
1569	tremando	trembling
1570	tremendo	tremendous
1571	trionfante	triumphant
1572	triste / contristato	sad
1573	tristemente	sadly
1574	tristezza (con) / mestizia (con)	with sadness
1575	turbato	disturbed / distracted
1576	umile / modestamente	humble / modest
1577	umore (con)	with humour
1578	umoristico	humorous
1579	uniforme	uniform / equable
1580	urlando / gridando	shouting / screaming
1581	vagamente / vago	vague
1582	valore (con)	with valour
1583	valoroso / valente	valorous
1584	vaporoso / evanescente	vaporous
1585	veemente / irruente	vehement
1586	veemenza (con)	with vehemence
1587	vellutato	velvety
1588	venerazione (con)	with veneration
1589	venusto / vezzoso	pretty
1590	vezzeggiando	fondling
1591	vibrando / vibrante	vibrant
1592	vigore (con)	with vigour
1593	vigoroso / robusto	vigorous
1594	violento / prepotente	violent / overbearing
1595	violenza (con)	with violence
1596	virtuosità (con) / virtuoso	with virtuosity / virtuoso
1597	vispo	brisk
1598	vistoso / sgargiante	showy
1599	vittorioso / vincitore	victorious
1600	vivacità (con) / vivezza (con)	with liveliness / with animation
1601	vivido / esuberante	vivid
1602	vivo / vivente	alive / lively

tragikomisch	tragi-comique	1563
mit Ruhe	avec tranquillité	1564
ruhig / ruhevoll	tranquillement / tranquille	1565
verändert / verklärt	transfiguré	1566
durchsichtig	transparent	1567
verschwörerisch	en conspirant	1568
zitternd	tremblant	1569
furchtbar	effrayant	1570
triumphierend	triomphal	1571
traurig	triste	1572
in trauriger Weise	tristement	1573
mit Traurigkeit	avec tristesse	1574
verstört / verwirrt	troublé	1575
demütig / dürftig / bescheiden	humble / modestement	1576
mit Humor	avec humour	1577
humoristisch	humoristique	1578
gleichmäßig / einheitlich	uniforme	1579
schreiend / aufschreiend	en hurlant / en criant	1580
unbestimmt	vaguement / vague	1581
mit Tapferkeit / mit Bedeutung	avec vaillance	1582
tapfer	vaillant / valeureux	1583
dunstig	vaporeux	1584
heftig	véhément / emporté	1585
mit Heftigkeit / mit Vehemenz	avec véhémence	1586
samtartig	velouté	1587
mit Verehrung	avec vénération	1588
reizvoll / hübsch / hold	joli	1589
hätschelnd	en cajolant	1590
vibrierend	en vibrant / vibrant	1591
mit Lebenskraft	avec vigueur	1592
kräftig / kraftvoll	vigoureux / robuste	1593
gewaltsam / anmaßend	violent	1594
mit Gewalt	avec violence	1595
mit Virtuosität / virtuos	avec virtuosité / virtuose	1596
voll Lebendigkeit	plein de vivacité	1597
auffallend	voyant	1598
siegreich	victorieux	1599
mit Lebhaftigkeit	avec vivacité / avec entrain	1600
sehr lebhaft / überschwänglich	exubérant	1601
lebendig	vif / vivant	1602

1603	voglia (con) / desio (con)	with desire / wishful
1604	volando / volante / volteggiando	flying / flying away
1605	volontà (con) / volenteroso	with will / willing
1606	volubile / incostante	fickle
1607	volubilità (con)	with fickleness
1608	voluttuoso	voluptuous
1609	zelo (con) / zelante	with zeal / zealous

	Diversi	**Miscellany**
1610	abbastanza / assai	enough / quite
1611	ab initio (L) / ab inizio	from the beginning
1612	a cappella	unaccompanied vocal music
1613	accanto	beside
1614	accompagnando	accompanying
1615	acuto	shrill
1616	a due	in two
1617	a due volte / due volte	twice
1618	a fior di labbro	on the tip of the tongue
1619	al fine	to the end
1620	all'improvvista	improvised
1621	all'ottava	at the octave
1622	alla breve	minim beat
1623	alla coda	to the coda / to the final part
1624	alla meglio	as well as possible
1625	alquanto	some / rather
1626	al rigore di tempo	strictly in time
1627	al segno	to the sign
1628	al suo posto	on his place
1629	al tempo precedente	at the preceding pace
1630	allargato	broadened
1631	alternando	alternating / alternatively
1632	alternato	alternate
1633	altrimenti	otherwise
1634	altro	other
1635	anche	too / also

mit Lust / wünschend	avec envie / avec désir	1603
fliegend	en volant / volant	1604
mit Willen / willig	avec volonté / de bonne volonté	1605
unbeständig / flatterhaft	volage	1606
mit Unbeständigkeit	avec volubilité	1607
wollüstig	voluptueux	1608
mit Eifer / eifrig	avec zèle / zélé	1609

Verschiedenes	**Divers**	
genug / genügend / ziemlich	assez / suffisamment	1610
von Anfang an	du début	1611
ohne Instrumente	sans instruments / style de chapelle	1612
neben	à côté	1613
begleitend	en accompagnant	1614
scharf	aigu	1615
in zwei Zählzeiten / zu zweit	à deux	1616
zweimal	deux fois	1617
fast unvernehmlich	du bout des lèvres	1618
bis zum Ende	à la fin	1619
unvorbereitet / improvisiert	improvisé	1620
in der Oktave	à l'octave	1621
in halben Noten	à la blanche	1622
zum Anhang / bis zum Schlussteil	à la partie finale	1623
so gut es geht	le mieux possible	1624
etwas / ziemlich	quelque peu	1625
streng im Takt	rigoureusement en mesure	1626
bis zum Zeichen	au signe	1627
an seiner Stelle	à sa place	1628
ins vorige Zeitmaß zurückkehrend	au mouvement précédent	1629
verbreitert	élargi	1630
abwechselnd / alternierend	en alternant	1631
abgewechselt	alterné	1632
sonst / anderenfalls	autrement	1633
anderer	autre	1634
auch	aussi	1635

1636	ancora	still / again
1637	ancora una volta	once again
1638	aperto / sfogato	open
1639	appena	scarcely
1640	approssimativo	approximately
1641	appuntino	done neatly
1642	assolutamente	absolutely / continously
1643	assoluto	absolute
1644	assordante	ear-deafening
1645	attacca	"attack!" / begin / go on
1646	attacca subito	immediate attack
1647	bastante / sufficiente	sufficient
1648	ben / bene	well
1649	bicordo	bichord
1650	breve / corto	short / brief
1651	cadenzale / cadenzante	cadential / cadencing
1652	cambiando / cangiando / mutando	changing
1653	che	that / who / which / what
1654	circa	about
1655	coda *f*	"tail" / final part
1656	coinvolto	involved
1657	colla voce / con la voce	with the voice
1658	colpo *m*	stroke
1659	come	as / how / like
1660	come al principio	as the beginning
1661	come prima / di sopra	as before
1662	come sopra	as above
1663	come stà	as it is
1664	come una cadenza	like a cadenza
1665	cominciando	beginning
1666	con / col / colla / coi / colle	with / with the
1667	con un dito	with one finger
1668	concertante	concertante
1669	conciso / stringato	concise
1670	contano	count
1671	continua	go on
1672	continuo / continuamente	continuous

noch / wieder	encore	1636
noch einmal	encore une fois	1637
offen	ouvert	1638
kaum / knapp	à peine	1639
annähernd	approximatif	1640
ganz richtig / genau	bien comme il faut	1641
durchaus / unbedingt	absolument	1642
absolut	absolu	1643
ohrenbetäubend	assourdissant	1644
„falle ein" / beginne	attaque / commence	1645
anknüpfen / unmittelbar anschließen	enchaîner	1646
genügend	suffisant	1647
gut	bien	1648
Doppelgriff	à doubles cordes	1649
kurz	bref / court	1650
kadenzierend	cadentiel	1651
wechselnd	en changeant	1652
welcher / welche / welches	que	1653
ungefähr	environ	1654
„Schwanz" *m* / Anhang *m* / Schlussteil *m*	„queue" *f* / partie finale *f*	1655
einbezogen / verwickelt in etwas	engagé	1656
mit der Stimme	avec la voix	1657
Schlag *m* / Stoß *m*	coup *m*	1658
wie / wie bei	comme	1659
wie anfangs / wie beim Eingang	comme au début	1660
wie vorher / wie früher	comme avant	1661
wie oben	comme plus haut	1662
wie es dasteht	tel quel	1663
wie eine Kadenz	comme une cadence	1664
anfangend	en commençant	1665
mit / mit dem / - der / - den	avec / avec le / - la / - les	1666
mit einem Finger	avec un doigt	1667
konzertierend / konzertant	concertant	1668
bündig / knapp	concis	1669
zählen Sie (bei Pausen)	comptez	1670
setzen Sie fort	continuez	1671
ununterbrochen / durchgehend	continu / continuellement	1672

1673	contro	against
1674	da	from
1675	da capo / daccapo / dal principio	from the beginning
1676	da capo al fine	from the beginning to the end
1677	da capo al segno	from the beginning to the sign
1678	dal principio alla fine	throughout
1679	dal segno	from the sign
1680	dal segno al fine	from the sign to the end
1681	dappertutto	everywhere
1682	da qui	from here
1683	davanti	in front
1684	dietro / indietro	back / backwards
1685	di colpo / repente	sudden
1686	di nuovo	once more / again
1687	diritto / retto	right / straight
1688	diverso	different
1689	divisi / diviso	divided
1690	dopo / poi	after / afterwards
1691	doppio	double
1692	durante	during
1693	eccessivamente	excessively
1694	eccetto	except
1695	eccezione *f*	exception
1696	enormemente	enormously
1697	equabilmente	equitably
1698	estremamente	extremely
1699	facoltativo	optional
1700	fate vibrare / lasciate vibrare	make vibrate
1701	fine *f*	end
1702	finito	finished
1703	fino al / sino al	up to / to the / until
1704	fino al segno	up to the sign
1705	già	already
1706	giustamente	suitably
1707	gli altri	the others
1708	gli stessi	the same
1709	gradatamente / gradualmente	gradually
1710	gran / grande	great / much / big

gegen	contre	1673
von	depuis	1674
von vorne / von Anfang an	du début	1675
wieder von Anfang an bis zum Schluss	du début à la fin	1676
wieder von Anfang an bis zum Zeichen	du début au signe	1677
durchweg	du début à la fin	1678
vom Zeichen	du signe	1679
vom Zeichen bis zum Schluss	du signe à la fin	1680
überall	partout	1681
von hier ab	depuis ici	1682
vorne / davor	devant	1683
hinten / zurück / rückwärts	derrière / en arrière	1684
plötzlich	tout à coup	1685
nochmals / von neuem	à nouveau	1686
gerade	droit	1687
verschieden	différent	1688
geteilt	divisé	1689
dann / anschließend / nach	après / ensuite	1690
doppelt	double	1691
während	durant / pendant	1692
übermäßig	excessivement	1693
ausgenommen	excepté	1694
Ausnahme *f*	exception *f*	1695
in enormer Weise	énormément	1696
in gleichförmiger Weise / auf dieselbe Art	équitablement	1697
äußerst	extrèmement	1698
wahlfrei / beliebig	facultatif	1699
vibrieren lassen / klingen lassen	laissez vibrer	1700
Schluss *m*	fin *f*	1701
beendet	terminé	1702
bis zu / bis zum	jusqu'au	1703
bis zum Zeichen	jusqu'au signe	1704
schon / bereits	déjà	1705
angemessen	justement	1706
die Übrigen	les autres	1707
dieselben	les mêmes	1708
stufenweise	graduellement	1709
groß / viel	grand	1710

1711	il più …	the most …
1712	il più possibile	as much as possible
1713	imitando	imitating
1714	immutato / inalterato	unchanged
1715	improvvisamente / improvviso	suddenly
1716	in fuori / in evidenza	bring out / bring forward
1717	in giù / giù	below
1718	in luogo di	in place of
1719	in mancanza di	in the absence of
1720	in maniera / in modo	in a … way / in a … manner
1721	in nessun caso	in no case
1722	in primo piano	in the foreground
1723	in rilievo / prominente	pointed out
1724	in risalto	to emphasize
1725	insieme / assieme	together
1726	in su	above
1727	lasciar vibrare	let sound / let vibrate
1728	levate i sordini	remove the mutes
1729	loco (L) / al luogo	sounding as written
1730	lungo / a lungo	long
1731	luogo *m* / posto *m*	place
1732	ma	but
1733	ma non tanto / ma non troppo	but not too much
1734	massimo	greatest
1735	medesimo / stesso / istesso	same / the same
1736	meno	less
1737	metà *f*	half
1738	mezzo / mezza	half
1739	mezza forza	half strength
1740	minimo	minimum
1741	misto	mixed
1742	misurato	measured
1743	moltissimo	very much
1744	molto / di molto / assai	much / very
1745	moto *m* / movimento *m*	motion
1746	multiplo	multiple
1747	muta / cambia	change
1748	nascosto	hidden
1749	nel / nella	in the

das meiste / äußerst …	le plus …	1711
so viel wie möglich	le plus possible	1712
nachahmend	en imitant	1713
unverändert	inchangé	1714
plötzlich	soudain	1715
außerhalb / hervortretend / hervor	en dehors / en évidence	1716
nach unten / abwärts / unten	en bas	1717
an Stelle von	au lieu de	1718
in Ermangelung von	à défaut de	1719
in … Weise	de façon / de manière	1720
keinesfalls / in keinem Fall	en aucun cas	1721
im Vordergrund	au premier plan	1722
hervorgehoben	en valeur / relevé / en relief	1723
hervorbringen / hervorstechend	mettre en valeur	1724
zusammen	ensemble	1725
aufwärts / nach oben / oben	en haut	1726
klingen lassen	laisser vibrer / résonner	1727
Dämpfer abnehmen	enlever la sourdine	1728
an seinem Platz (Oktavierung aufgehoben)	à sa place	1729
lang / in langer Weise	long / longuement	1730
Stelle *f* / Ort *m*	endroit *m* / lieu *m*	1731
aber / jedoch	mais	1732
aber nicht zu sehr	mais pas trop	1733
(der) größte	maximum	1734
derselbe / dieselbe / dasselbe	la même chose / même (le)	1735
weniger	moins	1736
Hälfte *f*	moitié *f*	1737
halb	demi / demie	1738
halbe Kraft	demi force	1739
(der) kleinste	minimum	1740
gemischt	mélangé / mixte	1741
gemessen	mesuré	1742
sehr viel	énormément	1743
viel / sehr / gar	très / beaucoup	1744
Bewegung *f*	mouvement *m*	1745
vielfach	multiple	1746
verändere	change	1747
verborgen / versteckt	caché	1748
im / in	dans le / dans la	1749

1750	nello (allo) stesso modo	in the same way
1751	nessuno	no one / nobody
1752	niente / nulla	nothing / not at all
1753	non	not
1754	non molto	not much / not very
1755	non tanto	not very / not so
1756	non tenuto	not held
1757	non troppo	not too much
1758	obbligato / obbligatorio	obligatory / compulsory
1759	ogni / ciascuno	every / each
1760	ogni volta	every time
1761	omesso	omitted
1762	ordinario / usuale	ordinary
1763	ossia / oppure / ovvero	otherwise / or / else
1764	per	for / to
1765	per finire	to end / in order to finish
1766	per l'ultima volta	for the last time
1767	per tutta la durata	for the whole length
1768	però	however
1769	pieno	full
1770	più / di più	more
1771	più che / più del	more then
1772	piuttosto	rather
1773	poco / scarso / piccolo	little / few / small
1774	poco a poco	little by little
1775	poco a poco meno	gradually less
1776	poco a poco più	gradually more
1777	poco meno	a little less
1778	poco più	a little more
1779	poi segue	then follows
1780	possibile	(as) possible
1781	possibilmente	if possible
1782	precedente / anteriore	preceding
1783	prima	before
1784	prima che / prima di	before
1785	prossimo	next
1786	qua / qui	here
1787	qualche / alcune	some
1788	quanto	as much as
1789	quasi	almost /nearly / as if

auf dieselbe Art	de la même façon	1750
niemand / kein	personne / aucun	1751
nichts / gar nichts	rien / du tout	1752
nicht	ne....pas	1753
nicht viel / nicht sehr	pas beaucoup	1754
nicht zu sehr	pas trop	1755
nicht gehalten	non tenu	1756
nicht zu viel	pas trop	1757
obligat / verpflichtend / bindend	obligé / obligatoire	1758
jede / jeder / jedes	chaque / chacun	1759
jedes Mal	chaque fois	1760
unterlassen	omis	1761
gewöhnlich / üblich	habituel	1762
oder / oder auch	ou bien	1763
für / durch	pour	1764
zum Schluss	pour finir	1765
zum letzten Mal	pour la dernière fois	1766
für die ganze Dauer	pendant toute la durée	1767
dennoch / jedoch	pourtant	1768
mit vollem Ton / voll	plein	1769
mehr	plus / davantage	1770
mehr als	plus que / plus du	1771
eher / lieber	plutôt	1772
wenig / knapp / klein	peu / petit	1773
allmählich	peu à peu	1774
allmählich weniger	de moins en moins	1775
allmählich mehr	de plus en plus	1776
etwas weniger	un peu moins	1777
etwas mehr	un peu plus	1778
sodann folgt	puis poursuit	1779
möglich	possible	1780
möglichst	si cela est possible	1781
vorhergehend / im Vorigen	précédent / antérieur	1782
früher / vorher / zuvor	avant	1783
bevor	avant que / avant de	1784
nächste / nächstfolgend	prochain	1785
hier	ici	1786
einige	quelque (s)	1787
so viel wie	autant que	1788
fast / beinahe / wie / als ob	presque	1789

1790	rigorosamente	rigorously
1791	rispettare il testo	respect the text
1792	ritornando / tornando	returning
1793	se	if
1794	se bisogna	if necessary
1795	segno *m*	sign / mark
1796	segue	it follows
1797	seguite	follow
1798	sempre / costantemente	always
1799	sempre lo stesso	always the same
1800	senza	without
1801	senza cambiare	without changing
1802	senza correre	without hurrying
1803	senza fermarsi / senza interruzioni	without interruptions
1804	senza replica	without repetition
1805	senza strumenti	without instruments
1806	separato	separated
1807	si leva / si toglie	take away
1808	simile / lo stesso	similar
1809	sin / sino	until
1810	solito	usual
1811	solo / soli / assolo	alone
1812	soltanto	only / just
1813	sommo	highest
1814	sopra	on / upon
1815	soprattutto	mainly / above all
1816	sordina *f* / sordino *m*	mute / damper / muffle
1817	sotto	under
1818	sovente / spesso	often
1819	spostamento *m*	shift
1820	strettamente	strictly
1821	su / sul / sulla	on / on the
1822	subito / immediatamente	at once / immediately
1823	tace / tacesi / taci	remain silent / be quiet
1824	tacet (L)	silent
1825	tale	such
1826	tantino	a little bit

in strenger Weise	rigoureusement	1790
den Text respektieren	respecter le texte	1791
zurückkommend / zurückkehrend	en revenant	1792
wenn / falls / sofern	si	1793
wenn nötig	si nécessaire	1794
Zeichen *n*	signe *m*	1795
es folgt	ça suit	1796
folgen Sie	suivez	1797
immer / stets / ständig	toujours / constamment	1798
stets das Gleiche	toujours le (la) même	1799
ohne	sans	1800
ohne zu wechseln	sans changer	1801
ohne davonzurennen	sans courir	1802
durchgehend / ohne Unterbrechung	sans s'arrêter / sans interruptions	1803
ohne Wiederholung	sans reprise	1804
ohne Instrumente	sans instruments	1805
getrennt	séparé	1806
man nehme weg	on enlève	1807
gleich	semblable / pareil	1808
bis / zu	jusque	1809
gewohnt / auf gewohnte Weise	habituel	1810
allein	seul	1811
nur	seulement	1812
höchst	suprême	1813
auf / über / oben	dessus	1814
vor allem / überhaupt	surtout	1815
Dämpfer *m*	sourdine *f*	1816
unter	dessous / sous	1817
oft / oftmals / häufig	souvent	1818
Verschiebung *f*	déplacement *m*	1819
sehr genau	strictement	1820
auf / auf der / auf die / auf das	sur / sur le / sur la	1821
sofort / unmittelbar / sogleich	immédiatement / tout de suite	1822
schweige / nicht mitwirken / pausiere	tais-toi	1823
schweigen / nicht mitwirken / pausieren	se taire	1824
solch	tel	1825
ein bißchen	un tantinet	1826

1827	tanto	so / so much / many
1828	tempo precedente	preceding tempo
1829	tenendo	holding
1830	tenete / mantenete	keep on
1831	tenuto	held
1832	trillato	shaken
1833	triplo	triple
1834	troppo	too much
1835	troppo poco	not enough
1836	tutta	all
1837	tutta la forza	all the force
1838	tutte / tutti	everybody
1839	tutto	all
1840	udibile	audible
1841	uguale / eguale	equal
1842	ultima volta	last time
1843	ultimo / ultima	last
1844	un'altra volta	another time
1845	una volta	once
1846	unico	unique / sole
1847	unito / unitamente / nello stesso tempo	together / at the same time
1848	un pochettino / un pochino	a very little
1849	un poco	a little / somewhat
1850	un poco più	a little more
1851	variabile / variante	variable / varying
1852	variato	varied
1853	vicendevole	alternate
1854	vide (L)	see
1855	…volta	…times
1856	volta subito	turn the page immediately
1857	volti	turn
1858	vuoto	empty

Teoria musicale — Music theory

1859	a due voci	two voices
1860	a forma aperta	through composed

so viel / so sehr	tant / autant	1827
voriges Zeitmaß	tempo précédent	1828
haltend	en tenant	1829
halten Sie	tenez / gardez / maintenez	1830
gehalten / ausgehalten	tenu / lourré	1831
getrillert	trillé	1832
dreifach	triple	1833
zu viel	trop	1834
nicht genug	trop peu	1835
die ganze	toute	1836
die ganze Kraft	de toutes ses forces	1837
alle	toutes / tous	1838
all / alles / ganz	tout	1839
hörbar	audible	1840
gleich / gleichmäßig	égal	1841
letztes Mal	dernière fois	1842
letzter / letzte	dernier / dernière	1843
ein anderes Mal	une autre fois	1844
einmal	une fois	1845
einzig	unique	1846
gleichzeitig / zusammen	uni / en même temps	1847
ein klein wenig	un petit peu	1848
ein wenig / etwas	un peu	1849
ein wenig mehr	un peu plus	1850
veränderlich	variable	1851
variiert / verändert	varié	1852
abwechselnd	alternativement	1853
siehe	vois	1854
…fach / …mal	…fois	1855
sofort umblättern	tournez aussitôt	1856
blättere um	tournez	1857
leer	vide	1858

Musiktheorie — Théorie musicale

zweistimmig	à deux voix	1859
durchkomponiert	de forme ouverte	1860

1861	a più voci / a molte parti	in many parts
1862	a quattro voci	four voices
1863	a tre voci	three voices
1864	abbellimento *m*	embellishment
1865	abbellito	embellished
1866	abbreviatura *f* / abbreviazione *f*	abbreviation
1867	accento *m*	stress / accent
1868	accento principale	main accent
1869	accento secondario	secondary accent
1870	acciaccatura *f*	crushed note / short appoggiatura
1871	acciaccatura doppia *f*	slide
1872	accidente *m* / alterazione *f*	accidental / alteration
1873	accollatura *f*	brace / bracket
1874	accordo *m*	chord
1875	accordo di passaggio *m*	passing chord
1876	accordo di settima di dominante *m*	dominant seventh chord
1877	accordo perfetto *m*	common chord
1878	accordo spezzato *m*	broken chord
1879	agogica *f*	agogic
1880	alterato	altered
1881	altezza del suono *f*	pitch / pitch level
1882	anacrusi *f*	anacrusis
1883	analisi *f*	analysis
1884	andamento *m*	fugal episode
1885	antecedente *m*	antecedent
1886	anticipazione *f*	anticipation
1887	appoggiatura *f*	grace-note
1888	appoggiatura doppia *f*	double appoggiatura
1889	armatura di chiave *f*	key signature
1890	armonia *f*	harmony
1891	armonico	harmonic
1892	arpeggio *m*	arpeggio / battery
1893	arsi *f*	arsis
1894	ascendente	ascending
1895	atonale	atonal

mehrstimmig	à plusieurs voix / à plusieurs parties	1861
vierstimmig	à quatre voix	1862
dreistimmig	à trois voix	1863
Verzierung *f*	agrément *m* / broderie *f*	1864
verziert	ornementé	1865
Kürzung *f* / Verkürzung *f*	abréviation *f*	1866
Akzent *m* / Betonung *f* / Schwerpunkt *m*	accent *m*	1867
Hauptbetonung *f*	accent principal *m*	1868
Nebenbetonung *f*	accent secondaire *m*	1869
kurzer Vorschlag *m* / Quetschung *f*	appogiature brève *f* / pincé étouffé *m*	1870
Schleifer *m*	coulé *m*	1871
Versetzungszeichen *n* / Vorzeichen *n* / Alteration *f*	altération *f* / accident *m*	1872
Klammer *f*	accolade *f*	1873
Akkord *m*	accord *m*	1874
Durchgangsakkord *m*	accord de passage *m*	1875
Dominantseptakkord *m*	accord de séptième de dominante *m*	1876
Dreiklang *m*	accord parfait *m*	1877
gebrochener Akkord *m*	accord brisé *m*	1878
Agogik *f*	agogique *f*	1879
verändert / alteriert	altéré	1880
Tonhöhe *f*	hauteur du son *f*	1881
Anakrusis *f* / Auftakt *m*	anacrouse *f*	1882
Analyse *f*	analyse *f*	1883
Fugen-Zwischenspiel *n* / längeres Fugenthema *n*	divertissement *m*	1884
Dux *m* / Führer *m*	antécédent *m*	1885
Antizipation *f* / Vorausnahme *f*	anticipation *f*	1886
Vorschlag *m*	appoggiature *f*	1887
Doppelvorschlag *m*	appoggiature double *f*	1888
Tonartvorzeichnung *f* / Vorzeichen *n*	armure de la clé *f* / armature *f*	1889
Harmonie *f*	harmonie *f*	1890
harmonisch	harmonique	1891
Arpeggio *n*	arpège *m*	1892
Arsis *f* / Hebung *f*	arsis *f*	1893
aufsteigend	ascendant	1894
atonal	atonal	1895

1896	aumentato / eccedente	raised / augmented
1897	aumentazione *f* / aggravamento *m*	augmentation
1898	autentico	authentic
1899	basso cifrato m / basso numerato *m*	figured bass
1900	basso continuo	through-bass
1901	basso ostinato *m*	ground bass
1902	battuta *f*	beat / bar
1903	battuta composta *f*	compound time
1904	battuta semplice *f*	simple time
1905	bemolle *m*	flat
1906	bequadro *m*	natural
1907	binario	binary
1908	bitonalità *f*	bitonality
1909	bordone *m*	bourdon
1910	cadenza *f*	cadenza / cadence
1911	cadenza evitata *f* / cadenza d'inganno *f*	delusive cadence / deceptive cadence (Am.)
1912	cadenza finale *f*	final cadenza
1913	cadenza imperfetta *f*	imperfect cadence / half-close
1914	cadenza perfetta *f*	perfect cadence / authentic cadence
1915	cadenza plagale *f*	plagal cadence
1916	cadenza sospesa *f*	delayed cadence
1917	cambiamento di tempo *m* / cambio di misura *m*	change of time / change of meter
1918	cambio di tonalità *m*	key change
1919	canto fermo *m*	cantus firmus
1920	cesura *f*	caesura
1921	chiave *f*	clef
1922	chiave di baritono *f*	baritone clef
1923	chiave di basso *f*	bass clef
1924	chiave di contralto *f*	alto clef
1925	chiave di do *f*	C clef
1926	chiave di mezzosoprano *f*	mezzo-soprano clef
1927	chiave di soprano *f*	soprano clef

übermäßig / hochalteriert	augmenté	1896
Vergrößerung *f* (der Zeitwerte)	augmentation *f*	1897
authentisch	authentique	1898
bezifferter Bass *m* / Generalbass *m*	basse chiffrée f	1899
Generalbass *m*	basse continue *f*	1900
Basso ostinato *m* / Ostinato *m*	basse obstinée *f* / basse contrainte *f*	1901
Schlag *m* / Takt *m* / Taktschlag *m*	mesure *f*	1902
zusammengesetzter Takt *m*	mesure composée *f*	1903
einfacher Takt	mesure simple *f*	1904
B *n* / Erniedrigungszeichen *n*	bémol *m*	1905
Auflösungszeichen *n*	bécarre *m*	1906
zweiteilig	binaire	1907
Bitonalität *f*	bitonalité *f*	1908
Bordun *m*	bourdon *m*	1909
Kadenz *f*	cadence *f*	1910
Trugschluss *m*	cadence rompue *f*	1911
Schlusskadenz *f*	cadence finale *f*	1912
Halbschluss *m*	cadence suspendue *f* / demi-cadence *f*	1913
authentische Kadenz *f* / vollkommene Kadenz *f* / Ganzschluss *m*	cadence parfaite *f*	1914
plagale Kadenz *f*	cadence plagale *f*	1915
unvollkommene Kadenz *f* / Halbkadenz *f*	cadence suspendue *f* / cadence interrompue *f*	1916
Taktwechsel *m*	changement de mesure *m* / changement de temps *m*	1917
Tonartwechsel *m*	changement de tonalité *m*	1918
Cantus firmus *m*	cantus firmus *m*	1919
Zäsur *f*	césure *f*	1920
Schlüssel *m*	clé *f* / clef *f*	1921
Baritonschlüssel *m*	clé de fa troisième ligne *f*	1922
Bassschlüssel *m*	clé de fa quatrième ligne *f*	1923
Altschlüssel *m*	clé d'ut troisième ligne *f*	1924
C-Schlüssel *m*	clé d'ut *f*	1925
Mezzosopranschlüssel *m*	clé d'ut seconde ligne *f*	1926
Sopranschlüssel *m*	clé d'ut première ligne *f*	1927

1928	chiave di tenore *f*	tenor clef
1929	chiave di violino *f*	treble clef
1930	chiusa del trillo *f*	termination of trill
1931	cifrare	to figure
1932	cifratura *f*	figuring / figuration
1933	circolo delle quinte *m*	circle of fifths
1934	codetta *f*	tail / flag
1935	comma *m*	comma
1936	conclusione *f*	conclusion
1937	condotta delle parti *f*	linear construction
1938	condotta delle voci *f*	part-writing / voice-leading
1939	congiunto	by step / conjunct
1940	consonanza *f*	consonance
1941	contrappunto *m*	counterpoint
1942	contrappunto fiorito *m* / contrappunto florido *m*	florid counterpoint
1943	controsoggetto *m*	counter subject
1944	contrattempo *m*	syncopation
1945	controcanto m / controtema *m*	counter voice / counter part / counter melody
1946	corona *f*	pause / fermata
1947	cromatico	chromatic
1948	cromatismo *m*	chromaticism
1949	dattilo *m*	dactyl
1950	dettato *m*	dictation
1951	dettato musicale *m*	music dictation
1952	diatonico	diatonic
1953	diatonismo *m*	diatonicism
1954	diesis *m*	sharp
1955	diminuito	diminished
1956	diminuzione *f*	diminution
1957	discendente	descending
1958	dissonanza *f*	dissonance
1959	dodecafonia *f*	twelve-tone music
1960	dominante *f*	dominant
1961	dominante di passaggio *f* / dominante secondaria *f*	secondary dominant
1962	doppia stanghetta *f*	double bar

Tenorschlüssel *m*	clé d'ut quatrième ligne *f*	1928
Violinschlüssel *m*	clé de sol *f*	1929
Nachschlag *m*	gruppetto final *m* / terminaison *f*	1930
beziffern	chiffrer	1931
Bezifferung *f*	chiffrage *f*	1932
Quintenzirkel *m*	cycle des quintes *m*	1933
Notenfahne *f* / Fähnchen *n*	crochet *m*	1934
Komma *n*	comma *m*	1935
Schlusssatz *m* / Abschluss *m* / Beschluss *m*	conclusion *f*	1936
Linienführung *f*	construction linéaire *f*	1937
Stimmführung *f*	conduite des voix *f*	1938
schrittweise / stufenweise	conjoint	1939
Konsonanz *f*	consonance *f*	1940
Kontrapunkt *m*	contrepoint *m*	1941
„blühender" Kontrapunkt *m*	contrepoint fleuri *m*	1942
Kontrasubjekt *n* / Gegenthema *n* / Gegensatz *m*	contresujet *m*	1943
Gegenzeit *f* (Betonung auf dem schlechten Taktteil)	contre-temps *m*	1944
Gegenstimme *f*	contre-chant *m*	1945
Fermate *f*	point d'arrêt *m* / point d'orgue *m*	1946
chromatisch	chromatique	1947
Chromatik *f*	chromatisme *m*	1948
Daktylos *m*	dactyle *m*	1949
Diktat *n*	dictée *f*	1950
Musikdiktat *n*	dictée musicale *f*	1951
diatonisch	diatonique	1952
Diatonik *f*	diatonisme *m*	1953
Kreuz *n* / Erhöhungszeichen *n*	dièse *m*	1954
vermindert	diminué	1955
Verkleinerung *f* (der Notenwerte)	diminution *f*	1956
absteigend	descendant	1957
Dissonanz *f*	dissonance *f*	1958
Zwölftontechnik *f*	dodécaphonisme *m*	1959
Dominante *f*	dominante *f*	1960
Zwischendominante *f*	dominante de passage *f*	1961
Doppelstrich *m*	double barre *f*	1962

1963	doppio bemolle *m*	double flat
1964	doppio diesis *m*	double sharp
1965	dorico	dorian
1966	duina *f*	duplet
1967	durata del suono *f*	sound duration
1968	enarmonico	enharmonic
1969	entrata *f*	entry
1970	eolio	aeolian
1971	episodio *m*	episode
1972	esacordo *m*	hexachord
1973	esposizione *f*	exposition
1974	falsa relazione *f*	false relation
1975	falso bordone *m*	faburden / fauxbourdon
1976	figura *f*	figure
1977	figurato	figured
1978	fioritura *f*	embellishment
1979	fondamentale	fundamental
1980	forma *f*	form
1981	forma binaria *f*	binary form
1982	forma ciclica *f*	cyclic form
1983	forma ternaria *f*	ternary form
1984	frase *f*	phrase
1985	fraseggio *m*	phrasing
1986	frigio	phrygian
1987	fugato	in fugal style
1988	funzione *f*	function
1989	gambo *m*	stem
1990	giambo *m*	iamb
1991	giusto	perfect
1992	grado *m*	degree
1993	gruppetto m / groppo *m*	turn
1994	gruppo di suoni m / gruppo di note *m*	note cluster / tone cluster
1995	hemiolia *f*	hemiola
1996	imitazione *f*	imitation
1997	imperfetto	imperfect
1998	in battere	downbeat
1999	in levare / levata *f*	up beat
2000	intavolatura *f*	tablature
2001	intervallo *m*	interval

Doppel-B *n*	double bémol *m*	1963
Doppelkreuz *n*	double dièse *m*	1964
dorisch	dorien	1965
Duole *f*	duolet *m*	1966
Tonlänge *f* / Tondauer *f*	durée du son *f*	1967
enharmonisch	enharmonique	1968
Einsatz *m*	entrée *f*	1969
äolisch	éolien	1970
Episode *f* / Zwischensatz *m*	épisode *m*	1971
Hexachord *n*	hexacorde *m*	1972
Exposition *f*	exposition *f*	1973
Querstand *m*	fausse relation *f*	1974
Fauxbourdon *m*	faux-bourdon *m*	1975
Figur *f*	figure *f*	1976
figuriert	figuré	1977
Blume *f* (Verzierung)	fioriture *f*	1978
wesentlich	fondamental	1979
Form *f* / Gestalt *f*	forme *f*	1980
zweiteilige Form *f*	forme binaire *f*	1981
zyklische Form *f*	forme cyclique *f*	1982
dreiteilige Form *f*	forme ternaire *f*	1983
Phrase *f*	phrase *f*	1984
Phrasierung *f*	phrasé	1985
phrygisch	phrygien	1986
fugenartig	fugué	1987
Funktion *f*	fonction *f*	1988
Notenhals *m*	hampe *f* / queue de la note *f*	1989
Jambus *m*	jambus *m*	1990
richtig	juste	1991
Stufe *f* / Schritt *m*	degré *m*	1992
Doppelschlag *m*	doublé *m* / double cadence *f*	1993
Tontraube *f* / Tonballung *f*	groupe de sons *m* / groupe de notes *m*	1994
Hemiole *f*	hemiolios *m*	1995
Imitation *f* / Nachahmung *f*	imitation *f*	1996
unvollkommen	imparfait	1997
abtaktig	frappé	1998
Aufschlag *m* / Auftakt *m*	sur la levée / levée *f*	1999
Tabulatur *f*	tablature *f*	2000
Intervall *n* / Abstand *m*	intervalle *m*	2001

2002	intonazione *f*	intonation / pitch
2003	ionico	ionian
2004	legatura *f*	slur
2005	legatura di fraseggio *f*	phrase mark
2006	legatura di valore *f*	tie
2007	lidio	lydian
2008	maggiore	major
2009	mano guidoniana *f*	guidonian hand
2010	mediante *f*	mediant
2011	melodia *f*	melody / tune
2012	melodico	melodic
2013	metrico	metric(al)
2014	metro *m*	metre
2015	mettere il punto di valore	to dot
2016	minore	minor
2017	misolidio	mixolydian
2018	misura *f*	bar / measure / mensuration
2019	modale	modal
2020	modalità *f*	modality
2021	modo *m*	mode / modus
2022	modo ecclesiastico *m*	church mode
2023	modulare	to modulate
2024	modulazione *f*	modulation
2025	modulazione di transizione *f*	temporary modulation
2026	monodia *f* / monofonia *f*	monody / monophony
2027	mordente *m*	mordent / shake
2028	mordente inferiore *m*	mordent
2029	mordente superiore *m*	inverted mordent / mordent with note above
2030	motivo *m*	motif
2031	motivo conduttore *m* / motivo ricorrente *m*	leading motif
2032	moto contrario *m*	contrary motion
2033	moto obliquo *m*	oblique motion
2034	moto retto *m*	parallel motion
2035	movimento *m* / tempo *m*	movement
2036	movimento parallelo *m*	parallel movement
2037	neuma *m*	neuma / neume
2038	nota *f*	note
2039	nota ausiliare *f*	auxiliary note

Intonation *f* / Stimmung *f* / Tongebung *f*	intonation *f*	2002
ionisch	ionien	2003
Bindebogen *m*	liaison *f*	2004
Phrasierungsbogen *m*	signe de liaison du phrasé *m*	2005
Haltebogen *m*	signe de tenue *m*	2006
lydisch	lydien	2007
Dur	majeur	2008
Guidonische Hand *f*	main guidonienne *f*	2009
Mediante *f*	médiante *f*	2010
Melodie *f*	mélodie *f*	2011
melodisch	mélodique	2012
metrisch	métrique	2013
Metrum *n*	mètre *m*	2014
punktieren	pointer	2015
Moll / klein (Intervall)	mineur	2016
mixolydisch	mixo-lydien	2017
Takt *m* / Mensur *f* / Metrum *n*	mesure *f*	2018
modal	modal	2019
Modalität *f*	modalité *f*	2020
Tongeschlecht *n* / Modus *m*	mode *m*	2021
Kirchentonart *f*	mode ecclésiastique *m*	2022
modulieren	moduler	2023
Modulation *f*	modulation *f*	2024
Ausweichung *f*	modulation passagère *f*	2025
Monodie *f* / Einstimmigkeit *f*	monodie *f*	2026
Mordent *m*	mordant *m* / battement *m*	2027
Mordent *m*	mordant *m* / pincé *m*	2028
Pralltriller *m* / Schneller *m* / Praller *m*	mordant supérieur *m*	2029
Motiv *n*	motif *m*	2030
Leitmotiv *n*	motif conducteur *m* / idée fixe *f*	2031
Gegenbewegung *f*	mouvement contraire *m*	2032
Seitenbewegung *f*	mouvement oblique *m*	2033
Parallelbewegung *f*	mouvement parallèle *m*	2034
Satz *m*	mouvement *m*	2035
Parallelführung *f*	mouvement parallèle *m*	2036
Neumen *f pl*	neume *f*	2037
Note *f*	note *f*	2038
Nebennote *f*	note secondaire *f*	2039

2040	nota cambiata *f*	changing note
2041	nota di passaggio *f*	passing note
2042	nota principale *f*	essential note
2043	nota puntata *f*	dotted note
2044	notazione *f*	notation
2045	notina *f*	cue note
2046	numero di battute *m*	bar number / measure number
2047	obbligato	obbligato
2048	omofonia *f*	homophony
2049	orchestrazione *f*	orchestration
2050	orizzontale	horizontal
2051	ornamento *m* / adornamento *m*	ornament
2052	parallele nascoste *f pl*	hidden consecutives
2053	parallelo	parallel
2054	parte estrema *f* / voce estrema *f*	outer part
2055	parte inferiore *f* / voce inferiore	lower part / lowest part
2056	parte intermedia *f* / voce intermedia *f*	middle part / inner part
2057	parte melodica *f*	melody part
2058	parte superiore *f* / voce superiore *f*	upper part / top part
2059	passaggio *m*	passage / transition
2060	pausa *f* / silenzio *m*	rest
2061	pausa generale *f* / vuoto *m*	general pause
2062	pedale d'armonia *m*	pedal point
2063	pentagramma *m*	staves / system
2064	pèntatonico	pentatonic
2065	periodo *m*	period
2066	plagale	plagal
2067	policoralità *f* / polifonia policorale *f*	polychoral music
2068	polifonia *f*	polyphony
2069	polimetria *f*	polymetre
2070	poliritmica *f*	polyrhythm
2071	politonalità *f*	polytonality

Wechselnote *f* / Wechselton *m*	cambiata *f* / note changée *f*	2040
Durchgangsnote *f* / Durchgangston *m*	note de passage *f*	2041
Hauptnote *f*	note principale *f*	2042
punktierte Note *f*	note pointée *f*	2043
Notation *f* / Notenschrift *f*	notation *f*	2044
Stichnote *f*	petite note *f*	2045
Taktzahl *f*	nombre de mesures *m*	2046
obligat	obligé	2047
Homophonie *f*	homophonie *f*	2048
Orchestration *f* / Orchestrierung *f*	orchestration *f*	2049
waagrecht / horizontal	horizontal	2050
Verzierung *f* / Ornament *n*	ornement *m* / broderie *f*	2051
verdeckte Parallelen *f Pl*	parallèles cachées *f pl*	2052
parallel	parallèle	2053
Außenstimme *f*	voix extrême *f* / partie extrême *f*	2054
Unterstimme *f*	voix inférieure *f* / partie inférieure *f*	2055
Mittelstimme *f* / Innenstimme *f*	voix intermédiaire *f* / voix intérieure *f*	2056
Melodiestimme *f*	partie mélodique *f*	2057
Oberstimme *f*	voix supérieure *f* / partie supérieure *f* / partie de dessus *f*	2058
Passage *f* / Durchgang *m* / Überleitung *f*	passage *m* / transition *f*	2059
Pause *f*	pause *f* / silence *m*	2060
Generalpause *f*	pause générale *f*	2061
Orgelpunkt *m*	pédale inférieure *f*	2062
Liniensystem *n* / Fünfliniensystem *n*	portée *f*	2063
pentatonisch	pentatonique	2064
Periode *f*	période *f*	2065
plagal	plagal	2066
Mehrchörigkeit *f*	pluralité des chœurs *f*	2067
Polyphonie *f* / Mehrstimmigkeit *f*	polyphonie *f*	2068
Polymetrik *f*	polymétrie *f*	2069
Polyrhythmik *f*	polyrythmie *f*	2070
Polytonalität *f*	polytonalité *f*	2071

2072	ponte *m*	bridge
2073	posizione fondamentale *f*	fondamental position
2074	posizione lata *f*	open / extended position
2075	posizione stretta *f*	close position
2076	preparazione *f*	preparation
2077	prima frase *f*	first phrase
2078	primo tema *m* / tema principale *m*	main theme
2079	primo tempo *m*	first movement
2080	principale	main
2081	progressione *f*	progression
2082	proposta *f*	antecedent
2083	puntato	dotted
2084	punto di valore *m*	dot
2085	punto doppio *m*	double dot
2086	quartina *f*	quadruplet
2087	quarto tempo *m*	fourth movement
2088	quintina *f*	quintuplet
2089	quinto tempo *m*	fifth movement
2090	raddoppio *m*	doubling
2091	realizzazione *f*	realization
2092	relativo / affine	relative
2093	relazione *f* / affinità *f*	relationship
2094	retrogrado	retrograde
2095	rigo *m* / linea *f*	line
2096	ripetizione *f* / ripresa *f*	repetition / repeat
2097	ripresa *f* / riesposizione *f*	repeat / recapitulation / return
2098	risoluzione *f*	resolution
2099	risposta *f* / conseguente *m*	answer / consequent
2100	risposta reale *f*	real answer
2101	risposta tonale *f*	tonal answer
2102	ritardo *m*	suspension / retardation
2103	ritmo *m*	rhythm
2104	ritmo lombardo *m*	scotch snap
2105	ritornello *m*	refrain
2106	riverso	backwards
2107	rivolto *m* / rovescio *m*	inversion
2108	salmodia *f*	psalmody
2109	scala *f*	scale

Überleitung *f*	transition *f* / pont *m*	2072
Grundstellung *f*	position fondamentale *f*	2073
weite Lage *f*	position large *f*	2074
enge Lage *f*	position serrée *f*	2075
Vorbereitung *f*	préparation *f*	2076
Vordersatz *m*	proposition *f*	2077
Hauptthema *n*	thème principal *m*	2078
erster Satz *m* / Kopfsatz *m*	premier mouvement *m*	2079
Haupt-...	principal	2080
Fortschreitung *f*	progression *f*	2081
Proposta *f*	proposition *f* / antécédent *m*	2082
punktiert	pointé	2083
Punkt *m*	point *m*	2084
Doppelpunkt *m*	double point *m*	2085
Quartole *f*	quartolet *m*	2086
vierter Satz *m*	quatrième mouvement *m*	2087
Quintole *f*	quintolet *m*	2088
fünfter Satz *m*	cinquième mouvement *m*	2089
Verdopplung *f*	redoublement *m*	2090
Aussetzung *f* (eines bezifferten Basses)	réalisation *f*	2091
verwandt / bezüglich (Paralleltonart)	relatif	2092
Verwandtschaft *f*	relation *f*	2093
krebsgängig / rückwärtsgehend	rétrograde	2094
Linie *f*	ligne *f*	2095
Wiederholung *f*	répétition *f* / reprise *f*	2096
Reprise *f* / Wiederkehr *f*	reprise *f* / réexposition *f*	2097
Auflösung *f* (einer Dissonanz)	résolution *f*	2098
Antwort *f* / Comes *m*	réponse *f* / conséquent *m*	2099
reale Antwort *f*	réponse réelle *f*	2100
tonale Antwort *f*	réponse tonale *f*	2101
Verzögerung *f* / Vorhalt *m*	retard *m*	2102
Rhythmus *m*	rythme *m*	2103
lombardischer Rhythmus *m*	rythme lombard *m*	2104
Refrain *m* / Kehrreim *m*	refrain *m*	2105
von rückwärts	à la renverse	2106
Umkehrung *f*	inversion *f*	2107
Psalmodie *f*	psalmodie *f*	2108
Tonleiter *f*	gamme *f*	2109

2110	scala esatonale *f*	whole-tone scale
2111	secondario	secondary
2112	secondo tema *m* / tema secondario *m*	second theme / secondary subject
2113	secondo tempo *m*	second movement
2114	segno d'espressione *m*	expression mark
2115	segno dinamico *m*	dynamic sign / dynamic mark
2116	segno di ripetizione *m* / segno di ritornello *m*	repeat sign
2117	semitono *m*	semitone
2118	sensibile *f*	leading note / leading tone
2119	sequenza *f*	sequence
2120	serie *f*	series / row
2121	sesta napolitana *f*	neapolitan sixth
2122	sestina *f*	sextuplet
2123	settima di dominante *f*	dominant seventh
2124	settimina *f*	septuplet
2125	sincope *f*	syncopation
2126	sistema tonale *m*	tonal system / tone system
2127	soggetto *m*	subject
2128	solfeggio *m*	tonic sol-fa
2129	solmisazione *f*	solmization
2130	sostituzione enarmonica *f*	enharmonic change
2131	sottodominante *f*	subdominant
2132	sovrapposizione *f*	superimposition
2133	spazio *m*	space
2134	stanghetta *f* / barra *f*	beam / bar-line / ligature
2135	stretta *f*	stretto
2136	stretto *m*	stretto
2137	strofa *f*	verse
2138	strumentazione *f*	instrumentation
2139	struttura *f* / costruzione *f*	structure / construction
2140	successione *f*	succession
2141	successioni parallele *f pl*	consecutives
2142	suono *m*	sound
2143	suono fondamentale *m*	fundamental / tonic
2144	suono simpatico *m*	sympathetic tone
2145	suoni armonici *m pl* / flautato	harmonics

Ganztonleiter *f*	gamme par tons *f*	2110
neben	secondaire	2111
Seitenthema *n*	second thème *m* / thème secondaire *m*	2112
zweiter Satz *n*	deuxième mouvement *m*	2113
Vortragsbezeichnung *f* / Ausdrucksbezeichnung *f*	signe d'interprétation *m* / signe d'expression *m*	2114
dynamisches Zeichen *n*	signe dynamique *m*	2115
Wiederholungszeichen n	signe de répétition *m*	2116
Halbton *m*	demi-ton *m*	2117
Leitton *m*	sensible *f*	2118
Sequenz *f*	sequence *f*	2119
Reihe *f* / Tonreihe *f*	série *f*	2120
neapolitanische Sexte *f*	sixte napolitaine *f*	2121
Sextole *f*	sextolet *m*	2122
Dominantseptime *f*	septième de dominante *f*	2123
Septole *f*	septolet *m*	2124
Synkope *f*	syncope *f*	2125
Tonsystem *n*	système tonal *m*	2126
Subjekt *n* / Dux *m*	sujet *m*	2127
Solfeggio *n*	solfège *m*	2128
Solmisation *f*	solmisation *f*	2129
enharmonische Verwechslung *f*	substitution enharmonique *f*	2130
Subdominante *f*	sous-dominante *f*	2131
Schichtung *f*	superposition *f*	2132
Zwischenraum *m*	interligne *m*	2133
Notenbalken *m* / Taktstrich *m*	barre de mesure *f*	2134
schneller Schlussteil *m*	strette *f*	2135
Engführung *f*	strette *f*	2136
Strophe *f*	strophe *f* / couplet *m*	2137
Instrumentierung *f*	instrumentation *f*	2138
Aufbau *m* / Struktur *f*	construction *f* / structure *f*	2139
Folge *f*	succession *f*	2140
Parallelen *f Pl*	successions parallèles *f pl*	2141
Klang *m* / Schall *m*	son *m*	2142
Grundton *m* / Tonika *f*	son fondamental *m*	2143
Eigenton *m*	vibration sympathique *f*	2144
Obertöne *m Pl* / Flageolett-Töne *m pl*	sons harmoniques *m pl*	2145

2146	suoni naturali *m pl*	natural notes / natural tones
2147	suoni parziali *m pl*	partials
2148	sviluppo *m* / svolgimento *m*	development
2149	taglio addizionale *m* / righetta *f*	leger line
2150	tema *m*	theme
2151	temperamento *m*	equal temperament
2152	tempo *m*	speed / time / pace / metre
2153	tempo *m*	time signature
2154	tempo binario *m* / tempo pari *m*	duple time
2155	tempo debole *m*	off-beat / weak beat
2156	tempo forte *m*	strong beat / accentuated beat
2157	tempo ternario *m* / tempo dispari *m*	triple time
2158	ternario	ternary
2159	terza picarda *f*	picardy third
2160	terzina *f*	triplet
2161	terzo tempo *m*	third movement
2162	tesi *f*	thesis
2163	tetracordo *m*	tetrachord
2164	tonale	tonal
2165	tonalità *f*	tonality
2166	tonalità affine *f*	related key
2167	tonalità relativa *f*	related key
2168	tonica *f*	tonic / key-note
2169	tono *m*	tone / key
2170	tono intero *m*	whole tone
2171	tono naturale *m*	pure tone
2172	tono secondario *m*	neighbour note
2173	transizione *f*	transition
2174	trasporto *m*	transposition
2175	trattato d'armonia *m*	theory of harmony
2176	tratto d'unione *m*	cross / beam
2177	triade *f*	triad
2178	trillo *m*	trill / shake
2179	tritono *m*	tritone
2180	ultimo tempo *m* / ultimo movimento *m*	last movement

Naturtöne *m Pl*	sons ouverts *m pl* / sons naturels *m pl*	2146
Teiltöne *m Pl*	sons partiels *m pl*	2147
Entwicklung *f* / Durchführung *f*	développement *m*	2148
Hilfslinie *f*	ligne supplémentaire *f*	2149
Thema *n*	thème *m*	2150
Temperatur *f* / temperierte Stimmung *f*	tempérament *m*	2151
Zeitmaß *n* / Zählzeit *f*	temps *m* / mesure *f*	2152
Taktart *f*	indication de la mesure *f*	2153
gerader Takt *m*	mesure binaire *f*	2154
schwacher Taktteil *m* / schlechter Taktteil *m*	temps faible *m*	2155
starker Taktteil *m* / schwerer Taktteil *m*	temps fort *m*	2156
ungerader Takt *m*	mesure ternaire *f*	2157
dreiteilig	ternaire	2158
picardische Terz *f*	tierce picarde *f*	2159
Triole *f*	triolet *m*	2160
dritter Satz *m*	troisième mouvement *m*	2161
Thesis *f* / Senkung *f*	thésis *f*	2162
Tetrachord *m*	tétracorde *m*	2163
tonal	tonal	2164
Tonalität *f* / Tonart *f*	tonalité *f*	2165
verwandte Tonart *f*	tonalité voisine *f*	2166
Paralleltonart *f*	tonalité relative *f*	2167
Tonika *f* / Grundton *m*	tonique *f*	2168
Ton *m* / Tonart *f*	ton *m* / tonalité *f*	2169
Ganzton *m*	ton entier *m*	2170
reiner Ton *m*	ton naturel *m*	2171
Nebenton *m*	ton concomittant *m*	2172
Übergang *m* / Durchgang *m*	transition *f*	2173
Transposition *f* / Transponierung *f*	transposition *f*	2174
Harmonielehre *f*	traité d'harmonie *m*	2175
Notenbalken *m* / Querbalken *m*	barre transversale *f*	2176
Dreiklang *m*	triade *f*	2177
Triller *m*	trille *m* / tremblement *m*	2178
Tritonus *m*	triton *m*	2179
Schlusssatz *m*	dernier mouvement *m*	2180

2181	unisono (all') *m*	in unison
2182	valore *m*	value
2183	valore della nota *m*	note value
2184	valore della pausa *m*	rest value
2185	veloce passaggio di note *m*	run / quick passage
2186	verticale	vertical
2187	voce di ripieno *f* / parte di ripieno *f*	filling-in part
2188	voce principale *f*	principal part / principal voice

	Note	**Notes**
2189	Do *m*	C
2190	Do diesis *m*	C sharp
2191	Do bemolle *m*	C flat
2192	Do doppio diesis *m*	C double sharp
2193	Do doppio bemolle *m*	C double flat
2194	Re *m*	D
2195	Re diesis *m*	D sharp
2196	Re bemolle *m*	D flat
2197	Re doppio diesis *m*	D double sharp
2198	Re doppio bemolle *m*	D double flat
2199	Mi *m*	E
2200	Mi diesis *m*	E sharp
2201	Mi bemolle *m*	E flat
2202	Mi doppio diesis *m*	E double sharp
2203	Mi doppio bemolle *m*	E double flat
2204	Fa *m*	F
2205	Fa diesis *m*	F sharp
2206	Fa bemolle *m*	F flat
2207	Fa doppio diesis *m*	F double sharp
2208	Fa doppio bemolle *m*	F double flat
2209	Sol *m*	G
2210	Sol diesis *m*	G sharp
2211	Sol bemolle *m*	G flat
2212	Sol doppio diesis *m*	G double sharp
2213	Sol doppio bemolle *m*	G double flat
2214	La *m*	A
2215	La diesis *m*	A sharp

im Einklang *m*	à l'unisson *m*	2181
Wert *m*	valeur *f*	2182
Notenwert *m*	valeur de la note *f*	2183
Pausenwert *m*	valeur de la pause *f*	2184
Lauf *m*	passage rapide de notes *m*	2185
senkrecht / vertikal	vertical	2186
Füllstimme *f*	voix de remplissage *f* / parties de remplissage *f pl*	2187
Hauptstimme *f*	partie principale *f* / voix principale *f*	2188

Noten	**Notes**	
C *n*	Do / Ut *m*	2189
Cis *n*	Do dièse *m*	2190
Ces *n*	Do bémol *m*	2191
Cisis *n*	Do double dièse *m*	2192
Ceses *n*	Do double bémol *m*	2193
D *n*	Ré *m*	2194
Dis *n*	Ré dièse *m*	2195
Des *n*	Ré bémol *m*	2196
Disis *n*	Ré double dièse *m*	2197
Deses *n*	Ré double bémol *m*	2198
E *n*	Mi *m*	2199
Eis *n*	Mi dièse *m*	2200
Es *n*	Mi bémol *m*	2201
Eisis *n*	Mi double dièse *m*	2202
Eses *n*	Mi double bémol *m*	2203
F *n*	Fa *m*	2204
Fis *n*	Fa dièse *m*	2205
Fes *n*	Fa bémol *m*	2206
Fisis *n*	Fa double dièse *m*	2207
Feses *n*	Fa double bémol *m*	2208
G *n*	Sol *m*	2209
Gis *n*	Sol dièse *m*	2210
Ges *n*	Sol bémol *m*	2211
Gisis *n*	Sol double dièse *m*	2212
Geses *n*	Sol double bémol *m*	2213
A *n*	La *m*	2214
Ais *n*	La dièse *m*	2215

2216	La bemolle *m*	A flat
2217	La doppio diesis *m*	A double sharp
2218	La doppio bemolle *m*	A double flat
2219	Si *m*	B
2220	Si diesis *m*	B sharp
2221	Si bemolle *m*	B flat
2222	Si doppio diesis *m*	B double sharp
2223	Si doppio bemolle *m*	B double flat

	Valori delle note	**Time value of notes**
2224	intero *m* / semibreve *f*	semibreve (E) / whole note (Am.)
2225	metà *f* / minima *f*	minim (E) / half note (Am.)
2226	quarto *m* / semiminima *f*	crotchet (E) / quarter note (Am.)
2227	ottavo *m* / croma *f*	quaver (E) / eighth note (Am.)
2228	sedicesimo *m* / semicroma *f*	semiquaver (E) / sixteenth note (Am.)
2229	trentaduesimo *m* / biscroma *f*	demisemiquaver (E) / thirty-second note (Am.)
2230	sessantaquattresimo *m* / semibiscroma *f*	hemidemisemiquaver (E) / sixty-fourth note (Am.)
2231	pausa di semibreve *f*	semibreve rest (E) / whole note rest (Am.)
2232	pausa di minima *f*	minim rest (E) / half note rest (Am.)
2233	pausa di semiminima *f*	crotchet rest (E) / quarter note rest (Am.)
2234	pausa di croma *f*	quaver rest (E) / eighth note rest (Am.)
2235	pausa di semicroma *f*	semiquaver rest (E) / sixteenth note rest (Am.)
2236	pausa di biscroma *f*	demisemiquaver rest (E) / thirty-second note rest (Am.)
2237	pausa di semibiscroma *f*	hemidemisemiquaver rest (E) / sixty-fourth note rest (Am.)

As *n*	La bémol *m*	2216
Aisis *n*	La double dièse *m*	2217
Ases *n*	La double bémol *m*	2218
H *n*	Si *m*	2219
His *n*	Si dièse *m*	2220
B *n*	Si bémol *m*	2221
Hisis *n*	Si double dièse *m*	2222
Heses *n*	Si double bémol *m*	2223

Notenwerte **Valeur des notes**

Ganze *f*	ronde *f*	2224
Halbe *f*	blanche *f*	2225
Viertel *f*	noire *f*	2226
Achtel *f*	croche *f*	2227
Sechzehntel *f*	double croche *f*	2228
Zweiunddreißigstel *f*	triple croche *f*	2229
Vierundsechzigstel *f*	quadruple croche *f*	2230
ganze Pause *f*	pause *f*	2231
halbe Pause *f*	demi-pause *f*	2232
Viertelpause *f*	soupir *m*	2233
Achtelpause *f*	demi-soupir *m*	2234
Sechzehntelpause *f*	quart de soupir *m*	2235
Zweiunddreißigstelpause *f*	huitième de soupir *m*	2236
Vierundsechzigstelpause *f*	seizième de soupir *m*	2237

	Intervalli	**Intervals**
2238	unisono *m*	unison (E) / prime (Am.)
2239	seconda *f*	second
2240	terza *f*	third
2241	quarta *f*	fourth
2242	quinta *f*	fifth
2243	sesta *f*	sixth
2244	settima *f*	seventh
2245	ottava *f*	octave
2246	nona *f*	ninth
2247	decima *f*	tenth

	Generi e forma	**Genres and forms**
2248	alba *f*	aubade (song at dawn)
2249	allemanda *f*	allemande / almand
2250	antifona *f*	antiphon
2251	arabesca *f*	arabesque
2252	aria *f*	air / aria
2253	aria concertante *f*	concert aria
2254	aria d'opera *f*	operatic aria
2255	aria di bravura *f*	bravura aria
2256	aria di coloratura *f*	coloratura aria
2257	aria di corte *f*	court song
2258	arietta *f*	short aria
2259	arioso *m*	aria-like
2260	baccanale *f*	bacchanal
2261	bagatella *f*	bagatelle
2262	ballata *f*	ballad
2263	balletto *m*	ballet
2264	balletto di corte *m*	court dance
2265	ballo tedesco *m* / danza tedesca *f*	German dance
2266	barcarola *f*	barcarole
2267	bassa danza *f*	basse danse
2268	battaglia *f*	battle
2269	bergamasca *f*	bergamask
2270	bourrée *f*	bourée / buree / borry
2271	brando *m*	branle

Intervalle | Intervalles

Deutsch	Français	Nr.
Prime *f*	unisson *m*	2238
Sekunde *f*	seconde *f*	2239
Terz *f*	tierce *f*	2240
Quarte *f*	quarte *f*	2241
Quinte *f*	quinte *f*	2242
Sexte *f*	sixte *f*	2243
Septime *f*	septième *f*	2244
Oktave *f*	octave *f*	2245
None *f*	none *f*	2246
Dezime *f*	dixième *f*	2247

Gattungen und Formen | Genres et formes

Deutsch	Français	Nr.
Tagelied *n*	aube *f* / aubade *f*	2248
Allemande *f*	allemande *f*	2249
Antiphon *f*	antienne *f*	2250
Arabeske *f*	arabesque *f*	2251
Arie *f*	air *m*	2252
Konzertarie *f*	air de concert *m*	2253
Opernarie *f*	air d'opéra *m*	2254
Bravourarie *f*	air de bravoure *m*	2255
Koloraturarie *f*	air avec colorature *m* / air à vocalises *m*	2256
höfisches Lied *n*	air de cour *m*	2257
kleine Arie *f*	ariette *f*	2258
wie eine Arie	comme une aria	2259
Bacchanal *n*	bacchanale *f*	2260
Bagatelle *f*	bagatelle *f*	2261
Ballade *f*	ballade *f*	2262
Ballett *n*	ballet *m*	2263
höfischer Tanz *m*	ballet de cour *m*	2264
Deutscher Tanz *m*	danse allemande *f*	2265
Barkarole *f*	barcarolle *f*	2266
Basse danse *f*	basse danse *f*	2267
Schlacht *f*	bataille *f*	2268
Bergamasker Tanz *m*	bergamasque *f*	2269
Bourrée *f*	bourrée *f*	2270
Branle *m*	branle m / bransle *m*	2271

2272	brindisi *m* / ditirambo *m*	drinking song
2273	bolero *m*	bolero
2274	burlesca *f*	burlesque
2275	burletta *f*	little jest
2276	cabaletta *f*	cabaletta
2277	caccia *f*	hunt
2278	canaria *f*	canary
2279	canone *m*	canon
2280	cantata *f*	cantata
2281	cantata da camera *f*	chamber cantata
2282	cantata da chiesa *f*	church cantata
2283	cantata profana *f*	secular cantata
2284	cantata su un corale *f*	choral cantata
2285	cantico *m*	canticle
2286	cantilena *f*	cantilena
2287	canto carnascialesco *m*	carnival song
2288	canto di lavoro *m*	work song
2289	canto di Natale *m*	Christmas song
2290	canto funebre *m*	dirge
2291	canto gitano *m*	gipsy song
2292	canto goliardico *m*	student song
2293	canto gregoriano *m*	plainsong (Gregorian chant)
2294	canto nuziale *m*	bridal song (wedding song)
2295	canzone *f*	song
2296	canzone della sera *f*	evening song
2297	canzone infantile *f*	nursery song
2298	canzone moderna *f* / canzonetta *f*	song / pop song
2299	canzone popolare *f*	folk song
2300	canzonetta *f*	canzonet
2301	capriccio *m*	capriccio
2302	carmagnola *f*	carmagnole
2303	carola *f*	carol
2304	cassazione *f*	cassation
2305	cavatina *f*	cavatina
2306	ciaccona *f*	chaconne
2307	commedia musicale *f*	musical
2308	commedia per musica *f*	musical comedy

Trinklied *n*	chanson à boire *f* / chanson bacchique *f*	2272
Bolero *m*	boléro *m*	2273
Burleske *f*	burlesque *f*	2274
kleine Posse *f*	petite farce *f*	2275
Cabaletta *f*	cabalette *f*	2276
Jagd *f*	chasse *f*	2277
Canarie *f*	canarie *f*	2278
Kanon *m*	canon *m*	2279
Kantate *f*	cantate *f*	2280
Kammerkantate *f*	cantate de chambre *f*	2281
Kirchenkantate *f*	cantate d'église *f*	2282
weltliche Kantate *f*	cantate profane *f*	2283
Choralkantate *f*	cantate sur un choral *f*	2284
Gesang *m* / (Kirchen-)Lied *n*	cantique *m*	2285
Kantilene *f*	cantilène *f*	2286
Karnevalslied *n*	chanson de carnaval *f*	2287
Arbeitslied *n*	chant de travail *m*	2288
Weihnachtslied *n*	chant de Noël *m*	2289
Grabgesang *m*	chant funèbre *m*	2290
Zigeunerlied *n*	chant gitan *m*	2291
Studentenlied *n*	chanson d'étudiant *m*	2292
Gregorianischer Choral *m*	plain-chant *m* / chant grégorien *m*	2293
Brautlied *n*	chant nuptial *m*	2294
Lied *n* / Kanzone *f*	chanson *f*	2295
Abendlied *n*	chant du soir *m*	2296
Kinderlied *n*	chanson enfantine *f*	2297
Schlager *m*	chanson à la mode *f* / chansonnette *f*	2298
Volkslied *n*	chanson populaire *f*	2299
Kanzonette *f*	canzonette *f*	2300
Capriccio *n*	caprice *m*	2301
Carmagnole *f* / Revolutionsgesang *m*	carmagnole *f*	2302
Carole *f*	carole *f*	2303
Kassation *f*	cassation *f*	2304
Kavatine *f*	cavatine *f*	2305
Chaconne *f*	chaconne *f*	2306
Musical *n*	comédie musicale *f*	2307
lyrische Komödie *f*	comédie lyrique *f*	2308

2309	concerto *m*	concerto
2310	concerto con quattro strumenti solisti *m*	quadruple concerto
2311	concerto doppio *m*	double concerto
2312	concerto per orchestra *m*	concerto for orchestra
2313	concerto per organo *m*	organ concerto
2314	concerto per pianoforte *m*	piano concerto
2315	concerto per violino *m*	violin concerto
2316	concerto sacro *m*	sacred concerto
2317	concerto sinfonico *m*	symphony concert
2318	concerto triplo *m*	triple concerto
2319	concerto vocale *m*	vocal concert
2320	consolazione *f*	consolation
2321	contraddanza *f*	country dance
2322	corale *m*	choral / chorale
2323	corrente *f*	courante
2324	cotillon *m*	cotillon
2325	czarda(s) *f*	czardas
2326	danza concertante *f*	concert dance
2327	danza delle streghe *f*	witches' dance
2328	danza dei morti *f* / danza macabra *f*	dance of death
2329	danza gitana *f*	gipsy dance
2330	danza popolare *f* / danza folcloristica *f*	folk dance
2331	danza rustica *f*	peasant dance
2332	danza slava *f*	Slavic dance
2333	danza spagnola *f*	Spanish dance
2334	danza ungherese *f*	Hungarian dance
2335	decimino *m*	work for ten players
2336	divertimento *m*	divertimento
2337	dramma lirico *m*	operatic / lyric drama
2338	dramma musicale *m*	music drama
2339	duetto *m* / duo *m*	duet
2340	egloga *f*	eclogue
2341	elegia *f*	elegy
2342	epilogo	epilogue
2343	fanfara *f*	fanfare / flourish
2344	fantasia *f*	fantasia / fancy

Konzert *n*	concerto *m*	2309
Quadrupelkonzert *n*	quadruple concerto *m*	2310
Doppelkonzert *n*	double concerto *m*	2311
Konzert für Orchester *n*	concerto pour orchestre *m*	2312
Orgelkonzert *n*	concerto pour orgue *m*	2313
Klavierkonzert *n*	concerto pour piano *m*	2314
Violinkonzert *n*	concerto pour violon *m*	2315
geistliches Konzert *n*	concert de musique sacrée *m*	2316
Sinfoniekonzert *n*	concert symphonique *m*	2317
Tripelkonzert *n*	triple concerto *m*	2318
Gesangskonzert *n*	concert vocal *m*	2319
Consolation *f* / Tröstung *f*	consolation *f*	2320
Kontretanz *m*	contredanse *f*	2321
Choral *m*	choral *m*	2322
Courante *f*	courante *f*	2323
Kotillon *m*	cotillon *m*	2324
Csárdás *m*	csardas *f*	2325
konzertanter Tanz *m*	danse concertante *f*	2326
Hexentanz *m*	dance des sorcières *f*	2327
Totentanz *m*	danse macabre *f*	2328
Zigeunertanz *m*	danse gitane *f*	2329
Volkstanz *m*	danse folklorique *f* / danse populaire *f*	2330
Bauerntanz *m*	danse champêtre *f* / danse paysanne *f* / villageoise *f*	2331
slawischer Tanz *m*	danse slave *f*	2332
spanischer Tanz *m*	danse espagnole *f*	2333
ungarischer Tanz *m*	danse hongroise *f*	2334
Dezett *n*	dixtuor *m*	2335
Divertimento *n* / „Unterhaltung" *f*	divertissement *m*	2336
lyrisches Drama *n*	drame lyrique *m*	2337
Musikdrama *n*	drame musical *m*	2338
Duett *n* / Duo *n*	duo *m*	2339
Hirtengedicht *n* / Ekloge *f*	églogue *f*	2340
Elegie *f*	élégie *f*	2341
Epilog *m* / Ausklang *m*	épilogue *m*	2342
Fanfare *f* / Tusch *m*	fanfare *f*	2343
Fantasie *f*	fantaisie *f*	2344

2345	farandola *f*	farandole
2346	farsa *f*	farce
2347	finale *m*	finale
2348	foglio d'album *m*	album leaf
2349	follia *f*	folia
2350	francese *f*	French dance
2351	fuga *f*	fugue
2352	fughetta *f*	fughetta
2353	furlana *f* / forlana *f*	forlana / furlana
2354	gagliarda *f*	galliard
2355	galanteria *f*	galanteries
2356	galoppo *m*	galop
2357	gavotta *f*	gavotte
2358	giga *f*	jig
2359	girotondo *m*	round dance
2360	gopak *m*	gopak
2361	improvviso *m*	impromptu
2362	inglese *f*	English dance
2363	inno *m*	hymn / anthem / hymn of praise
2364	inno nazionale *m*	national anthem
2365	interludio *m*	interlude
2366	intermezzo *m* / intermedio *m*	interlude
2367	intrada *f* / entrata *f*	intrada
2368	introduzione *f*	introduction
2369	invenzione *f*	invention
2370	istampita *f* / estampida *f*	estampie
2371	lai *m*	lay
2372	lamento *m*	lament
2373	lancieri *m pl*	lanciers
2374	landa *f*	lands
2375	lavolta *f* / volta *f*	volta
2376	leggenda *f*	legend
2377	litania *f*	litany
2378	madrigale *m*	madrigal
2379	maggiolata *f*	may song
2380	marcia *f*	march
2381	marcia funebre *f*	funeral march
2382	marcia nuziale *f*	wedding march
2383	marcia trionfale *f*	triumphal march
2384	marinesca *f*	sailor-like dance

Farandole *f*	farandole *f*	2345
Farce *f* / Posse *f*	farce *f*	2346
Schlussstück *n*	final *m*	2347
Albumblatt *n*	feuille d'album *f*	2348
Folia *f*	folie *f*	2349
Française *f*	française *f*	2350
Fuge *f*	fugue *f*	2351
Fughette *f* / kleine Fuge *f*	fughette *f*	2352
Forlana *f* / Friauler *m*	forlane *f*	2353
Gagliarde *f*	gaillarde *f*	2354
Galanterie *f*	galanteries *f pl*	2355
Galopp *m*	galop *m*	2356
Gavotte *f*	gavotte *f*	2357
Gigue *f*	gigue *f*	2358
Reigen *m*	ronde *f*	2359
Hopak *m*	gopak *m*	2360
Impromptu *n*	impromptu *m*	2361
Anglaise *f*	anglaise *f*	2362
Hymne *f* / Lobgesang *m*	hymne *m*	2363
Nationalhymne *f*	hymne national *m*	2364
Zwischenspiel *n*	entr'acte *m* / interlude *m*	2365
Zwischenspiel *n*	intermède *m*	2366
Intrade *f*	entrée *f*	2367
Einleitung *f*	introduction *f*	2368
Invention *f*	invention *f*	2369
Estampie *f*	estampie *f*	2370
Leich *m*	lai *m*	2371
Klage *f*	lamentation *f*	2372
Lancers *m Pl*	lanciers *m pl* / quadrille à la cour *f*	2373
Lande *f*	lande *f*	2374
Volta *f*	volte *f*	2375
Legende *f*	légende *f*	2376
Litanei *f*	litanie *f*	2377
Madrigal *n*	madrigal *m*	2378
Mailied *n*	chant de mai *m*	2379
Marsch *m*	marche *f*	2380
Trauermarsch *m*	marche funèbre *f*	2381
Hochzeitsmarsch *m*	marche nuptiale *f*	2382
Triumphmarsch *m*	marche triomphale	2383
Matelote *f* / Matrosentanz *m*	marinière *f* / matelote *f*	2384

2385	mascherata *f*	masque
2386	mattinata *f*	morning music / aubade
2387	mazurca *f*	mazurka
2388	melodramma *m*	melodrama
2389	messa *f*	mass
2390	messa dei defunti *f* / Requiem *m* / messa di (da) Requiem *f*	mass for the dead / requiem mass
2391	minuetto *m*	minuet
2392	mistero *m*	liturgical drama
2393	momento musicale *m*	"musical moment"
2394	monodramma *m*	monodrama
2395	moresca *f*	morris dance
2396	moto perpetuo *m* / perpetuum mobile (L)	perpetual motion
2397	mottetto *m*	motet
2398	nenia *f* / lamento funebre *m*	nenia / funeral lament
2399	ninna nanna *f*	lullaby / cradle song
2400	nonetto *m*	nonet
2401	notturno *m*	nocturne
2402	novelletta *f*	novelette
2403	ochetus *m*	hocket
2404	offertorio *m*	offertory
2405	opera *f*	opera
2406	opera buffa *f*	comic opera
2407	opera comica *f*	comic opera
2408	opera corale *f*	choral work
2409	opera seria *f*	serious opera
2410	operetta *f*	operetta
2411	oratorio *m*	oratorio
2412	ottetto *m*	octet
2413	ouverture *f* / sinfonia *f*	overture
2414	ouverture d'opera *f*	operatic overture
2415	ouverture da concerto *f*	concert overture
2416	parafrasi *f*	paraphrase
2417	parodia *f*	parody
2418	passacaglia *f*	passacaglia
2419	passepied *m*	passepied
2420	passione *f*	passion
2421	pasticcio *m*	pasticcio / pastiche
2422	pastorale *f*	pastoral

Maskenspiel *n* / Maskerade *f*	mascarade *f*	2385
Morgenständchen *n*	aubade *f*	2386
Mazurka *f*	mazurka *f*	2387
Melodram *n* / Melodrama *n*	mélodrame *m*	2388
Messe *f*	messe *f*	2389
Totenmesse *f* / Requiem *n*	messe des morts *f*	2390
Menuett *n*	menuet *m*	2391
liturgisches Drama *n*	drame liturgique *m*	2392
„musikalischer Augenblick“ *m* / Moment musical *m*	moment musical *m*	2393
Monodram *n*	monodrame *m*	2394
Moreske *f* / Moriskentanz *m*	mauresque *f*	2395
durchlaufend bewegt	mouvement perpétuel *m*	2396
Motette *f*	motet *m*	2397
Nänie *f* / Totenklage *f*	nénie *f*	2398
Wiegenlied *n*	berceuse *f*	2399
Nonett *n*	nonet *m*	2400
Notturno *n* / Nachtstück *n*	nocturne *m*	2401
Novellette *f*	novelette *f*	2402
Hoketus *m*	hoquet *m*	2403
Offertorium *n*	offertoire *m*	2404
Oper *f*	opéra *m*	2405
heitere Oper *f*	opéra bouffe *m*	2406
komische Oper *f*	opéra comique *m*	2407
Chorwerk *n*	œuvre chorale *f*	2408
ernste Oper *f*	opéra sérieux *m*	2409
Operette *f*	opérette *f*	2410
Oratorium *n*	oratorio *m*	2411
Oktett *n*	octuor *m*	2412
Ouvertüre *f*	ouverture *f*	2413
Opernouvertüre *f*	ouverture d'opéra *f*	2414
Konzertouvertüre *f*	ouverture de concert *f*	2415
Paraphrase *f* / Umspielung *f*	paraphrase *f*	2416
Parodie *f*	parodie *f*	2417
Passacaglia *f*	passacaille *f*	2418
Passepied *m*	passepied *m*	2419
Passion *f*	passion *f*	2420
Flickoper *f*	pastiche *m*	2421
Pastorale *f* / Hirtenstück *n*	pastorale *f* / pastourelle *f*	2422

2423	pavana *f* / padovana *f*	pavan
2424	perigordino *m*	perigourdine
2425	pezzo caratteristico *m*	character piece
2426	pezzo da concerto *m*	concert piece
2427	pezzo lirico *m*	lyric piece
2428	poema *f*	poem
2429	poema sinfonico *m*	symphonic poem
2430	polacca *f*	polonaise
2431	polca *f*	polka
2432	postludio *m*	postlude
2433	pot-pourri *m*	pot-pourri / medley
2434	preambulo *m*	preamble
2435	preludio *m*	prelude
2436	prologo *m*	prologue
2437	quadriglia *f*	quadrille
2438	quartetto *m*	quartet
2439	quartetto d'archi *m*	string quartet
2440	quintetto *m*	quintet
2441	quintetto per (di) fiati *m*	wind quintet
2442	quodlibet *m* / messanza *f*	quodlibet
2443	rapsodia *f*	rhapsody
2444	recitativo *m*	recitative
2445	recitativo accompagnato *m*	accompanied recitative
2446	recitativo secco *m*	recitative with continuo accompaniment ("dry")
2447	ricercare *m*	ricercar
2448	rigaudon *m*	rigadoon
2449	ritornello *m*	ritornello
2450	romanza *f*	romance
2451	romanza senza parole *f*	song without words
2452	rondò *m*	rondo
2453	salmo *m*	psalm
2454	sarabanda *f*	sarabande
2455	sardana *f*	sardana
2456	scherzino *m* / scherzetto *m*	little scherzo
2457	scozzese *f*	Scottish dance
2458	serenata *f*	serenade
2459	sestetto *m*	sextet
2460	settimino *m*	septet
2461	siciliana *f*	siciliana
2462	sinfonia *f*	symphony

Pavane *f*	pavane *f*	2423
Perigourdine *f*	périgourdine *f*	2424
Charakterstück *n*	pièce de charactère *f*	2425
Konzertstück *n*	morceau de concert *m*	2426
Lyrisches Stück *n*	pièce lyrique *f*	2427
Poem *n* / Gedicht *n*	poème *m*	2428
sinfonische Dichtung *f*	poème symphonique *m*	2429
Polonaise *f*	polonaise *f*	2430
Polka *f*	polka *f*	2431
Nachspiel *n*	postlude *m*	2432
Potpourri *n*	pot-pourri *m*	2433
Präambel *f*	préambule *m*	2434
Präludium *n* / Vorspiel *n*	prélude *m*	2435
Prolog *m*	prologue *m*	2436
Quadrille *f*	quadrille *f*	2437
Quartett *n*	quatuor *m*	2438
Streichquartett *n*	quatuor à cordes *m*	2439
Quintett *n*	quintette *m*	2440
Bläserquintett *n*	quintette à vent *m*	2441
Quodlibet *n*	quodlibet *m* / fricassée *f*	2442
Rhapsodie *f*	rhapsodie *f*	2443
Rezitativ *n*	récitatif *m*	2444
begleitetes Rezitativ *n*	récitatif accompagné *m*	2445
Rezitativ nur mit Continuo („trocken") *n*	récitatif seulement avec continuo ("sec") *m*	2446
Ricercar *n*	ricercare *m*	2447
Rigaudon *m*	rigaudon *m*	2448
Ritornell *n*	ritournelle *f*	2449
Romanze *f*	romance *f*	2450
Lied ohne Worte *n*	romance sans paroles *f*	2451
Rondo *n*	rondo *m* / rondeau *m*	2452
Psalm *m*	psaume *m*	2453
Sarabande *f*	sarabande *f*	2454
Sardane *f*	sardane *f*	2455
kleines Scherzo *n*	petit scherzo *m*	2456
Ecossaise *f* (schottischer Tanz)	écossaise *f*	2457
Ständchen *n*	sérénade *f*	2458
Sextett *n*	sextuor *m*	2459
Septett *n*	septuor *m*	2460
Siciliano *m*	sicilienne *f*	2461
Sinfonie *f*	symphonie *f*	2462

No.	Italiano	English
2463	sinfonia concertante *f*	sinfonia concertante
2464	sogno *m*	dream
2465	sonata *f*	sonata
2466	sonata da camera *f*	chamber sonata
2467	sonata da chiesa *f*	church sonata
2468	sonata per pianoforte *f*	piano sonata
2469	sonatina *f*	sonatina
2470	stanza *f*	stanza
2471	studio *m*	study
2472	studio da concerto *m*	concert study
2473	studio di virtuosità *m*	virtuosity / virtuoso study
2474	studio trascendentale *m*	transcendental study
2475	suite francese *f*	French suite
2476	suite inglese *f*	English suite
2477	tarantella *f*	tarantella
2478	tema con variazioni *m*	theme with variations
2479	tenzone *m*	tenson
2480	terzetto *m* / trio *m*	trio
2481	tirolese *f*	tyrolienne
2482	tortiglione *m*	tourdion
2483	tragedia lirica *f*	lyric tragedy
2484	umoresca *f*	humoresque
2485	valzer *m*	waltz
2486	valzer viennese *m*	Viennese waltz
2487	variazione *f*	variation
2488	versetto *m*	verset
2489	vespri *m pl*	vespers
2490	villanella *f* / villanesca *f*	villanella
2491	zingaresca *f*	gipsy dance

Konzertante Sinfonie *f*	symphonie concertante *f*	2463
Träumerei *f* / Traum *m*	rêverie *f* / rêve *m*	2464
Sonate *f*	sonate *f*	2465
Kammersonate *f*	sonate de chambre *f*	2466
Kirchensonate *f*	sonate d'église *f*	2467
Klaviersonate *f*	sonate pour piano *f*	2468
Sonatine *f*	sonatine *f*	2469
Stanza *f*	stance *f*	2470
Etüde *f*	étude *f*	2471
Konzertetüde *f*	étude concertante *f* / étude de concert *f*	2472
virtuose Etüde *f*	étude de virtuosité *f*	2473
Transzendentaletüde *f*	étude transcendentale *f*	2474
Französische Suite *f*	suite française *f*	2475
Englische Suite *f*	suite anglaise *f*	2476
Tarantella *f*	tarentelle *f*	2477
Thema mit Variationen *n*	thème avec variations *m*	2478
Tenzone *f*	tenson *m*	2479
Terzett *n* / Trio *n*	trio *m*	2480
Tiroler Ländler *m* / Tiroler Lied *n*	tyrolienne *f*	2481
Tourdion *m*	tordion *m*	2482
Lyrische Tragödie *f*	tragédie lyrique *f*	2483
Humoreske *f*	humoresque *f*	2484
Walzer *m*	valse *f*	2485
Wienerwalzer *m*	valse viennoise *f*	2486
Variation *f* / Veränderung *f*	variation *f*	2487
Versett *n*	verset *m*	2488
Vesper *f*	vêpres *f pl*	2489
Villanella *f*	villanesque *f*	2490
Zigeunertanz *m* / Zigeunerlied *n*	tzigane *f*	2491

Le seguenti composizioni musicali portano lo stesso nome in tutte le lingue.

The following compositions bear the same term in all languages.

2492 Alabado
2493 Alalá
2494 Alborada
2495 Alegrias
2496 Angelito
2497 Aragonaise
2498 Arioso
2499 Ayre
2500 Baborák
2501 Badinage
2502 Badinerie
2503 Batuque
2504 Bergerette
2505 Bluette
2506 Brunette
2507 Bulerias
2508 Cachucha
2509 Calata
2510 Cancan
2511 Cantigas
2512 Catch
2513 Cebell
2514 Chiarantana
2515 Cinquepace
2516 Colinda
2517 Concertino
2518 Concerto grosso
2519 Contrás
2520 Corrido
2521 Cueca
2522 Cumbia
2523 Danzón
2524 Diferencia
2525 Doina
2526 Double
2527 Dumka
2528 Duo
2529 Extravaganza
2530 Fado
2531 Fandango
2532 Farruca
2533 Flamenco
2534 Frottola
2535 Furiant
2536 Giustiniana
2537 Glee
2538 Greghesca
2539 Guajira
2540 Guaracha
2541 Habanera
2542 Halling
2543 Hey
2544 Highland fling
2545 Hornpipe
2546 Horo
2547 Hupfauf
2548 Jabadao
2549 Jabo
2550 Jacara
2551 Jaleo
2552 Jarabe
2553 Jota
2554 Koleda
2555 Kolo
2556 Kujawiak
2557 Ländler
2558 Lesginka
2559 Lied
2560 Loure
2561 Malagueña
2562 Manfredina
2563 Manseque
2564 Manta
2565 Monferrina

Die folgenden musikalischen Kompositionen tragen in allen Sprachen den gleichen Namen.

Les compositions musicales suivantes portent le même nom dans toutes les langues.

2566 Muñeira
2567 Murciana
2568 Musette
2569 Oberek
2570 Obertas
2571 Ode
2572 Palotas
2573 Partita
2574 Passamezzo
2575 Pastourelle
2576 Penillion
2577 Petenera
2578 Piva
2579 Polo
2580 Polska
2581 Redowa
2582 Reel
2583 Rejdovak
2584 Réjouissance
2585 Requiem
2586 Rheinländer
2587 Rispetto
2588 Romanesca
2589 Ronda
2590 Rondeau
2591 Rondeña
2592 Rueda
2593 Ruggiero
2594 Saeta
2595 Sainete
2596 Saltarello
2597 Scherzo
2598 Schuhplattler
2599 Sevillana
2600 Shanty
2601 Sinfonietta
2602 Singspiel
2603 Soleà
2604 Solfeggetto
2605 Springtanz
2606 Stornello
2607 Strambotto
2608 Strathspey
2609 Styrienne
2610 Suite
2611 Tambourin
2612 Tiento
2613 Tirana
2614 Toccata
2615 Tombeau
2616 Tonadilla
2617 Tourbillon
2618 Trepak
2619 Tresca
2620 Trescone
2621 Trezza
2622 Trio
2623 Trotto
2624 Tumba
2625 Varsovienne
2626 Vaudeville
2627 Veneziana
2628 Villancico
2629 Villotta
2630 Virelai
2631 Voluntary
2632 Zamacueco
2633 Zapateado
2634 Zarzuela
2635 Zortzico

Il linguaggio di ogni giorno — Every day language

Verbi — Verbs

	Verbi	Verbs
2636	abbassare	to lower
2637	abbassare l'intonatura / abbassare l'accordatura	to tune down
2638	abbellire	to embellish
2639	abbreviare	to shorten
2640	accelerare	to accelerate
2641	accentuare	to stress
2642	accompagnare	to accompany
2643	accordare	to tune
2644	adattare	to adapt
2645	affrettare	to hasten
2646	aggiungere	to add
2647	allargare	to widen
2648	allontanarsi	to go away
2649	allungare	to lengthen
2650	alterare	to alter
2651	alternare	to alternate
2652	alzare	to raise
2653	alzare l'intonatura / alzare l'intonazione	to tune up
2654	ampliare	to enlarge
2655	animare	to animate
2656	annunciare	to announce
2657	applaudire	to applaud
2658	aprire	to open
2659	armonizzare	to harmonize
2660	arpeggiare	to play arpeggios
2661	articolare	to articulate
2662	ascoltare	to listen
2663	aspettare	to wait
2664	aumentare	to augment
2665	balbettare	to stammer
2666	ballare	to dance
2667	battere	to beat
2668	battere il tempo	to beat the time
2669	borbottare	to mumble

Die tägliche Sprache — Le langage de tous les jours

Verben — Verbes

senken / erniedrigen	baisser / abaisser	2636
herunterstimmen / tiefer stimmen	baisser l'accord / baisser l'intonation	2637
verschönern	embellir	2638
abkürzen	abréger	2639
beschleunigen	accélérer	2640
betonen	accentuer	2641
begleiten	accompagner	2642
einstimmen / stimmen	accorder	2643
bearbeiten	adapter	2644
beeilen	hâter	2645
hinzufügen	ajouter	2646
erweitern	élargir	2647
sich entfernen	s'éloigner	2648
verlängern	allonger	2649
alterieren	altérer	2650
alternieren / abwechseln	alterner	2651
erhöhen	hausser	2652
hinaufstimmen / höher stimmen	monter l'intonation / monter l'accord	2653
erweitern	agrandir	2654
beleben	animer	2655
ankündigen / ansagen	annoncer	2656
klatschen	applaudir	2657
öffnen	ouvrir	2658
harmonisieren	harmoniser	2659
arpeggieren	arpéger	2660
deutlich aussprechen	articuler	2661
zuhören / anhören / horchen	écouter	2662
warten	attendre	2663
vergrößern / steigern	augmenter	2664
stottern	balbutier	2665
tanzen	danser	2666
schlagen	battre	2667
Takt schlagen	battre la mesure	2668
murmeln	grommeler	2669

2670	brontolare	to grumble
2671	bussare	to knock
2672	buttare	to throw
2673	cadere / cascare	to fall down
2674	calare	to let down
2675	calmare	to calm
2676	cambiare / mutare	to change
2677	cantare	to sing
2678	capire	to understand
2679	cedere	to give in
2680	cercare	to seek / to look for
2681	chiaccherare	to chat
2682	chiedere	to ask
2683	chiudere	to shut / to close
2684	commuovere	to move
2685	comporre	to compose
2686	concatenare	to link together
2687	concentrarsi	to concentrate
2688	contare	to count
2689	continuare	to continue
2690	copiare	to copy
2691	coprire	to cover
2692	correggere	to correct
2693	creare	to create
2694	crescere	to grow
2695	criticare	to criticize
2696	dare dei concerti	to give concerts
2697	declamare	to declaim
2698	dedicare	to dedicate
2699	descrivere	to describe
2700	dimenticare	to forget
2701	diminuire	to diminish
2702	dirigere	to conduct
2703	dividere	to divide
2704	elaborare / rifinire	to elaborate
2705	elogiare / lodare	to praise
2706	entrare	to enter / to appear
2707	entrare in scena	to appear on stage
2708	esagerare	to exagerate
2709	eseguire	to perform

brummen	grogner	2670
klopfen	frapper	2671
werfen	jeter	2672
fallen / stürzen	tomber	2673
sinken / herablassen	faire descendre	2674
beruhigen	calmer	2675
wechseln / ändern	changer	2676
singen	chanter	2677
verstehen	comprendre	2678
nachgeben / nachlassen	céder	2679
suchen	chercher	2680
plaudern / tratschen	bavarder	2681
fragen	demander	2682
schließen / abschließen	fermer	2683
rühren	émouvoir	2684
komponieren	composer	2685
anknüpfen	enchaîner	2686
sich konzentrieren	se concentrer	2687
zählen	compter	2688
fortsetzen / fortfahren	continuer	2689
kopieren / abschreiben	copier	2690
bedecken	couvrir	2691
korrigieren	corriger	2692
erschaffen	créer	2693
wachsen / zunehmen / anwachsen	croître / grandir	2694
tadeln / kritisieren	critiquer	2695
konzertieren	donner des concerts	2696
deklamieren	déclamer	2697
widmen	dédier	2698
beschreiben	décrire	2699
vergessen	oublier	2700
vermindern / abnehmen	diminuer	2701
dirigieren	diriger	2702
teilen	diviser	2703
ausarbeiten	élaborer / fignoler	2704
loben	louer	2705
eintreten	entrer	2706
auftreten	entrer en scène	2707
übertreiben	exagérer	2708
ausführen / vortragen	exécuter	2709

2710 esercitare — to practise
2711 esordire — to make one’s début
2712 espirare — to breathe out
2713 esprimere — to express
2714 essere fuori tempo — to be out of tempo
2715 essere in ritardo — to be late
2716 esultare — to exult
2717 fare — to make / to do
2718 felicitare — to congratulate
2719 fermare — to stop
2720 festeggiare — to celebrate
2721 finire — to finish
2722 fischiare — to whistle
2723 forzare — to force
2724 fraseggiare — to phrase
2725 frenare — to hold back / to brake
2726 graduare — to shade / to graduate
2727 grattare — to scratch
2728 gridare — to shout / to scream
2729 guidare / condurre — to lead / to guide
2730 imitare — to imitate
2731 imparare — to learn
2732 improvvisare — to improvise
2733 incominciare / attaccare — to begin / to strike up
2734 incrociare — to cross
2735 indicare — to indicate
2736 insegnare — to teach
2737 insistere — to insist
2738 interpretare — to interpret / to perform
2739 interrompere — to interrupt
2740 inspirare — to inhale
2741 intonare — to intone
2742 introdurre — to introduce
2743 invertire — to invert
2744 lavorare — to work
2745 legare — to tie / to slur
2746 leggere — to read
2747 marcare — to mark
2748 mentire — to lie
2749 mettere — to put

üben	exercer	2710
debütieren	débuter	2711
ausatmen	expirer	2712
ausdrücken	exprimer	2713
aus dem Takt sein	être hors du tempo	2714
zu spät kommen	être en retard	2715
jubeln	exulter	2716
machen / tun	faire	2717
beglückwünschen / gratulieren	féliciter	2718
abbrechen / anhalten	arrêter	2719
feiern	fêter	2720
enden	finir	2721
pfeifen	siffler	2722
forcieren	forcer	2723
phrasieren	phraser	2724
bremsen	freiner	2725
abstufen	nuancer / graduer	2726
kratzen	gratter	2727
schreien / aufschreien	crier	2728
führen	guider / conduire	2729
imitieren / nachahmen	imiter	2730
lernen	apprendre	2731
improvisieren / extemporieren	improviser	2732
anfangen / einsetzen / beginnen	commencer / attaquer	2733
kreuzen	croiser	2734
zeigen	indiquer	2735
lehren / unterrichten	enseigner	2736
beharren	insister	2737
interpretieren	interpréter	2738
unterbrechen	interrompre	2739
einatmen	inspirer	2740
anstimmen	entonner	2741
einführen / einleiten	introduire	2742
umkehren	inverser	2743
arbeiten	travailler	2744
binden	lier	2745
lesen	lire	2746
markieren	marquer	2747
lügen	mentir	2748
setzen / legen / stellen	mettre	2749

2750	mettere in scena	to stage
2751	migliorare	to improve
2752	misurare	to measure
2753	moderare	to moderate
2754	modificare	to modify
2755	mostrare	to show
2756	muoversi	to move
2757	orchestrare	to orchestrate
2758	parlare / dire	to speak / to talk / to say
2759	partecipare	to take part
2760	passare	to pass
2761	pensare	to think
2762	perfezionarsi	to improve
2763	plagiare	to plagiarize
2764	portare	to carry / to fetch
2765	posare / porre	to lay down
2766	precipitare	to precipitate / to hurry
2767	pregare	to beg / to pray
2768	preludiare	to prelude
2769	prendere	to take
2770	preparare	to prepare
2771	presentare	to present
2772	prestare	to lend
2773	progredire	to progress
2774	prolungare	to prolong
2775	pronunciare	to pronounce
2776	proporre	to propose
2777	provare	to try
2778	raccontare	to tell
2779	raccorciare / ridurre	to shorten / to reduce
2780	raddoppiare	to double
2781	raggruppare	to group
2782	rallentare	to slow down
2783	recitare	to recite
2784	registrare / incidere	to record / to tape
2785	rendere	to give back
2786	respirare	to breathe
2787	restare / rimanere	to stay / to remain
2788	richiamare	to recall

inszenieren	mettre en scène	2750
verbessern	améliorer	2751
messen	mesurer	2752
mäßigen	modérer	2753
abändern	modifier	2754
zeigen	montrer	2755
sich bewegen	se mouvoir / remuer	2756
orchestrieren	orchestrer	2757
sprechen / sagen	parler / dire	2758
teilnehmen	participer	2759
überleiten / übergehen	passer	2760
denken	penser	2761
sich vervollkommnen / sich weiterbilden	se perfectionner	2762
abschreiben / plagiieren	plagier	2763
tragen / bringen	porter	2764
niederlegen / hinlegen	poser	2765
überstürzen	précipiter	2766
bitten / beten	prier	2767
präludieren	préluder	2768
nehmen	prendre	2769
vorbereiten	préparer	2770
vorstellen	présenter	2771
leihen	prêter	2772
fortschreiten	progresser	2773
verlängern	prolonger	2774
aussprechen	prononcer	2775
vorschlagen	proposer	2776
probieren / versuchen	essayer	2777
erzählen	raconter	2778
verkürzen	réduire / raccourcir	2779
verdoppeln	doubler	2780
zusammenstellen	grouper	2781
verlangsamen	ralentir	2782
vortragen / vorzutragen	réciter	2783
(auf Tonträger) aufnehmen / mitschneiden	enregistrer / graver	2784
zurückgeben	rendre	2785
atmen	respirer	2786
bleiben / verweilen	rester	2787
zurückrufen	rappeler	2788

2789	ricominciare	to recommence / to start again
2790	ricordarsi	to remember
2791	ridere	to laugh
2792	riflettere	to think over
2793	rilassarsi / distendersi	to relax
2794	rimbalzare	to bounce
2795	rimbombare	to resound
2796	rinforzare	to reinforce
2797	rinviare	to adjourn / to put off
2798	ripetere	to rehearse / to repeat
2799	riprendere	to retake
2800	risolvere	to resolve
2801	rispondere	to answer
2802	risuonare	to replay
2803	ritardare	to delay
2804	ritenere	to hold back
2805	ritmare	to emphasize the rhythm
2806	rovesciare	to upset / to overturn
2807	saltare	to jump
2808	saltare al posto di un'altro	to understudy / to take over a part
2809	sapere / conoscere	to know
2810	sbagliare / equivocarsi	to mistake / to make a mistake
2811	scrivere	to write
2812	scrivere delle note / scrivere della musica	to notate
2813	seguire	to follow
2814	semplificare	to simplify
2815	sentire	to feel / to hear
2816	separare	to separate
2817	sfiorare	to touch lightly
2818	singhiozzare	to sob
2819	smettere / cessare	to stop
2820	smorzare	to subdue
2821	soffiare	to blow
2822	sognare	to dream
2823	sopprimere	to suppress
2824	sorridere	to smile
2825	sospirare	to sigh
2826	sostituire / rimpiazzare	to substitute

wieder beginnen	recommencer	2789
sich erinnern	se souvenir	2790
lachen	rire	2791
nachdenken / überdenken	réfléchir	2792
lockern / entspannen	se relaxer / se détendre	2793
zurückprallen	rebondir	2794
dröhnen / widerhallen	retentir	2795
verstärken	renforcer	2796
verschieben / vertagen	renvoyer / ajourner	2797
proben / wiederholen	répéter	2798
wieder anfangen / wieder aufnehmen	reprendre	2799
auflösen	résoudre	2800
antworten	répondre	2801
erneut spielen	rejouer	2802
verzögern	retarder	2803
zurückhalten	retenir	2804
rhythmisieren	rhythmer	2805
umkehren	renverser	2806
springen / überspringen	sauter	2807
einspringen	remplacer au pied levé	2808
wissen / kennen	savoir / connaître	2809
(sich) irren / sich täuschen	se tromper / faire une faute	2810
schreiben	écrire	2811
notieren / Noten schreiben	noter / écrire de la musique	2812
folgen	suivre	2813
vereinfachen	simplifier	2814
hören / fühlen	ressentir	2815
trennen	séparer	2816
streifen	effleurer	2817
schluchzen	sangloter	2818
aufhören	cesser	2819
dämpfen	atténuer	2820
blasen	souffler	2821
träumen	rêver	2822
aufheben	supprimer	2823
lächeln	sourir	2824
seufzen	soupirer	2825
ersetzen	substituer / remplacer	2826

2827	sparire	to disappear
2828	spegnere	to extinguish
2829	spiegare	to explain
2830	spingere	to push
2831	staccare	to undo
2832	stare	to stay
2833	stonare / steccare	to be out of tune / to waver in pitch / to strike a false note
2834	strappare	to tear
2835	strimpellare	to strum
2836	strumentare	to score
2837	studiare	to study
2838	suddividere	to subdivide
2839	suggerire	to prompt
2840	suonare / toccare	to play / to touch
2841	suonare a memoria	to play by heart
2842	suonare a orecchio	to play by ear
2843	suonare a prima vista / leggere a prima vista	to play at sight / to sight-read
2844	tacere	to be silent
2845	tagliare	to cut
2846	tenere	to keep / to hold
2847	tenere il tempo	to keep time
2848	terminare / concludere	to end
2849	tirare	to pull
2850	togliere / levare	to take away / to remove
2851	tornare / ritornare	to return
2852	trascinare / trascicare	to drag
2853	trasportare / spostare	to transpose
2854	trattare	to treat
2855	tremare	to tremble
2856	trovare	to find
2857	udire	to hear
2858	unire / congiungere	to connect / to join
2859	urlare	to howl
2860	variare	to vary
2861	vedere / guardare	to see / to look
2862	vibrare	to vibrate
2863	vociare	to yell
2864	voltare / girare	to turn

verschwinden	disparaître	2827
auslöschen	éteindre	2828
erklären	expliquer	2829
stoßen / treiben	pousser	2830
abstoßen / lostrennen	détacher	2831
bleiben	rester	2832
detonieren / falsch spielen	détonner / jouer faux	2833
reißen	arracher	2834
klimpern	tapoter	2835
instrumentieren	instrumenter	2836
studieren / lernen	étudier	2837
unterteilen	subdiviser	2838
vorsagen / soufflieren	souffler	2839
spielen / greifen / berühren	jouer / toucher	2840
auswendig spielen	jouer par cœur	2841
nach Gehör spielen	jouer d'oreille	2842
vom Blatt spielen	déchiffrer / jouer à vue	2843
schweigen	se taire	2844
schneiden	couper	2845
halten / aushalten	tenir	2846
Takt halten	garder la mesure	2847
beendigen / abschließen	terminer	2848
ziehen	tirer	2849
wegnehmen	enlever / lever / ôter	2850
zurückkommen / zurückkehren	revenir	2851
schleppen	traîner	2852
transponieren	transposer	2853
behandeln	traiter	2854
zittern	trembler	2855
finden	trouver	2856
hören	entendre	2857
verbinden / anschließen	unir / joindre	2858
heulen	hurler	2859
abändern / verändern	varier	2860
sehen / schauen	voir / regarder	2861
vibrieren / schwingen / erklingen	vibrer	2862
grölen / brüllen	vociférer	2863
umblättern / wenden	tourner	2864

	Piccola raccolta di parole	**A small collection of words**
2865	abbonamento *m*	subscription
2866	accademia di musica *f*	music school / college
2867	abbondante	abundant
2868	abile	able
2869	accessori *m pl*	accessories / props
2870	accentuazione *f*	accentuation
2871	accompagnamento *m*	accompaniment
2872	accordato	tuned
2873	accordatura *f*	tuning
2874	acustica *f*	acoustics
2875	acustica ambientale *f*	acoustics (of a hall/room)
2876	addio!	farewell!
2877	adesso / ora	now
2878	agenzia di concerti *f*	concert agency
2879	allievo *m* / allieva *f* / alunno *m* / alunna *f*	pupil
2880	almeno	at least
2881	altezza *f*	height
2882	alto	high
2883	amante della musica *m + f* / melomane *m + f*	music lover
2884	a mente / a memoria	by heart
2885	annotazione *f*	annotation
2886	antico	antique
2887	antologia *f*	anthology
2888	apice *m* / punto culminante *m*	climax / apex
2889	apparecchi imitanti voci animali *m pl*	animal sound-effects
2890	applauso *m*	applause
2891	archi *m pl*	string section
2892	arrangiamento *m* / adattamento *m*	arrangement / adaptation
2893	arte *f*	art
2894	artistico	artistic / artistry
2895	ascoltatore *m* / ascoltatrice *f*	listener
2896	ascolto *m*	hearing
2897	assordante	deafening
2898	attacco *m*	cue

Kleine Wörtersammlung	**Petite collection de mots**	
Abonnement *n*	abonnement *m*	2865
Musikhochschule *f* / Musikakademie *f*	école supérieure de musique *f*	2866
reichlich	abondant	2867
geschickt / fähig zu	habile	2868
Requisiten *n Pl*	accessoires *m pl*	2869
Betonung *f*	accentuation *f*	2870
Begleitung *f*	accompagnement *m*	2871
gestimmt	accordé	2872
Stimmung (eines Instrumentes) *f*	accordage *m*	2873
Akustik *f*	acoustique *f*	2874
Raumakustik *f*	acoustique ambiante *f* / acoustique d'un local *f*	2875
Lebe wohl!	adieu!	2876
jetzt	maintenant	2877
Konzertagentur *f*	agence de concerts	2878
Schüler *m* / Schülerin *f*	élève *m + f*	2879
wenigstens	au moins	2880
Höhe *f*	hauteur *f*	2881
hoch	haut	2882
Musikliebhaber *m* / Musiklieb-haberin *f*	amateur de musique *m* / mélomane *m + f*	2883
auswendig	par cœur	2884
Anmerkung *f* / Notiz *f*	annotation *f* / notice *f*	2885
altertümlich	antique / ancien	2886
Sammelwerk *n*	anthologie *f*	2887
Höhepunkt *m*	point culminant *m*	2888
Tierstimmeneffekte *m Pl*	effects d'animaux *m pl*	2889
Beifall *m*	applaudissement *m*	2890
Streicher *m Pl*	cordes *f pl*	2891
Arrangement *n* / Bearbeitung *f*	arrangement *m* / adaptation *f*	2892
Kunst *f*	art *m*	2893
künstlerisch	artistique	2894
Hörer *m* / Hörerin *f*	auditeur *m* / auditrice *f*	2895
Gehör *n*	écoute *m*	2896
betäubend	assourdissant	2897
Einsatz *m*	entrée *f*	2898

2899	attento	attentive
2900	attenzione!	take care!
2901	atto *m*	act
2902	audizione *f*	audition
2903	autore *m*	author
2904	avanzato	advanced
2905	bacchetta *f*	stick / baton
2906	ballo *m* / danza *f*	dance
2907	ballo di società *m* / ballo di sala *m*	ballroom dance
2908	bambino prodigio *m*	infant prodigy
2909	banda *f* / fanfara *f*	brass band / wind band
2910	banda di ottoni *f*	brass band
2911	banda militare *f*	military band
2912	barocco *m*	baroque
2913	basso	low / bass
2914	basta!	that's enough!
2915	bellezza *f*	beauty
2916	bello / bella	beautiful
2917	biglietto *m* / ingresso *m*	ticket
2918	biglietto in omaggio *m*	complimentary ticket
2919	bis (L)	encore
2920	botteghino *m* / biglietteria *f*	box office
2921	brano *m* / pezzo *m*	piece
2922	bravissimo!	very good!
2923	cacofonia *f*	cacophony
2924	calcare le scene	to tread the stage
2925	cambiamento *m*	change
2926	cambio di scena *m*	change of set
2927	camerino *m*	green-room
2928	canzone a successo *f*	hit
2929	capolavoro *m*	masterpiece
2930	cappella *f*	chapel
2931	caratteristico	characteristic
2932	carnevale *m*	carnival
2933	carta da musica *f*	music-paper
2934	cartellone *m*	poster / playbill
2935	casa editrice di musica *f*	music publishing house
2936	catalogo *m*	catalogue / catalog

aufmerksam	attentif	2899
Achtung! / pass auf!	attention!	2900
Akt *m* / Aufzug *m*	acte *m*	2901
Probespiel *n*	audition *f* / essai *m*	2902
Autor *m*	auteur *m*	2903
fortgeschritten	avancé	2904
Taktstock *m* / Dirigentenstab *m*	baguette *f*	2905
Tanz *m*	danse *f*	2906
Gesellschaftstanz *m*	danse de societé *f* / danse de salon *f*	2907
Wunderkind *n*	enfant prodige *m*	2908
Blasmusik *f* / Fanfare *f*	fanfare *f* / corps de musique *m*	2909
Blechblasorchester *n*	fanfare de cuivres *f*	2910
Militärkapelle *f*	musique militaire *f* / harmonie *f*	2911
Barock *m*	baroque *m*	2912
niedrig / tief	bas	2913
genug!	assez!	2914
Schönheit *f*	beauté *f*	2915
schön	beau / belle	2916
Eintrittskarte *f*	billet *m* / billet d'entrée *m*	2917
Freikarte *f*	billet de faveur *m* / billet gratuit *m*	2918
noch einmal! / Zugabe! *f*	encore!	2919
Theaterkasse *f* / Konzertkasse *f*	bureau de location *m*	2920
Stück *n*	morceau *m* / pièce *f*	2921
sehr gut!	très bien!	2922
Kakophonie *f* / Missklang *m*	cacophonie *f*	2923
auf die Bühne gehen	monter sur les planches	2924
Abwechslung *f* / Änderung *f*	changement *m*	2925
Umbau *m*	changement de décor *m*	2926
Künstlerzimmer *n*	foyer des artistes *m*	2927
Erfolgsschlager *m*	tube *m*	2928
Meisterwerk *n*	chef-d'œuvre *m*	2929
Kapelle *f*	chapelle *f*	2930
charakteristisch	caractéristique	2931
Karneval m / Fastnacht *f* / Fasching *m*	carnaval *m*	2932
Notenpapier *n*	papier à musique *m*	2933
Plakat *n* / Spielplan *m*	affiche *f*	2934
Musikverlag *m*	maison d'édition musicale *f*	2935
Verzeichnis *n*	catalogue *m*	2936

2937	celebre / famoso	famous
2938	centro uditivo *m*	listening centre
2939	certo / sicuro	certain / sure
2940	chiesa *f*	church
2941	chiuso	closed
2942	ciclo *m*	cycle
2943	cielo *m*	sky
2944	classico	classic
2945	classicismo *m*	classicism
2946	collaborazione *f*	collaboration
2947	collezione *f* / raccolta *f*	collection
2948	colore *m* / colorito *m* / timbro *m*	tone-colour / timbre / colour
2949	colto	cultivated
2950	commedia *f*	comedy
2951	comparsa *m + f* / figurante *m + f*	bit player / extra
2952	complesso *m*	ensemble
2953	completamente / totalmente	completely
2954	completo	complete
2955	composizione *f*	composition
2956	comprimario *m*	supporting role
2957	comune	common
2958	concerto *m*	concert / recital
2959	concerto privato *m*	house concert / private concert
2960	concorso musicale *m*	musical competition / musical contest
2961	conservatorio *m*	conservatoire / conservatory
2962	consonante *f*	consonant
2963	contenuto *m*	contents
2964	continuità *f*	continuity
2965	contrario *m*	contrary
2966	contrasto *m*	contrast
2967	coreografia *f*	choreography
2968	corpo di ballo *m*	chorps de ballet
2969	corretto	correct
2970	cosa *f*	thing
2971	costume *m*	costume / dress
2972	creativo	creative

berühmt	célèbre / fameux	2937
Hörzentrum *n*	centre auditif *m*	2938
gewiss / sicher	certain / sûr	2939
Kirche *f*	église *f*	2940
geschlossen	fermé	2941
Zyklus *m*	cycle *m*	2942
Himmel *m*	ciel *m*	2943
klassisch	classique	2944
Klassik *f*	classicisme *m*	2945
Mitwirkung *f*	collaboration *f*	2946
Sammlung *f*	collection *f* / recueil *m*	2947
Klangfarbe *f* / Tonfarbe *f* / Farbe *f* / Schattierung *f*	timbre *m* / couleur *f* / nuance *f*	2948
gebildet	cultivé	2949
Komödie *f*	comédie *f*	2950
Komparse *m* / Komparsin *f* / Statist *m* / Statistin *f*	figurant *m* / figurante *f*	2951
Ensemble *n*	ensemble *m*	2952
in vollständiger Weise / gänzlich	complètement / entièrement	2953
vollständig	complet	2954
Komposition *f* / Vertonung *f*	composition *f*	2955
Nebenrolle *f*	rôle secondaire *m*	2956
gemeinsam	commun	2957
Konzert *n*	concert *m* / récital *m*	2958
Hauskonzert *n*	concert privé *m*	2959
Musikwettbewerb *m*	concours de musique *m* / compétition musicale *f* / concours musical *m*	2960
Konservatorium *n*	conservatoire *m*	2961
Konsonant *m*	consonne *f*	2962
Inhalt *m*	contenu *m*	2963
Kontinuität *f*	continuité *f*	2964
Gegenteil *n*	contraire *m*	2965
Kontrast *m*	contraste *m*	2966
Choreographie *f*	chorégraphie *f*	2967
Ballettkorps *n*	corps de ballet *m*	2968
korrekt	correct	2969
Ding *n*	chose *f*	2970
Kostüm *n*	costume *m*	2971
schöpferisch	créatif	2972

2973	critica *f*	criticism
2974	debutto *m* / esordio *m*	début
2975	dedica *f*	dedication
2976	destra (a)	right (on the)
2977	dialogo *m*	dialogue
2978	diapason *m*	tuning fork
2979	diapason à fiato *m*	pitch pipe
2980	diapason da camera *m*	concert pitch
2981	dietro le quinte	behind the scenes
2982	difetto *m*	fault
2983	differenza *f*	difference
2984	difficile	difficult
2985	difficoltà *f*	difficulty
2986	dilettante *m*	dilettante / amateur / layman
2987	dinamica *f*	dynamics
2988	direttore ospite *m*	guest conductor
2989	direzione *f*	management
2990	diritti d'autore *m pl*	royalties
2991	diritti d'esecuzione *m pl*	performing rights
2992	diritto d'autore *m*	copyright
2993	discoteca *f*	discotheque
2994	discreto	discreet
2995	disposizione dell'orchestra *f*	orchestral layout
2996	distanza *f*	distance
2997	distribuzione *f*	cast
2998	diteggiatura *f*	fingering
2999	divertente	funny / amusing
3000	dramma *m*	drama
3001	durata *f*	duration
3002	eccellente	excellent
3003	eccetera / etc	and so on
3004	ecco	here
3005	edizione *f*	edition / issue
3006	edizione completa *f*	complete edition
3007	educazione dell'orecchio *f* / ascolto *m*	aural training
3008	effetto *m*	effect / result
3009	efficace	effective

Kritik *f*	critique *f*	2973
Debüt *n*	début *m*	2974
Widmung *f*	dédicace *f*	2975
rechts	droite (á)	2976
Dialog *m*	dialogue *m*	2977
Stimmgabel *f*	diapason à branches *m*	2978
Stimmpfeife *f*	diapason à bouche *m*	2979
Kammerton *m*	diapason de chambre *m*	2980
hinter der Bühne	derrière les coulisses	2981
Fehler *m* / Mangel *m*	défaut *m*	2982
Unterschied *m*	différence *f*	2983
schwierig / schwer	difficile	2984
Schwierigkeit *f*	difficulté *f*	2985
Dilettant *m* / Liebhaber *m* / Laie *m*	dilettante *m* / amateur *m*	2986
Dynamik *f*	dynamique *f* / nuances *f pl*	2987
Gastdirigent *m*	chef invité *m*	2988
Direktion *f* / Leitung *f*	direction *f*	2989
Tantiemen *f Pl*	droits d'auteur *m pl* / tantièmes *m pl*	2990
Aufführungsrecht *n*	droits d'execution *m pl*	2991
Urheberrecht *n*	droit d'auteur *m*	2992
Diskothek *f*	discothèque *f*	2993
ziemlich gut / diskret	passable / discret	2994
Orchesteranordnung *f*	disposition de l'orchestre *f*	2995
Abstand *m* / Distanz *f*	distance *f*	2996
Besetzung *f*	distribution *f*	2997
Fingersatz *m* / Applikatur *f*	doigté *m*	2998
unterhaltend / vergnüglich	divertissant / amusant	2999
Drama *n*	drame *m*	3000
Dauer *f* / Spieldauer *f*	durée *f*	3001
ausgezeichnet	excellent	3002
und so weiter / usw.	et ainsi de suite	3003
hier / da	voici / voilà	3004
Ausgabe *f* / Auflage *f*	édition *f* / tirage *m*	3005
Gesamtausgabe *f*	édition complète *f*	3006
Gehörbildung *f*	éducation de l'oreille *f*	3007
Effekt *m* / Wirkung *f* / Eindruck *m*	effet *m*	3008
wirkungsvoll	efficace	3009

3010	eguaglianza *f*	equality
3011	entrata *f*	entrance
3012	entrata degli artisti *f*	the stage door
3013	epoca *f*	epoch / era
3014	esaurito / completo / pienone *m*	sold out / full house
3015	esecuzione *f*	performance
3016	esempio *m*	example
3017	esercizio *m*	exercise
3018	esercizio per le dita *m*	finger exercise
3019	esordiente *m + f* / principiante *m + f*	beginner
3020	esposizione *f*	exhibition
3021	espressionismo *m*	expressionism
3022	estensione *f*	range / extension
3023	estetica *f*	aesthetics
3024	estratto *m*	excerpt
3025	eterno	eternal
3026	eufonia	euphony
3027	euritmia *f*	eurhythmics
3028	facile	easy
3029	facilità *f*	facility
3030	fantasma *m* / spettro *m*	ghost / apparition
3031	favola *f* / fiaba *f*	fairy tale / fable
3032	fedele all'originale	faithful to the original
3033	felice	happy / merry
3034	festa *f* / gala *m*	holiday / festival / party / gala
3035	festival musicale *m*	music festival
3036	fiasco *m*	failure / flop
3037	fiati *m pl*	wind section
3038	fiato *m*	breath
3039	figurazione *f*	figuration
3040	filarmonica / filarmonico	philharmonic
3041	filo *m*	thread / wire
3042	finto	feigned
3043	foglio *m*	sheet
3044	folclore *m*	folklore
3045	folletto *m*	elf
3046	fonetica *f*	phonetics

Deutsch	Français	Nr.
Gleichheit *f*	égalité *f*	3010
Eingang *m* / Eintritt *m* / Orchestereinsatz *m*	entrée *f*	3011
Künstlereingang m	entrée des artistes *f*	3012
Epoche *f* / Zeitabschnitt *m*	époque *f*	3013
ausverkauft / vergriffen	épuisé / complet	3014
Ausführung *f* / Vortrag *m*	exécution *f*	3015
Beispiel *n*	exemple *m*	3016
Übung *f*	exercice *m*	3017
Fingerübung *f*	exercice pour les doigts *m*	3018
Anfänger *m* / Anfängerin *f*	débutant *m* / débutante *f*	3019
Ausstellung *f*	exposition *f*	3020
Expressionismus *m*	expressionisme *m*	3021
Umfang *m* / Raum *m* / Ausdehnung *f*	étendue *f*	3022
Ästhetik *f*	esthétique *f*	3023
Ausschnitt *m* / Auszug *m*	extrait *m*	3024
ewig	éternel	3025
Euphonie *f* / Wohlklang *m*	euphonie *f*	3026
Eurhythmie *f*	eurythmie *f*	3027
leicht	facile	3028
Leichtigkeit *f*	facilité *f*	3029
Gespenst *n* / (Geister-) Erscheinung *f*	fantôme *m* / apparition *f*	3030
Fabel *f* / Märchen *n*	fable *f* / conte *m*	3031
werkgetreu	fidèle à l'original	3032
glücklich	heureux	3033
Fest *n* / Gala *f*	fête *f* / gala *m*	3034
Musikfest(spiel) *n*	festival de musique *m*	3035
Misserfolg *m* / Durchfall *m*	échec *m* / four *m*	3036
Bläser *m Pl*	vents *m pl*	3037
Atem *m*	souffle *m*	3038
Darstellung *f*	figuration *f*	3039
philharmonisch	philharmonique	3040
Faden *m* / Garn *n* / Draht *m*	fil *m*	3041
vorgetäuscht / fingiert	simulé / feint	3042
Papierblatt *n* / Bogen *m*	feuille *f*	3043
Folklore *f*	folklore *m*	3044
Troll *m* / Poltergeist *m*	lutin *m* / follet *m*	3045
Phonetik *f* / Lautkunde *f*	phonétique *f*	3046

3047	foresta *f* / bosco *m*	forest
3048	formato *m*	format
3049	forza *f* / intensità sonora *f*	strength of tone / intensity
3050	fossa dell'orchestra *f* / golfo mistico *m*	orchestra box / orchestral pit
3051	frammento *m*	fragment
3052	fuori / all'aperto	outside / open air
3053	galleria *f* / loggione *m*	balcony / gallery
3054	generalmente	generally
3055	genere *m*	genre
3056	geniale	ingenious
3057	genio *m*	genius
3058	gesto *m* / cenno *m*	gesture / wave
3059	graduazione *f*	gradation
3060	gratis / gratuito	free / gratuitous
3061	gregoriano	Gregorian
3062	idea *f*	idea
3063	ideale	ideal
3064	il sipario si abbassa	the curtain goes down
3065	il sipario si alza	the curtain rises / goes up
3066	il sipario si apre	the curtain opens
3067	il sipario si chiude	the curtain closes
3068	illuminazione *f*	lighting
3069	immagine sonora *f*	sound picture
3070	impercettibile	imperceptible
3071	importante / considerevole	important
3072	impossibile	impossible
3073	impreciso / inesatto	inaccurate / inexact
3074	impreparato	unprepared
3075	impressionismo *m*	impressionism
3076	improvvisazione *f*	improvisation
3077	in bocca al lupo	good luck / break a leg
3078	inatteso	unexpected
3079	incerto	uncertain
3080	inchino *m*	bow / curtsey
3081	incompleto	incomplete
3082	indicazione metronomica *f*	metronome mark(ing)
3083	indipendenza *f*	independence

Wald *m* / Tann *m*	forêt *f* / bois *m*	3047
Format *n*	format *m*	3048
Intensität des Klanges *f*	intensité du son *f* / puissance *f*	3049
Orchestergraben *m*	fosse d'orchestre *f*	3050
Fragment *n* / Bruchstück *n*	fragment *m*	3051
draußen / im Freien	dehors / en plein air	3052
Galerie *f*	galerie *f* / poulailler *m* / paradis *m*	3053
im Allgemeinen	en général	3054
Gattung *f*	genre *m*	3055
genial	génial	3056
Genius *m* / Genie *n*	génie *m*	3057
Gebärde *f* / Geste *f*	geste *m*	3058
Abstufung *f*	graduation *f*	3059
gratis / unentgeltlich	gratuit	3060
gregorianisch	grégorien	3061
Idee *f*	idée *f*	3062
ideal / vollkommen	idéal	3063
der Vorhang fällt	le rideau se baisse	3064
der Vorhang hebt sich	le rideau se lève	3065
der Vorhang öffnet sich	le rideau s'ouvre	3066
der Vorhang schließt sich	le rideau se ferme	3067
Beleuchtung *f*	éclairage *m*	3068
Klangbild *n*	image sonore *f*	3069
unmerklich / unvernehmlich	imperceptible	3070
wichtig / bedeutend / beträchtlich	important / considerable	3071
unmöglich	impossible	3072
ungenau	imprécis / inexact	3073
unvorbereitet	non préparé	3074
Impressionismus *m*	impressionisme *m*	3075
Improvisation *f*	improvisation *f*	3076
Hals- und Beinbruch / toi, toi, toi	trois fois merde	3077
unerwartet	inattendu	3078
unsicher	incertain / douteux	3079
Verbeugung *f* / Verneigung *f*	révérence *f*	3080
unvollständig	incomplet	3081
Metronomangabe *f*	indication métronomique *f*	3082
Unabhängigkeit *f*	indépendance *f*	3083

3084	ineseguibile	unplayable
3085	inferiore	lower / inferior
3086	inizio *m* / principio *m*	beginning
3087	integrale *f*	complete works
3088	interpretazione *f*	interpretation
3089	interprete *m* + *f*	performer / interpreter
3090	interruzione *f* / pausa *f*	interruption / intermission
3091	intervallo *m*	intermission
3092	intesa *f*	agreement / entente
3093	intuizione *f*	intuition
3094	invariabile	invariable
3095	irregolare	irregular
3096	ispirazione *f*	inspiration
3097	larghezza *f*	width / breadth
3098	leggio *m*	music stand / desk
3099	legni *m pl* / strumentini *m pl*	woodwind
3100	legno *m*	wood
3101	lettera *f*	letter
3102	lezione *f*	lesson
3103	lezione collettiva *f*	group lesson
3104	libro *m* / volume *m*	book / volume
3105	luci della ribalta	limelights
3106	malgrado / nonostante	although / even
3107	maschera *f*	mask
3108	maschera *m*+*f*	usher *m* / usherette *f*
3109	mecenate *m*	maecenas / patron
3110	meraviglioso / stupendo	marvellous / wonderful
3111	messa in scena *f*	production / staging
3112	metronomo *m*	metronome
3113	modello *m*	model / pattern
3114	moderno	modern
3115	musa *f*	muse
3116	musica *f*	music
3117	musica a programma *f*	programme music
3118	musica a quarti di tono *f*	quarter-tone music
3119	musica aleatoria *f*	aleatoric music
3120	musica antica *f*	ancient music

unausführbar / unspielbar	inexécutable	3084
niedriger / unter	inférieur	3085
Anfang *m*	début *m* / commencement *m*	3086
Gesamtwerk	l'œuvre intégrale *f*	3087
Interpretation *f* / Gestaltung *f* / Deutung *f*	interprétation *f*	3088
Interpret *m* / Ausführender *m*	interprète *m* + *f*	3089
Unterbrechung *f*	interruption *f*	3090
Pause *f*	entracte *m*	3091
Einklang *m* / Übereinstimmung *f*	entente *f*	3092
Eingebung *f*	intuition *f*	3093
unveränderlich	invariable	3094
unregelmäßig	irrégulier	3095
Inspiration *f* / Einfall *m*	inspiration *f*	3096
Breite *f*	largeur *f*	3097
Notenpult *n* / Notenständer *m*	lutrin *m* / pupitre *m*	3098
Holzbläser *m Pl*	bois *m pl*	3099
Holz *n*	bois *m*	3100
Buchstabe *m* / Brief *m*	lettre *f*	3101
Lektion *f* / Unterricht *m*	leçon *f*	3102
Gruppenunterricht *m*	cours collectif *m*	3103
Buch *n* / Band *m*	livre *m* / volume *m*	3104
Rampenlicht	feux de la rampe	3105
trotzdem / ungeachtet	malgré	3106
Maske *f*	masque *m*	3107
Platzanweiser *m* / Platzanweiserin *f*	ouvreur *m* / ouvreuse *f*	3108
Mäzen *m* / Förderer *m*	mécène *m*	3109
wunderbar / erstaunlich	merveilleux / étonnant	3110
Inszenierung *f*	mise en scène *f*	3111
Metronom *m*	métronome *m*	3112
Muster *n* / Vorbild *n*	modèle *m*	3113
modern	moderne	3114
Muse *f*	muse *f*	3115
Musik *f*	musique *f*	3116
Programmmusik *f*	musique à programme *f*	3117
Vierteltonmusik *f*	musique en quarts de ton *f* / musique microtonale *f*	3118
aleatorische Musik *f*	musique aléatoire *f*	3119
alte Musik *f*	musique ancienne *f*	3120

3121	musica assoluta *f* / musica pura *f*	absolute music
3122	musica classica *f*	classical music
3123	musica concreta *f*	musique concrète
3124	musica contemporanea *f*	contemporary music
3125	musica corale *f* / musica per coro *f*	choral music
3126	musica d'ambiente *f*	mood music
3127	musica d'avanguardia *f*	avantgarde music
3128	musica da ballo *f*	dance music
3129	musica da caccia *f*	hunting music
3130	musica da camera *f*	chamber music
3131	musica da chiesa *f* / musica liturgica *f*	church music
3132	musica da consumo *f* / musica d'uso *f*	functional music
3133	musica da salotto *f*	salon music
3134	musica da tavola *f*	table music
3135	musica dell'avvenire *f*	music of the future
3136	musica descrittiva *f*	descriptive music
3137	musica di corte *f*	court music
3138	musica di gatti *f*	cater wauling / shivaree
3139	musica di sottofondo *f*	background music
3140	musica della Passione *f*	passion music
3141	musica di Natale	Christmas music
3142	musica di scena *f* / musica scenica *f*	incidental music
3143	musica dodecafonica *f*	dodecaphonic music / twelve-tone music
3144	musica drammatica *f*	dramatic music
3145	musica elettronica *f*	electronic music
3146	musica esotica *f*	exotic music
3147	musica familiare *f* / musica domestica *f*	domestic music
3148	musica funebre *f*	funeral music
3149	musica leggera *f*	light music / entertainment music
3150	musica lirica *f*	operatic music
3151	musica meccanica *f*	mechanical music
3152	musica militaire *f*	military music
3153	musica nella (della) strada *f*	street music

absolute Musik *f*	musique pure *f*	3121
klassische Musik *f* / E-Musik *f*	musique classique *f*	3122
konkrete Musik *f*	musique concrète *f*	3123
zeitgenössische Musik *f* / neue Musik *f*	musique contemporaine *f*	3124
Chormusik *f*	musique chorale *f*	3125
Stimmungsmusik *f*	musique d'ambiance	3126
avantgardistische Musik *f*	musique d'avant-garde *f*	3127
Tanzmusik *f*	musique de danse *f*	3128
Jagdmusik *f*	musique de chasse *f*	3129
Kammermusik *f*	musique de chambre *f*	3130
Kirchenmusik *f*	musique d'église *f* / musique liturgique *f*	3131
Gebrauchsmusik *f*	musique fonctionelle *f*	3132
Salonmusik *f*	musique de salon *f*	3133
Tafelmusik *f*	musique de table *f*	3134
Zukunftsmusik *f*	musique d'avenir *f*	3135
Programmmusik *f*	musique descriptive *f*	3136
Hofmusik *f*	musique de cour *f*	3137
Katzenmusik *f*	charivari *m*	3138
Hintergrundmusik *f*	musique de fond *f*	3139
Passionsmusik *f*	musique de la Passion *f*	3140
Weihnachtsmusik *f*	musique de Noël *f*	3141
Bühnenmusik *f*	musique de scène *f*	3142
Dodekaphonie *f* / Zwölftonmusik *f*	dodécaphonie *f* / musique dodécaphonique *f*	3143
dramatische Musik *f*	musique dramatique *f*	3144
elektronische Musik *f*	musique électronique *f*	3145
exotische Musik *f*	musique exotique *f*	3146
Hausmusik *f*	musique domestique *f*	3147
Trauermusik *f*	musique funèbre *f*	3148
leichte Musik *f* / Unterhaltungsmusik *f* / U-Musik *f*	musique légère *f*	3149
Opernmusik *f*	musique lyrique *f*	3150
mechanische Musik *f*	musique méchanique *f*	3151
Militärmusik *f*	musique militaire *f*	3152
Straßenmusik *f*	musique de rue *f*	3153

3154	musica orchestrale *f*	orchestral music
3155	musica per balletto *f*	ballet music
3156	musica per banda *f*	wind music / band music
3157	musica per film *f*	film music
3158	musica per la scuola *f*	school music
3159	musica per strumenti a corda *f*	music for strings
3160	musica per strumenti a fiato *f*	wind music
3161	musica popolare *f* / musica folcloristica *f*	folk music / popular music
3162	musica profana *f*	secular music
3163	musica puntillistica *f*	pointillist music
3164	musica religiosa *f*	religious music
3165	musica rinascimentale *f*	renaissance music
3166	musica sacra *f*	sacred music
3167	musica seria *f*	serious music
3168	musica seriale *f*	serial music
3169	musica sinfonica *f*	symphonic music
3170	musica sperimentale *f*	experimental music
3171	musica strumentale *f*	instrumental music
3172	musica turca *f*	Turkish music
3173	musica tzigana *f*	gipsy music
3174	musica vocale *f*	vocal music
3175	musicale	musical
3176	musicalità *f*	musicality
3177	musicista di professione *m + f*	professional musician
3178	musicologia *f*	musicology
3179	musicoterapia *f*	music therapy
3180	muto	dumb / mute
3181	narratore *m*	narrator
3182	naturale	natural
3183	necessario	necessary
3184	noioso	boring
3185	nostalgia *f*	homesickness
3186	nota falsa *f* / stecca *f*	wrong note / false note
3187	notevole	remarkable
3188	numero *m*	number
3189	nuova versione *f*	new version
3190	nuovo	new

Orchestermusik *f*	musique d'orchestre *f*	3154
Ballettmusik *f*	musique de ballet *f*	3155
Blasmusik *f* / Harmoniemusik *f*	musique pour harmonie *f*	3156
Filmmusik *f*	musique de film *f*	3157
Schulmusik *f*	musique scolaire *f*	3158
Musik für Streichinstrumente *f* / Musik für Saiteninstrumente *f*	musique pour instruments à cordes *f*	3159
Blasmusik *f*	musique pour instruments à vent *f*	3160
Volksmusik *f* / volkstümliche Musik *f*	musique folklorique *f* / musique populaire *f*	3161
weltliche Musik *f*	musique profane *f*	3162
punktuelle Musik *f*	pointillisme musical *m*	3163
geistliche Musik *f*	musique religieuse *f*	3164
Renaissancemusik *f*	musique de la Renaissance *f*	3165
Kirchenmusik *f*	musique sacrée *f*	3166
ernste Musik *f* / E-Musik *f*	musique sérieuse *f*	3167
serielle Musik *f*	musique sérielle *f*	3168
Orchestermusik *f*	musique symphonique *f*	3169
experimentelle Musik *f*	musique expérimentale *f*	3170
Instrumentalmusik *f*	musique instrumentale *f*	3171
Janitscharenmusik *f*	musique turque *f*	3172
Zigeunermusik *f*	musique tzigane *f*	3173
Vokalmusik *f*	musique vocale *f*	3174
musikalisch	musical	3175
Musikalität *f*	musicalité *f*	3176
Berufsmusiker *m* / Berufsmusikerin *f*	musicien professionel *m + f*	3177
Musikwissenschaft *f*	musicologie *f*	3178
Musiktherapie *f*	musicothérapie *f*	3179
stumm	muet	3180
Sprecher *m*	récitant *m*	3181
natürlich	naturel	3182
nötig	nécessaire	3183
langweilig	ennuyeux	3184
Heimweh *n*	nostalgie *f*	3185
falsche Note *f* / Misston *m*	fausse note *f* / canard *m*	3186
bemerkenswert	remarcable / notable	3187
Nummer *f* / Zahl *f*	numéro *m*	3188
Neufassung *f*	nouvelle version *f*	3189
neu	neuf	3190

3191	nuvola *f*	cloud
3192	omaggio *m*	homage
3193	onorario *m*	fee / salary
3194	opera *f* / opus (L)	work
3195	orchestra *f*	orchestra
3196	orchestra da ballo *f*	dance band
3197	orchestra da camera *f*	chamber orchestra
3198	orchestra d'archi *f*	string orchestra
3199	orchestra d'opera *f* / dell'opera *f*	opera orchestra
3200	orchestra da salotto *f*	salon orchestra
3201	orchestra della radio *f*	radio orchestra
3202	orchestra sinfonica *f*	symphony orchestra
3203	ordine *m*	order
3204	orecchio assoluto *m*	absolute pitch / perfect pitch
3205	organico (strumentale) *m*	instrumentation / ensemble
3206	organologia *f*	organology
3207	originale	original
3208	ottoni *m pl*	brass
3209	pagina *f*	page
3210	palco *m*	box
3211	palpito *n*	heart beat
3212	pantomima *f*	pantomime
3213	paragone *m* / confronto *m*	comparison
3214	parola *f*	word
3215	parrucca *f*	wig
3216	partitura *f* / spartito *m*	score
3217	partitura per il direttore *f*	full score
3218	partitura tascabile *f*	pocket score / miniature score
3219	passaggio *m* / passo *m*	passage
3220	passo *m*	step
3221	paura dinanzi al pubblico *f*	stage fright
3222	pedagogia *f*	pedagogy
3223	percettibile / percepibile	perceptible
3224	perfetto	perfect
3225	perfezione *f*	perfection
3226	pezzo imposto *m*	compulsory piece
3227	perpetuo	perpetual
3228	pettinatura *f* / acconciatura *f*	hairdo / hair style
3229	plagio *m*	plagiarism

Deutsch	Français	Nr.
Wolke *f*	nuage *m*	3191
Huldigung *f*	hommage *m*	3192
Gage *f*	cachet *m*	3193
Werk *n*	œuvre *f*	3194
Orchester *n*	orchestre *m*	3195
Tanzorchester *n*	orchestre de danse *m*	3196
Kammerorchester *n*	orchestre de chambre *m*	3197
Streichorchester *n*	orchestre à cordes *m*	3198
Opernorchester *n*	orchestre d'opéra *m* / de l'opéra *m*	3199
Salonorchester *n*	orchestre de salon *m*	3200
Rundfunkorchester *n*	orchestre de la radio *m*	3201
Sinfonieorchester *n*	orchestre symphonique *m*	3202
Ordnung *f* / Reihenfolge *f*	ordre *m*	3203
absolutes Gehör *n*	oreille absolue *f*	3204
Besetzung *f*	distribution *f*	3205
Musikinstrumentenkunde *f*	organologie *f*	3206
original	original	3207
Blechinstrumente *n Pl*	cuivres *m pl*	3208
Seite *f* / Blatt *n*	page *f*	3209
Loge *f*	loge *f*	3210
Herzschlag *m*	battement de coeur *m*	3211
Pantomime *f*	pantomime *f*	3212
Vergleich *m*	comparaison *f*	3213
Wort *n*	parole *f*	3214
Perücke *f*	perruque *f*	3215
Partitur *f*	partition *f*	3216
Dirigierpartitur *f*	partition de direction *f*	3217
Taschenpartitur *f*	partition de poche *f*	3218
Passage *f* / Stelle *f* / Tonfolge *f*	passage *m* / trait *m*	3219
Schritt *m*	pas *m*	3220
Lampenfieber *n*	trac *m*	3221
Pädagogik *f*	pédagogie *f*	3222
wahrnehmbar / hörbar	perceptible	3223
perfekt / vollkommen	parfait	3224
Vollendung *f*	perfection *f*	3225
Pflichtstück *m*	morceau imposé *m*	3226
fortwährend	perpétuel	3227
Frisur *f*	coiffure *f*	3228
Plagiat *n*	plagiat *m*	3229

3230	platea *f*	stalls
3231	podio *m* / pedana *f*	rostrum
3232	popolare	popular
3233	posizione *f*	position
3234	posto *m*	place / seat
3235	posto a sedere *m*	seat / place
3236	posto in piedi *m*	standing-room
3237	postumo	posthumous
3238	prassi d'esecuzione *f* / pratica d'esecuzione *f*	performing practice
3239	preclassicismo *m*	pre-classical period
3240	prefazione *f*	preface
3241	preghiera *f*	prayer
3242	preparato	prepared
3243	presenza *f*	presence
3244	prima *f*	first night / opening night
3245	prima esecuzione *f*	first performance
3246	prima esecuzione mondiale *f* / creazione *f*	world première
3247	prima edizione *f*	first edition
3248	prima volta	first time
3249	primitivo	primitive
3250	primo leggio *m*	principal
3251	primo violino *m* / spalla *f*	leader / concertmaster
3252	profano	profane / secular
3253	progetto *m*	project / plan
3254	programma *m*	programme / playbill
3255	progresso *m*	progress
3256	prolungamento *f*	prolongation
3257	promotore *m*	promoter
3258	proporzione *f*	proportion
3259	proscenio *m*	frontstage
3260	prossima volta *f*	next time
3261	prova *f* / ripetizione *f*	rehearsal / coaching
3262	prova generale *f*	final rehearsal
3263	provvisorio	provisional / temporary
3264	prudenza *f*	prudence
3265	pseudonimo *m*	pseudonym / pen-name

Parkett *n*	fauteuils d'orchestre *m pl* / parterre *m*	3230
Podium *n* / Podest *n*	podium *m* / estrade *f*	3231
volkstümlich / populär	populaire	3232
Lage *f* / Stellung *f*	position *f*	3233
Platz *m* / Sitz *m*	place *f*	3234
Sitzplatz *m*	place assise *f*	3235
Stehplatz *m*	place debout *f*	3236
hinterlassen / nachgelassen	posthume	3237
Aufführungspraxis *f*	pratique de l'exécution *f*	3238
Vorklassik *f*	période pré-classique *f*	3239
Vorwort *n* / Einleitung *f*	préface *f*	3240
Gebet *n*	prière *f*	3241
präpariert / vorbereitet	préparé	3242
Ausstrahlung *f*	rayonnement *m*	3243
Premiere *f* / erste Vorstellung *f*	première *f*	3244
Uraufführung *f*	première représentation *f*	3245
Welterstaufführung *f*	première exécution mondiale *f* / création *f*	3246
Erstdruck *m*	première édition *f*	3247
erstes Mal	première fois	3248
urtümlich / primitiv	primitif	3249
Stimmführer *m* / Stimmführerin *f*	chef de pupitre *m* / chef d'attaque *m*	3250
Konzertmeister *m* / Konzertmeisterin *f* /Primarius *m*	premier violon solo *m*	3251
profan / weltlich / laienhaft	profane	3252
Projekt *m*	projet *m*	3253
Programm *n*	programme *m*	3254
Fortschritt *m*	progrès *m*	3255
Verlängerung *f*	prolongation *f*	3256
Veranstalter *m*	promoteur *m*	3257
Verhältnis *n*	proportion *f*	3258
Vorbühne *f*	l'avant-scène *f*	3259
nächstes Mal	prochaine fois *f*	3260
Probe *f* / Korrepetition *f*	répétition *f*	3261
Generalprobe *f*	répétition générale *f*	3262
provisorisch / vorläufig	provisoire	3263
Vorsicht *f*	prudence *f*	3264
Pseudonym *n* / Künstlername *m*	pseudonyme *m*	3265

3266	pubblico *m* / pubblico	audience / public
3267	pulito / netto	clean / neat / tidy
3268	punta *f*	point
3269	quadro musicale *m* / immagine musicale *f*	tone painting / musical imagery
3270	quinte *f pl*	wings
3271	raccolta di canzoni *f* / canzoniere *m*	songbook
3272	radiodiffusione *f*	broadcasting
3273	rappresentazione *f* / recita *f*	performance
3274	realtà *f*	reality
3275	regia *f*	stage direction
3276	regola *f*	rule
3277	regolare	regular
3278	repertorio *m* / avviso teatrale *m*	repertory / repertoire playbill
3279	replica *f*	repeat performance
3280	respirazione *f* / respiro	breathing
3281	retro	back / backwards
3282	retroscena *m*	backstage
3283	revisione *f*	revision
3284	ribalta *f*	footlights
3285	richiamo *m*	curtain call
3286	ridotto *m*	foyer / lobby
3287	riduzione *f* / adattamento *m*	reduction
3288	riduzione per pianoforte *f*	piano score
3289	riflettore *m*	spotlight
3290	rima *f*	rhyme
3291	rimbombo *m*	echo effect
3292	Rinascimento *m*	Renaissance
3293	rinviato	postponed
3294	riposo *m*	rest
3295	ripieno *m* / violino di fila *m*	ripieno violinist / section violinist
3296	rituale	ritual
3297	riverbero *m*	reverberation
3298	rivista *f*	magazine / review
3299	romanticismo *m*	romanticism
3300	rotto / spezzato	broken
3301	ruolo *m* / parte *f*	role / part

Publikum *n* / öffentlich	public *m* / publique	3266
sauber / reinlich	propre / net	3267
Kopf *m* / Spitze *f*	pointe *f*	3268
Tonmalerei *f*	image musicale *f* / peinture sonore *f*	3269
Kulisse *f*	coulisses *f pl*	3270
Liedersammlung *f*	recueil de chansons *m*	3271
Rundfunk *m*	radiodiffusion *f*	3272
Aufführung *f* / Darbietung *f* / Vorstellung *f*	représentation *f*	3273
Realität *f*	réalité *f*	3274
Regie *f* / Spielleitung *f*	régie *f*	3275
Regel *f*	règle *f*	3276
regelmäßig	régulier	3277
Repertoire *n* / Spielplan *m*	répertoire *m* / affiche *f*	3278
Wiederholung *f*	reprise *f* / réplique *f*	3279
Atmung *f*	respiration *f*	3280
rückwärts	en arrière	3281
Hinterbühne *f*	coulisses *f pl*	3282
Revision *f*	révision *f*	3283
Rampe *f*	rampe *f*	3284
herausklatschen / hervorklatschen	rappel *m*	3285
Foyer *n*	foyer *m*	3286
Reduktion *f* / Übertragung *f*	réduction *f*	3287
Klavierauszug *m*	partition pour piano *f*	3288
Scheinwerfer *m*	projecteur *m*	3289
Reim *m*	rime *f*	3290
Halleffekt *m* / Echo *n*	effet d'écho *m*	3291
Renaissance *f*	Renaissance *f*	3292
verschoben	renvoyé	3293
Ruhe *f*	repos *m*	3294
Ripienist *m* / Tuttigeiger *m*	ripièniste *m* / violon de file *m*	3295
rituell	rituel	3296
Rückstrahlung *f*	réverbération *f*	3297
Revue *f* / Zeitschrift *f*	revue *f*	3298
Romantik *f*	romantisme *m*	3299
gebrochen / zerbrochen	cassé / brisé	3300
Rolle *f* / Partie *f*	rôle *m* / partie *f*	3301

3302	ruolo principale *m*	main part
3303	saggezza *f*	wisdom
3304	saggio *m*	concert / audition
3305	sala da ballo *f*	ball room
3306	sala da concerto *f*	concert-hall
3307	salto *m*	jump / leap / skip
3308	santo	saint / holy
3309	sbagliato / falso / errato	wrong
3310	sbaglio *m* / errore *m*	mistake / error
3311	scambio *m*	exchange
3312	scatola *f*	box
3313	scelta *f* / selezione *f*	choice / selection
3314	scena *f* / palcoscenico *m*	scene / stage
3315	scenario *m*	scenery / set
3316	scenografia *f*	scenography
3317	scherzo *m*	joke
3318	schizzo *m* / abbozzo *m*	sketch / draft
3319	scorretto	incorrect
3320	scrittura *f* / contratto *m*	engagement / contract
3321	scuola *f*	school
3322	scuola di balletto *f*	ballet school
3323	scuola di coro *f*	choir school
3324	scuola di musica *f*	music school
3325	scuola viennese *f*	Viennese school
3326	scusa (i)	sorry
3327	segnale d'intervallo *m*	interval sign
3328	seguito *m*	continuation
3329	semplificato / facilitato	simplified
3330	senso *m*	sense
3331	sfumatura *f* / dettaglio *m*	shading / detail
3332	sguardo *m* / occhiata *f*	look / glance
3333	sillaba *f*	syllable
3334	silenzio *m* / silenzio!	silence / keep quiet!
3335	simbolo *m*	symbol
3336	simultaneo / contemporaneamente	simultaneous / at the same time
3337	sinistra (a)	left
3338	sipariettto *m*	act curtain

Hauptrolle *f*	rôle principal *m*	3302
Weisheit *f*	sagesse *f*	3303
Vorspiel *n*	essai *m* / audition *f*	3304
Ballsaal *m*	salle de danse *f*	3305
Konzertsaal *m*	salle de concert *f*	3306
Sprung *m*	saut *m*	3307
heilig	saint	3308
falsch	faux	3309
Fehler *m* / Irrtum *m*	faute *f* / erreur *f*	3310
Tausch *m*	échange *m*	3311
Schachtel *f*	boîte *f*	3312
Wahl *f* / Auswahl *f*	choix *m* / sélection *f*	3313
Bühne *f* / Szene *f*	scène *f* / planches *f pl*	3314
Bühnenbild *n* / Ausstattung *f*	scénario *m* / décor *m*	3315
Bühnenmalerei *f*	l'art du décor *m* / scénographie *f*	3316
Scherz *m*	plaisanterie *f*	3317
Entwurf *m* / Skizze *f*	esquisse *f* / ébauche *f* / brouillon *m*	3318
unkorrekt / fehlerhaft	incorrect	3319
Engagement *n* / Vertrag *m*	engagement *m* / contrat *m*	3320
Schule *f*	école *f*	3321
Ballettschule *f*	école de ballet *f* / école de danse classique *f*	3322
Chorschule *f*	maîtrise *f*	3323
Musikschule *f*	école de musique *f*	3324
Wiener Schule *f*	école viennoise *f*	3325
Entschuldigung	pardon / je m'excuse	3326
Pausenzeichen *n*	signal d'entracte *m*	3327
Fortsetzung *f*	suite *f*	3328
vereinfacht / leichter gemacht	simplifié / facilité	3329
Sinn *m*	sens *m*	3330
Schattierung *f* / Detail *n*	nuance *f* / détail *m*	3331
Blick *m*	regard *m* / coup d'œil *m*	3332
Silbe *f*	syllabe *f*	3333
Schweigen *n* / Ruhe!	silence *m* / taisez-vous!	3334
Symbol *n*	symbole *m*	3335
gleichzeitig	simultané / en même temps	3336
links	gauche (á)	3337
Aktvorhang *m*	rideau d'avant-scène *m*	3338

3339	sipario *m* / telone *m*	curtain
3340	soffio *m* / alito *m*	breath / puff
3341	solista *m + f*	soloist
3342	sonorità *f*	sonority
3343	sordo	deaf
3344	sorpresa *f*	surprise
3345	sostituto *m* / sostituta *f*	stand in / understudy
3346	sotto la direzione di ...	under the direction of ...
3347	spada *f*	sword / épée
3348	speciale	special
3349	speranza *f*	hope
3350	spettacolo *m*	performance / show
3351	spia *f*	peep-hole
3352	squillo *m*	ring
3353	stagione *f*	season
3354	stagione concertistica *f*	concert season
3355	stagione teatrale *f*	season
3356	stampa *f*	press
3357	stampa musicale *f*	musical press
3358	stato d'animo *m* / atmosfera *f*	mood
3359	stella *f*	star
3360	stile *m*	style
3361	stonato / scordato	out of tune / mistuned
3362	storia della musica *f*	history of music
3363	storico	historical
3364	straordinario / eccezionale	extraordinary / exceptional
3365	strapuntino *m*	folding seat
3366	strumentale	instrumental
3367	strumentazione variabile *f*	alternative scoring
3368	strumento *m*	instrument
3369	strumento accompagnatore *m*	accompanying instrument
3370	strumenti ad arco *m pl*	bowed stringed instruments
3371	strumenti a corda *m pl*	stringed instruments
3372	strumenti a fiato *m pl*	wind instruments
3373	strumenti a fiato di legno *m pl* / i legni *m pl*	woodwind instruments
3374	strumenti a fiato di ottone *m pl* / gli ottoni *m pl*	brass instruments

Theatervorhang *m*	rideau *m*	3339
Blasen *n* / Luftstoß *m* / Hauch *m*	souffle *m*	3340
Solist *m* / Solistin *f*	soliste *m* + *f*	3341
Klangfülle *f*	sonorité *f*	3342
taub	sourd	3343
Überraschung *f*	surprise *f*	3344
Stellvertreter *m* / Stellvertreterin *f*	remplaçant *m* / remplaçante *f*	3345
unter der Leitung von ...	sous la direction de ...	3346
Schwert *n* / Degen *m*	épée *f*	3347
spezial	spécial	3348
Hoffnung *f*	espoir *m*	3349
Vorstellung *f* / Schauspiel *n*	spectacle *m*	3350
Guckloch *n*	judas *m*	3351
Schall *m*	sonnerie *f*	3352
Saison *f* / Jahreszeit *f*	saison *f*	3353
Konzertsaison *f*	saison de concerts *f*	3354
Spielzeit *f*	saison théâtrale *f*	3355
Presse *f*	presse *f*	3356
Notendruck *m*	typographie musicale *f* / presse musicale *f*	3357
Stimmung *f*	climat *m* / atmosphère *f*	3358
Stern *m*	étoile *f*	3359
Stil *m*	style *m*	3360
verstimmt	désaccordé	3361
Musikgeschichte *f*	histoire de la musique *f*	3362
historisch	historique	3363
außerordentlich / außergewöhnlich	extraordinaire / exceptionnel	3364
Klappsitz *m*	strapontin *m*	3365
instrumental	instrumental	3366
variable Besetzung *f*	instrumentation variable *f*	3367
Instrument *n*	instrument *m*	3368
Begleitinstrument *n*	instrument accompagnateur *m*	3369
Streichinstrumente *n Pl*	cordes *f pl* / instruments à cordes *m pl*	3370
Saiteninstrumente *n Pl*	instruments à cordes *m pl*	3371
Blasinstrumente *n Pl*	instruments à vent *m pl*	3372
Holzblasinstrumente *n Pl*	les bois *m pl*	3373
Blechblasinstrumente *n Pl*	les cuivres *m pl*	3374

3375	strumenti a percussione *m*	percussion instruments
3376	strumenti a pizzico *m pl*	plucked instruments
3377	strumenti a tastiera *m pl*	keyboard instruments
3378	strumenti traspositori *m pl*	transposing instruments
3379	strumento a tastiera *m*	keyboard instrument
3380	strumento di fondamento *m* / strumento di basso continuo *m*	continuo instrument
3381	strumento melodico *m*	melodic instrument
3382	strumento ritmico *m*	rhythmic instrument
3383	strumento solistico *m*	solo instrument
3384	successo *m*	success
3385	sulla scena	on the stage
3386	sullo sfondo	in the background
3387	superfluo	superfluous
3388	superiore	superior / upper
3389	supplemento *m* / complemento *m*	supplement
3390	supplente *m+f* / aggiunto *m*	substitute / stopgap
3391	talento *m*	talent
3392	teatrale	theatrical
3393	teatro *m*	theatre (E) / theater (Am.)
3394	tecnica *f*	technique
3395	tecnica delle dita *f*	finger action
3396	televisione *f*	television
3397	temperamento *m*	temperament
3398	temporale *m*	thunderstorm
3399	tensione *f*	tension
3400	teoria musicale *f*	theory of music
3401	teoria degli affetti *f*	theory of emotional expression
3402	testo *m*	text
3403	tetralogia *f*	tetralogy
3404	tip-tap *m*	tap dance / step dance
3405	traduzione *f*	translation
3406	tragedia *f*	tragedy
3407	trama *f* / intreccio *m*	action / plot
3408	trascrizione *f*	transcription
3409	trasmissione *f*	broadcast / telecast
3410	travestimento *m*	disguise

Schlaginstrumente *n Pl*	instruments à percussion *m pl*	3375
Zupfinstrumente *n Pl*	instruments à cordes pincées *m pl*	3376
Tasteninstrumente *n Pl*	instruments à clavier m *pl*	3377
transponierende Instrumente *n Pl*	instruments transpositeurs *m pl*	3378
Tasteninstrument *n*	instrument à clavier *m*	3379
Generalbassinstrument *n*	instrument jouant la partie de basse *m*	3380
Melodieinstrument *n*	instrument mélodique *m*	3381
Rhythmusinstrument *n*	instrument rythmique *m*	3382
Soloinstrument *n*	instrument solo *m* / instrument soliste *m*	3383
Erfolg *m*	succès *m*	3384
auf der Bühne	sur la scène	3385
im Hintergrund	sur le fond	3386
überflüssig	superflu	3387
über / höher / ober	supérieur	3388
Ergänzung *f*	supplément *m* / complément *m*	3389
Stellvertreter *m* / Aushilfe *f*	suppléant *m* / supplémentaire *m+f*	3390
Begabung *f*	talent *m*	3391
theatralisch	théâtral	3392
Theater *n*	théâtre *m*	3393
Technik *f*	technique *f*	3394
Fingertechnik *f*	technique des doigts *f*	3395
Fernsehen *n*	télévision *f*	3396
Temperatur *f* / Temperament *n*	tempérament *m*	3397
Gewitter *n*	orage *m*	3398
Spannung *f*	tension *f*	3399
Musiktheorie *f*	théorie musicale *f*	3400
Affekttheorie *f* / Affektenlehre *f*	théorie de l'expression des émotions *f*	3401
Text *m*	texte *m*	3402
Tetralogie *f*	tétralogie *f*	3403
Stepptanz *m*	claquettes *f pl*	3404
Übersetzung *f*	traduction *f*	3405
Tragödie *f*	tragédie *f*	3406
Handlung *f*	action *f*	3407
Transkription *f* / Übertragung *f*	transcription *f*	3408
Sendung *f*	émission *f*	3409
Verkleidung *f*	déguisement *m*	3410

3411	trilogia *f* / trittico *m*	trilogy / triptych
3412	tuono *m*	thunder
3413	udito *m*	hearing
3414	uscita *f*	exit
3415	varietà *f*	variety
3416	varietà *f*	vaudeville (theatre) / music hall
3417	vento *m*	wind
3418	veramente	really
3419	verismo *m*	verismo / realism
3420	versione *f*	version
3421	versione originale *f*	original version
3422	verso *m*	verse / line
3423	vicino / presso	near / close
3424	vista *f*	sight
3425	vocale *f*	vocal / vowel
3426	volontà *f*	will
3427	zingaro *m* / zingara *f*	gipsy

Il corpo umano — The human body

3428	anca *f*	haunch / hip
3429	articolazione *f*	joint
3430	avambraccio *m*	forearm
3431	bocca *f*	mouth
3432	braccio *m*	arm
3433	capelli *m pl*	hair
3434	collo *m*	neck
3435	cuore *m*	heart
3436	denti *m pl*	teeth
3437	diaframma *m*	diaphragm
3438	dito *m*	finger
3439	dorso della mano *m*	back of the hand
3440	faccia *f*	face
3441	falange *f*	phalanx
3442	faringe *f*	pharynx
3443	fronte *f*	forehead
3444	gamba *f*	leg
3445	ginocchio *m*	knee
3446	gola *f*	throat

Trilogie *f* / Triptychon *m*	trilogie *f* / triptyque *m*	3411
Donner *m*	tonnerre *m*	3412
Gehör *n*	ouïe *f*	3413
Ausgang *m*	sortie *f*	3414
Vielfältigkeit *f*	variété *f*	3415
Varieté *n*	variété *m* / café-concert *m*	3416
Wind *m*	vent *m*	3417
wirklich	vraiment	3418
Verismo *m* / Verismus *m*	vérisme *m*	3419
Version *f* / Fassung *f*	version *f*	3420
Urtext *m*	version originale *f*	3421
Vers *m*	vers *m*	3422
nahe	près	3423
Sicht *f*	vue *f*	3424
Vokal *m* / Selbstlaut *m*	vocal *f* / voyelle *f*	3425
Wille *m*	volonté *f*	3426
Zigeuner *m* / Zigeunerin *f*	bohémien *m*/-ne *f* / tzigane *m* + *f*	3427

Der menschliche Körper — **Le corps humain**

Hüfte *f*	hanche *f*	3428
Gelenk *n*	articulation *f*	3429
Unterarm *m*	avant-bras *m*	3430
Mund *m*	bouche *f*	3431
Arm *m* / Oberarm *m*	bras *m*	3432
Haare *n Pl*	cheveux *m pl*	3433
Hals *m*	cou *m*	3434
Herz *n*	coeur *m*	3435
Zähne *m Pl*	dents *f pl*	3436
Zwerchfell *n*	diaphragme *m*	3437
Finger *m*	doigt *m*	3438
Handrücken *m*	dos de la main *m*	3439
Gesicht *n*	visage *m*	3440
Fingerglied *n* / Fingerknochen *m*	phalange *f*	3441
Rachenhöhle *f*	pharynx *m*	3442
Stirn *f*	front *m*	3443
Bein *n*	jambe *f*	3444
Knie *n*	genou *m*	3445
Kehle *f* / Rachen *m*	gorge *f*	3446

3447	gomito *m*	elbow
3448	guancia *f*	cheek
3449	indice *m*	forefinger
3450	labbro *m*	lip
3451	laringe *f*	larynx
3452	lingua *f*	tongue
3453	mano *f*	hand
3454	mascella *f*	jaw
3455	mento *m*	chin
3456	mignolo *m*	little finger
3457	muscolo *m*	muscle
3458	naso *m*	nose
3459	nervo *m*	nerve
3460	nuca *f*	nape of the neck
3461	occhio *m*	eye
3462	orecchio *m*	ear
3463	osso *m*	bone
3464	palato *m*	palate
3465	palmo della mano *m*	palm of the hand
3466	pancia *f*	tummy
3467	petto *m*	breast
3468	piede *m*	foot
3469	pollice *m*	thumb
3470	polmoni *m pl*	lungs
3471	polpastrello *m*	fingertips
3472	polso *m*	pulse
3473	polso *m*	wrist
3474	sangue *m*	blood
3475	schiena *f* / dorso *m*	back
3476	sedere *m*	backside
3477	spalla *f*	shoulder
3478	stomaco *m*	stomach
3479	tallone *m*	heel
3480	testa *f*	head
3481	torace *m*	thorax
3482	trachea *f*	windpipe
3483	unghia *f*	nail
3484	vena *f*	vein

Ellbogen *m*	coude *m*	3447
Wange *f*	joue *f*	3448
Zeigefinger *m*	index *m*	3449
Lippe *f*	lèvre *f*	3450
Kehlkopf *m*	larynx *m*	3451
Zunge *f*	langue *f*	3452
Hand *f*	main *f*	3453
Kiefer *m* / Kinnlade *f*	mâchoire *f*	3454
Kinn *n*	menton *m*	3455
kleiner Finger *m*	petit doigt *m*	3456
Muskel *m*	muscle *m*	3457
Nase *f*	nez *m*	3458
Nerv *m*	nerf *m*	3459
Genick *n* / Nacken *m*	nuque *f*	3460
Auge *n*	œil *m*	3461
Ohr *n*	oreille *f*	3462
Knochen *m*	os *m*	3463
Gaumen *m*	palais *m*	3464
Handfläche *f*	paume de la main *f*	3465
Bauch *m*	ventre *m*	3466
Brust *f*	poitrine *f*	3467
Fuß *m*	pied *m*	3468
Daumen *m*	pouce *m*	3469
Lungen *f Pl*	poumons *m pl*	3470
Fingerkuppe *f*	bout du doigt *m*	3471
Puls *m*	pouls *m*	3472
Handgelenk *n*	poignet *m*	3473
Blut *n*	sang *m*	3474
Rücken *m*	dos *m*	3475
Gesäß *n*	derrière *m*	3476
Schulter *f* / Achsel *f*	épaule *f*	3477
Magen *m*	estomac *m*	3478
Ferse *f*	talon *m*	3479
Kopf *m*	tête *f*	3480
Brustkorb *m*	thorax *m*	3481
Luftröhre *f*	trachée *f*	3482
Nagel *m*	ongle *m*	3483
Ader *f*	veine *f*	3484

	I mestieri	**The professions**
3485	accompagnatore *m* / accompagnatrice *f*	accompanist
3486	accordatore *m* / accordatrice *f*	tuner
3487	arpista *m+f*	harpist
3488	arrangiatore *m* / arrangiatrice *f*	arranger
3489	artista *m+f*	artist
3490	attore *m* / attrice *f*	actor *m* / actress *f*
3491	ballerino *m* / ballerina *f*	dancer / ballerina
3492	batterista *m+f*	drummer
3493	cantante *m+f*	singer / vocalist
3494	chitarrista *m+f*	guitarist
3495	clarinettista *m+f*	clarinettist / clarinetist
3496	clavicembalista *m+f*	harpsichordist
3497	compositore *m* / compositrice *f*	composer
3498	concertista *m+f*	concert artist
3499	contrabbassista *m+f*	double bass player / bass player
3500	copista *m+f*	copyist
3501	coreografo *m+f*	choreographer
3502	coreologo *m+f*	choreologist
3503	corista *m+f*	chorus singer / chorister
3504	cornista *m+f*	horn player
3505	critico musicale *m+f*	music critic
3506	direttore d'orchestra *m+f*	conductor
3507	fagottista *m+f*	bassoonist
3508	flautista *m+f*	flutist / flautist
3509	incisore *m+f*	engraver
3510	insegnante *m+f* / professore *m* / professoressa *f*	teacher / professor
3511	liutaio *m+f*	violin maker

Die Berufe	**Les métiers**	
Begleiter *m* / Begleiterin *f*	accompagnateur *m* / accompagnatrice *f*	3485
Stimmer *m* / Stimmerin *f*	accordeur *m+f*	3486
Harfenist *m* / Harfenistin *f*	harpiste *m+f*	3487
Bearbeiter *m* / Bearbeiterin *f*	arrangeur *m+f*	3488
Künstler *m* / Künstlerin *f*	artiste *m+f*	3489
Schauspieler *m* / Schauspielerin *f*	acteur *m* / actrice *f* / comédien *m* / comédienne *f*	3490
Tänzer *m* / Tänzerin *f* / Ballett-tänzer *m* / Balletttänzerin *f*	danseur *m* / danseuse *f*	3491
Schlagzeuger *m* / Schlagzeugerin *f*	batteur *m+f*	3492
Sänger *m* / Sängerin *f*	chanteur *m* / chanteuse *f* / cantatrice *f*	3493
Gitarrist *m* / Gitarristin *f*	guitariste *m+f*	3494
Klarinettist *m* / Klarinettistin *f*	clarinettiste *m+f*	3495
Cembalist *m* / Cembalistin *f*	claveciniste *m+f*	3496
Komponist *m* / Komponistin *f* / Tondichter *m* / Tondichterin *f*	compositeur *m*	3497
ausübender Künstler *m* / ausübende Künstlerin *f*	concertiste *m+f*	3498
Kontrabassist *m* / Kontrabassistin *f*	contrebassiste *m+f*	3499
Kopist *m* / Kopistin *f*	copiste *m+f*	3500
Choreograph *m* / Choreographin *f*	chorégraphe *m+f*	3501
Choreologe *m* / Choreologin *f*	choréologue *m+f*	3502
Chorsänger *m* / Chorsängerin *f*	choriste *m+f*	3503
Hornist *m* / Hornistin *f*	corniste *m+f*	3504
Musikkritiker *m* / Musik-kritikerin *f*	critique musical *m+f*	3505
Dirigent *m* / Dirigentin *f* / Kapellmeister *m* / Kapellmeisterin *f*	chef d'orchestre *m+f*	3506
Fagottist *m* / Fagottistin *f*	basson *m+f*	3507
Flötist *m* / Flötistin *f*	flûtiste *m+f*	3508
Stecher *m* / Stecherin *f*	graveur *m* / graveuse *f*	3509
Lehrer *m* / Lehrerin *f* / Professor *m* / Professorin *f*	instituteur *m* / institutrice *f* / professeur *m+f*	3510
Geigenbauer *m* / Geigenbauerin *f*	luthier *m+f*	3511

3512	maestro di ballo *m+f*	ballet master
3513	musicista *m+f*	musician
3514	musicologo *m+f*	musicologist
3515	oboista *m+f*	oboist
3516	organista *m+f*	organist
3517	pianista *m+f*	pianist
3518	professore d'orchestra *m* / professoressa d'orchestra *f*	orchestralist
3519	regista *m+f*	director / producer
3520	ripetitore / maestro sostituto *m+f*	coach
3521	sassofonista *m+f*	saxophonist
3522	suggeritore *m* / suggeritrice *f*	prompter
3523	tecnico del suono	sound engineer
3524	timpanista *m+f*	timpanist
3525	tromba *m+f*	trumpeter / trumpetist
3526	trombone *m+f*	trombonist
3527	violinista *m+f*	violinist
3528	violista *m+f*	violist
3529	violoncellista / cellista *m+f*	cellist

Deutsch	Français	Nr.
Ballettmeister *m* / Ballettmeisterin *f*	maître de ballet *m* / maîtresse de ballet *f*	3512
Musiker *m* / Musikerin *f*	musicien *m* / musicienne *f*	3513
Musikwissenschaftler *m* / Musikwissenschaftlerin *f*	musicologue *m+f*	3514
Oboist *m* / Oboistin *f*	hautboiste *m+f*	3515
Organist *m* / Organistin *f*	organiste *m+f*	3516
Pianist *m* / Pianistin *f*	pianiste *m+f*	3517
Orchestermusiker *m* / Orchestermusikerin *f*	musicien d'orchestre *m* / musicienne d'orchestre *f*	3518
Regisseur *m* / Regisseurin *f* / Spielleiter *m* / Spielleiterin *f*	régisseur	3519
Korrepetitor *m* / Korrepetitorin *f*	répétiteur *m* / répétitrice *f*	3520
Saxophonist *m* / Saxophonistin *f*	saxophoniste *m + f*	3521
Souffleur *m* / Souffleuse *f*	souffleur *m* / souffleuse *f*	3522
Tonmeister *m* / Tonmeisterin *f*	ingénieur du son *m+f*	3523
Pauker *m* / Paukerin *f*	timbalier *m+f*	3524
Trompeter *m* / Trompeterin *f*	trompette *m+f*	3525
Posaunist *m* / Posaunistin *f*	trombone *m+f* / tromboniste *m+f*	3526
Geiger *m* / Geigerin *f*	violiniste *m+f*	3527
Bratschist *m* / Bratschistin *f*	altiste *m+f*	3528
Cellist *m* / Cellistin *f*	violoncelliste *m+f*	3529

Anhang
Appendice
Appendix
Appendice

Terminologie française	Terminologia francese
à peine ralenti	appena rallentato
à toute vitesse	a tutta velocità
animez progressivement	animate progressivamente
attaques profondes	attacchi profondi
au dessous du mouvement	più lento del tempo primo
aussi légèrement que possible	il più leggermente possibile
avec beaucoup d'entrain	con molto brio
avec de brusques oppositions d'extrême violence et de passionnée douceur	con repentinee opposizioni di estrema violenza e di dolcezza appassionata
avec plus d'abandon	con più abbandono
avec la même humeur du début	con lo stesso stato d'animo dell'inizio
avec un doux flottement	dolcemente fluente
avec un profond ennui	con una noia profonda
avec une douceur cachée	con una dolcezza nascosta
avec une élégance grave et lente	con una lenta e grave eleganza
avec une émotion naissante	con un'emozione nascente
avec une étrangeté subite	con una repentinea stranezza
avec une expression intense	con un'espressione intensa
avec une fausse douceur	con una falsa dolcezza
avec une grâce capricieuse	con una grazia capricciosa
avec une grâce dolente	con una grazia dolente
avec une grande douceur	con una grande dolcezza
avec une grande émotion	con una grande emozione
avec une joie de plus en plus tumultueuse	con una gioia sempre più tumultuosa
avec une joie voilée	con una gioia velata
avec une légèreté fantasque mais précise	con una leggerezza fantasiosa ma precisa
avec une passion naissante	con una passione nascente
avec une volupté dormante	con una voluttà dormente
baigné de pédales	bagnato di pedali
beaucoup de pédale en la changeant très souvent	molto pedale, cambiandolo spessissimo
bien égal	molto uguale

French specialist terms	Französische Fachausdrücke
hardly slower	kaum verlangsamt
very quickly	mit größter Geschwindigkeit
animate progressively	nach und nach beleben
deep touch	tiefe Anschläge
in a slower tempo	in langsamerem Zeitmaß
as lightly as possible	so leicht wie möglich
with much liveliness	mit viel Lebhaftigkeit / mit Schwung
with sudden contrasts of extreme violence and passionate softness	mit Gegensätzen äußerster Heftigkeit und leidenschaftlicher Sanftheit
with more abandon	mit mehr Hingabe
with the same mood as at the beginning	in der gleichen Stimmung wie am Anfang
smoothly flowing	sanft fließend
with profound boredom	mit tiefer Langeweile
with hidden gentleness	mit verborgener Sanftheit
with a dignified and slow elegance	mit würdevoller und langsamer Eleganz
with growing emotion	mit aufkommender Erregung
with sudden strangeness	mit plötzlicher Seltsamkeit
with an intense expression	mit intensivem Ausdruck
with false sweetness	mit falscher Sanftmut
with capricious grace	mit launischer Anmut
with plaintive grace	anmutig klagend
with great tenderness	mit großer Zartheit
with a great emotion	mit großer Gemütsbewegung
with ever-increasing tumultuous joy	mit immer stürmischerer Freude
with restrained joy	mit verhaltener Freude
with an odd lightness but precise	mit wunderlicher, aber präziser Leichtigkeit
with growing passion	mit aufkommender Leidenschaft
with sleepy voluptuousness	mit schläfriger Wollust
full of pedals	mit sehr viel Pedal
much pedal, very often changing	viel Pedal, sehr oft wechselnd
very even	sehr gleichmäßig

changer souvent (la pédale)	cambiare spesso (il pedale)
claque *f*	pubblico pagato per applaudire
claquement doux et mouillé	un colpetto dolce e bagnato
comme de loin	come da lontano
comme des souffles frais	come dei zeffiri freschi
comme un fond de paysage	come lo sfondo di un paesaggio
comme une causerie	come una conversazione
comme un cri	come un grido
comme une buée irisée	come un leggero vapore iridato
comme un murmure confus	come un mormorio confuso
comme une ombre mouvante	come un'ombra movente
comme un regret	come un rimpianto
comme un lointain tumulte	come un tumulto lontano
comme une sonnerie de cors	come uno squillo di corni
d'un air songeur et triste	in maniera sognante e triste
commencer un peu en dessous du movement	incominciare un poco sotto il tempo
d'un bout à l'autre	da capo fino in fondo
d'un petit pas égal	d'un piccolo passo uguale
d'un rhythme las	con un ritmo stanco (lasso)
d'un rhythme libre	il ritmo libero
d'un seul doigt	con un dito solo
d'une sonorité pleine	con una sonorità piena
dans le style d'une sarabande	nello stile di una sarabanda
dans un goût burlesque	in modo burlesco
dans un halo de pédales	in un alone di pedali
dans un murmure	in un mormorio
dans un sentiment intime	con un sentimento *i*ntimo
dans une sonorité claire	con una sonorità chiara
d'une voix vivante	a viva voce
dans une sonorité harmonieuse et lointaine	con una sonorità armoniosa e distante
de plus en plus brouillé	sempre più confuso
de plus loin	da più lontano
de très loin	da molto lontano
doucement contenu	dolcemente rattenuto
doucement timbré	dolcemente sonoro
durant tout le morceau	durante tutto il pezzo

change often (the pedal)	das Pedal oft wechselnd
professional clapper audience	bezahlter Beifallklatscher
damp and gentle tapping	weicher, verschwommener Anschlag
as from far away	wie aus der Ferne
like a fresh breeze	wie eine frische Brise
with a country background	wie ein ländlicher Hintergrund
like a chat	wie ein Geplauder
like a cry	wie ein Schrei
like a rainbow-coloured mist	wie ein regenbogenfarbiger Dunst
like a confusing murmur	wie ein verworrenes Gemurmel
like a moving shadow	wie ein gleitender Schatten
like a regret	wie ein Bedauern
like tumult from far away	wie ein Tumult aus der Ferne
like a sound of horns	wie Hörnerklang
wistfully and sad	nachdenklich und traurig
start in a little slower tempo	in einem etwas langsameren Zeitmaß beginnend
from the beginning to the end	vom Anfang bis zum Schluss
in little, even pace	mit einem kleinen, gleichmäßigen Schritt
in a tired rhythm	mit müdem Rhythmus
in a free rhythm	in freiem Rhythmus
with only one finger	nur mit einem Finger
with a full sound	mit einem vollen Klang
in the style of a sarabande	im Stil einer Sarabande
in a burlesque style	in burlesker Weise
with a gentle touch of pedals	mit einem Hauch von Pedal
in a murmur	gemurmelt
with intimate feeling	mit innigem Gefühl
with a clear sound	mit hellem Klang
with lively voice	mit lebhafter Stimme
with a harmonious sound from far away	mit einem harmonischen Klang aus der Ferne
more and more confused	immer wirrer
from further away	von weiter her
from very far away	von sehr weit her
gently restrained	sacht zurückgehalten
with a gentle timbre	mit einer sanften Klangfarbe
during the whole piece	während des ganzen Stücks

en animant toujours davantage	sempre più animando
en demi-teinte	in mezza tinta
en diminuant graduellement	diminuendo gradualmente
en donnant à la basse une sonorité cristalline et dégagée	dando al basso una sonorità cristallina e disinvolta
en général sans nuances	generalmente senza dinamica
en se rapprochant	avvicinandosi
enveloppé de pédales	avvolto di pedale
frapper les accords sans lourdeur	suonare gli accordi senza pesantezza
gardez la pédale	tenete il pedale
intimement doux	intimamente dolce
jamais assez	mai abbastanza
joyeusement animé	allegramente animato
joyeux et emporté	gioioso ed impetuoso
jusqu'à la fin en se perdant	perdendosi fino al fine
la ligne d'en haut	la voce superiore in fuori
la mesure précédente	la battuta precedente
la moitié moins vite	la metà meno svelto
le chant un peu en dehors	il canto un poco in fuori
le reste	il resto
le thème en dehors	il tema in rilievo
les arpèges serrés	gli arpeggi stretti
les petites notes doivent être frappées sur le temps	le notine in battere
lâchez	allentate
librement déclamé	liberamente declamato
marquez le thème	marcate il tema
mettre beaucoup de pédale	mettere molto pedale
pédale à chaque accord	pedale ad ogni accordo
pédale à chaque mesure	pedale ad ogni battuta
pédale forte sur chaque temps	il pedale destro su ogni battuta
petite reprise	piccola ripresa
plus lent qu'au début	più lento del principio
plus pénétrant	più penetrante
plutôt lent	piuttosto lento
point trop vite	non troppo presto

more and more animated	mehr und mehr belebt
with light colour	mit halber (schwacher) Färbung
gradually becoming softer	schrittweise leiser werdend
giving the bass a crystalline and unconstrained timbre	dem Bass einen kristalklaren und ungezwungenen Klang gebend
generally without shading	im Allgemeinen ohne Abstufungen
approaching	sich nähernd
enveloped by pedals	in Pedalklang gehüllt
sound in unison without any weight	die Akkorde ohne Gewicht anschlagen
keep the pedal down	das Pedal halten
intimately gentle	innig sanft
never enough	nie genug
joyfully animated	freudig belebt
gaily and impetuously	fröhlich und ungestüm
allowing to die out	sich bis zum Schluss verlierend
the upper voice stressed	die obere Stimme hervorgehoben
the preceding measure	der vorhergehende Takt
half the speed	halb so schnell
the melody a little stressed	die Melodie etwas hervorgehoben
the rest	der Rest
the theme stressed	das Thema hervorgehoben
the arpeggios hurried	die Arpeggien eng gedrängt
the small notes on the beat	die kleinen Noten auf den Schlag
let slacken	nachlassen
freely recited / declaimed	frei deklamiert
mark the theme	das Thema mit Nachdruck
use plenty of pedal	viel Pedal nehmen
pedal on each chord	Pedal auf jeden Akkord
pedal on each measure	Pedal auf jeden Takt
sustaining pedal on each time	rechtes Pedal auf jede Taktzeit
short reprise	kleine Reprise
more slowly than at the beginning	langsamer als am Anfang
more penetrating	durchdringender
rather slowly	eher langsam
not too fast	nicht zu schnell

presque plus rien	quasi più niente
profondément expressif	profondamente espressivo
rallentissez beaucoup	rallentato molto
relâche *f*	oggi riposo
reprendre sans refrapper	riprendere senza ribattere
respectez scrupuleusement ce doigté	rispettate scrupolosamente questa diteggiatura
retro	fuori moda
revenez au premier mouvement	tornate al tempo primo
revenir au tempo initial	tornare al tempo iniziale
rêveusement lent	lento sognante
richement coloré	riccamento colorito
sans accentuation	senza accenti
sans aucun	senza nessun
sans aucune accentuation	senza nessuna accentuazione
sans décomposer	senza decomporre
sans dureté	senza durezza
sans expression	senza espressione
sans hâte	senza fretta
sans interrompre	senza interrompere
sans lourdeur	senza pesantezza
sans nuances	senza dinamica
sans presser ni ralentir	senza accelerare ne rallentare
sans sécheresse	senza secchezza
sensiblement plus...	sensibilmente più…
sourdement agité	cupamente agitato
sourdine durant toute la pièce	la sordina durante tutto il pezzo
sortant de la brume	uscendo dalla foschia/nebbia
tout à fait	del tutto
très allant	con molto brio
très calme	molto calmo
très chaleureux	molto caloroso
très décidé	molto deciso
très effilé	molto sottile
très fondu	molto fuso
très franc	molto schietto
très intense	molto intenso

almost nothing anymore	beinahe nichts mehr
with deep expression	mit tiefem Ausdruck
slow down a lot	verlangsamen Sie sehr
no performance today	heute keine Vorstellung
take back without touching again	nochmals niederdrücken, ohne anzuschlagen
follow this fingering exactly	peinlich genau diesen Fingersatz beachten
oldfashioned	altmodisch
go back to the first tempo	zum ersten Zeitmaß zurückkehren
come back to the initial tempo	zum Anfangszeitmaß zurückkehren
dreamily slow	träumerisch langsam
richly coloured	reichlich gefärbt
without accentuation	ohne Betonung
without any	ohne jegliche
without any accentuation	ohne jegliche Betonung
without decomposing	ohne den Takt zu zerlegen
without hardness	ohne Härte
without expression	ohne Ausdruck
without haste	ohne Eile
without interrupting	ohne zu unterbrechen
without heaviness	ohne Schwerfälligkeit
no differences in the dynamics	ohne Unterschied in der Dynamik
neither hurry nor slow down	weder eilen noch verlangsamen
without dryness	ohne Trockenheit
considerably more...	spürbar mehr...
gloomily agitated	düster bewegt
soft pedal throughout the whole piece	Dämpfer während des ganzen Stücks
appearing out of the fog	aus dem Nebel auftauchend
entirely	ganz und gar
very lively	sehr lebhaft
very calm	sehr ruhig
very cordial	sehr warmherzig
very decided	sehr bestimmt
very slender	sehr schlank
very melted	sehr verschmolzen
very sincere	sehr aufrichtig
very intense	sehr intensiv

très lointain	molto lontano
uniformément articulé	uniformemente articolato
un peu appuyé	un poco appoggiato
un peu élargi	un poco allargato
un peu en dehors	un poco in fuori
un peu en valeur	un poco in risalto
un peu languissant	un poco languido
un peu plus lent qu'au début	un poco più lento dell'inizio
un peu plus à l'aise	un poco più comodo
un peu plus intense	un poco più intenso
un peu plus las	un poco più lasso
un peu plus vif	un poco più vivo
un tant-soit-peu	pochissimo / appena

Deutsche Fachausdrücke / Terminologia tedesca

aber immer fließend	ma sempre scorrevole
aber stets ernst und gewichtig	ma sempre serio e con molta importanza
abwechslungsreich	ricco di cambiamenti
allmählich abnehmen und ins erste Zeitmaß zurückgehen	diminuire poco a poco e ritornare al tempo primo
allmählich bewegter	poco a poco più mosso
allmählich etwas zurückhalten	progressivamente un poco ritenuto
allmählich ins schnelle Zeitmaß	passare poco a poco al tempo rapido
allmählich verbreitern	allargare poco a poco
ängstlich erregt	ansiosamente eccitato
Anmerkung für den Dirigenten	nota per il direttore d'orchestra
bedeutend langsamer	considerabilmente più lento
beständig zunehmen	aumentando costantemente (sempre crescendo)
bühnenreif	pronto per la scena
das gleiche Gleiten eines langsamen Walzers nachahmend	imitando il movimento scivolante di un valzer lento
die Begleitung fast durchweg leise	l'accompagnamento quasi sempre piano

very distant	sehr entfernt
evenly articulated	gleichmäßig artikuliert
somewhat supported	etwas gestützt
somewhat enlarged	etwas gedehnt
somewhat stressed	etwas herausgehoben
somewhat stressed	etwas hervorgehoben
somewhat languishing	etwas schmachtend
somewhat slower than at the beginning	etwas langsamer als am Anfang
somewhat comfortably	etwas gemächlicher
somewhat more intensively	etwas intensiver
somewhat more tired	etwas müder
somewhat more lively	etwas lebendiger
only just	ein ganz kleines bisschen

German specialist terms Terminologie allemande

but always flowing	mais toujours fluide
but always serious and weighty	mais toujours sérieux et avec beaucoup d'importance
full of changes	plein de changements
gradually diminishing and going back to the first tempo	diminuer peu à peu et revenir au premier mouvement
moving ahead little by little	peu à peu plus animé
gradually holding back a little	retenir un peu progressivement
gradually moving into the fast tempo	passer peu à peu au tempo rapide
gradually broadening	en élargissant peu à peu
anxiously excited	craintivement excité
note for the conductor	note pour le chef d'orchestre
considerably slower	considérablement plus lent
continually growing	en augmentant constamment
ready for the stage	prêt pour la scène
imitating the sliding motion of a slow waltz	en imitant le mouvement glissant d'une valse lente
almost always a soft accompaniment	l'accompagnement presque toujours piano

die Einleitung ein wenig breiter	l'introduzione un poco più ampia
die Taste tonlos niederdrücken	premere il tasto senza farlo suonare
dieser Teil ist durchweg sehr leise zu spielen	questa parte deve essere suonata sempre dolcemente
doch nie übereilt	ma mai precipitosamente
dreimal so langsam	tre volte più lento
durch die untere Oktave zu verstärken	da rinforzare con l'ottava inferiore
durchaus phantastisch und leidenschaftlich vorzutragen	eseguire in maniera fantasiosa e appassionata
durchweg die gleiche Geschwindigkeit	sempre la stessa velocità
durchweg mit dem Dämpferpedal zu spielen	sempre col pedale sinistro
durchweg sehr zart und schlicht	sempre dolcissimo e semplice
ein wenig voran	avanzare un poco
entsprechend / gemäß	adeguato / conformemente
erreicht / gewonnen	raggiunto
etwas fließender, aber sehr ausdrucksvoll	un poco più rapido ma molto espressivo
etwas unbeholfen vorzutragen	va interpretato in modo piuttosto goffo
fest und bestimmt beginnend, dann allmählich wieder etwas lebhafter	incominciare fermo e deciso poi nuovamente un poco animato
folgt sofort der nächste Satz	attacca subito il tempo seguente
frisch und munter	vivo e vegeto
gefühlvoll	pieno di sentimento
genau doppelt so schnell	esattamente due volte più rapido
Grillen	propositi capricciosi
hanebüchen	un poco rude / rozzo
Hauptzeitmaß	il tempo principale
hier ist ein festes Zeitmaß erreicht	quì è stato raggiunto un tempo costante
hier wieder eine Pause, jedoch nicht so lang wie die erste	quì nuovamente una pausa, però non così lunga come la prima
hinabstürzend / herabstürzend	precipitando
immer ein wenig abziehen	sempre un poco diminuendo

the introduction a little broader	l'introduction un peu plus ample
to press the key without making a sound	enfoncer la touche sans la faire parler
this part has to be performed throughout very softly	cette partie doit être jouée toujours très doucement
but never rushed	mais sans jamais bousculer
three times slower	trois fois plus lent
to be reinforced with the lower octave	doit être renforcé par l'octave inférieure
to be absolutely performed with fantasy and passion	à exécuter de façon fantasque et passionnée
always the same tempo throughout	jouer continuellement à la même vitesse
always to be played with the soft pedal	toujours avec la pédale gauche
always very sweetly and simple	toujours très doux et simple
to go ahead a little	avancer un peu
according to / in proportion to	selon / conforme
reached	atteint
a little more quickly but very expressive	un peu plus rapide, mais très expressif
to be performed in a rather clumsy way	à interpréter d'une façon un peu gauche
beginning firm and decided, then gradually again a little more lively	commencer d'une façon ferme et décidée, puis peu à peu à nouveau plus animé
the next movement follows immediately	enchaîner tout de suite le mouvement suivant
fresh and lively	frais et dispos
full of feelings	plein de sentiment
exactly twice as fast	exactement deux fois plus vite
whims / silly ideas	un petit vélo dans la tête (Cortot: propos capricieux)
a little rough	un peu rude / grossier
the main tempo	le tempo principal
here a steady tempo is reached	ici on atteint une vitesse constante
here again a rest, but not as long as the first one	ici une nouvelle pause, mais pas aussi longue que la première
tumbling	en précipitant (précipiter)
always diminishing a little	en diminuant toujours un peu

immer frei deklamierend	sempre declamando liberamente
immer gut gehalten	sempre ben tenuto
immer mehr zurückhalten	sempre più ritenuto
immer noch beschleunigen	ancora accelerando (accelerare sempre di più)
immer so leise als möglich	sempre il più piano possibile
immerfort, immerzu	sempre, continuamente
in das nächste Zeitmaß übergehen	passare al tempo seguente
in das Tempo des Anfangs übergehen	passare alla velocità del tempo iniziale
in ruhigem, gleichmäßigem Zeitmaß	con un'andatura calma e regolare
in sich hineinhorchend	ascoltandosi internamente
in starr durchlaufender eintöniger Bewegung	con un movimento continuamente rigido e monotono
in wechselnder Taktart	con un tempo mutevole
ins erste Zeitmaß übergehen	passare al tempo primo
ins Hauptzeitmaß zurückgehen	ritornare al tempo principale
jeden Lauf etwas langsam beginnen	incominciare ogni passaggio un poco lentamente
kleine Noten mitspielen	suonare anche le notine
lassen / weglassen	lasciare
merklich	sensibilmente più…
mit akzentuiertem Ton	con un tono ben accentuato
mit äußerster Zartheit	con la massima dolcezza
mit fröhlichem Ausdruck	con un'espressione allegra
mit gänzlich gedämpfter Stimme	a bassa voce
mit geheimnisvoll schwermütigem Ausdruck	con un'espressione piena di mistero e di malinconia
mit gesteigertem Ausdruck	con un'espressione crescente
mit gutem Humor	di buon umore
mit höchster Kraft	con la massima forza
mit innigem Ausdruck	con un sentimento intimo (interno)
mit inniger Empfindung	con un'intensa espressione interna (intima)
mit schmerzlichem Ausdruck	con un'espressione dolorosa

always declaiming freely	en déclamant toujours librement
always well held	toujours bien tenu
holding back more and more	retenir toujours plus
still accelerating	accélérer de plus en plus
always as soft as possible	toujours aussi piano que possible
always	continuellement, toujours
to go on the the next tempo	passer au tempo suivant
to go on to the speed of the initial tempo	dans le mouvement du début
with a quite steady tempo	dans un mouvement calme et régulier
listening to oneself inwardly	en s'écoutant intérieurement
with a stiff and monotonous movement	dans un mouvement toujours rigide et monotone
with a changing meter	en changeant de tempo
to go on into the first tempo	passer au premier tempo
to go on to the main tempo	revenir au tempo principal
to begin each passage a little more slowly	commencer chaque passage un peu lentement
also play the grace notes	jouer aussi les petites notes
to let	laisser
noticeably more…	sensiblement plus…
with an accentuated sound	avec un ton bien accentué
with extreme sweetness	avec la plus extrême tendresse
with a cheerful expression	avec une expression joyeuse
in a very low voice	à voix basse
with an expression full of mistery and melancholy	avec une expression pleine de mystère et de mélancolie
with increasing expression	avec une expression croissante
with good humor	de bonne humeur
with greatest power	avec la plus grande force
with intimate sentiments	dans un sentiment d'intimité expressive
with intense intimate feeling	dans un profond sentiment d'intimité
with grievous expression	avec une expression douloureuse

mit Schwermut und Trauer vorzutragen	eseguire con malinconia e tristezza
mit verständigem Pedalgebrauch	con un uso ragionevole del pedale
mit viel innerlicher Bewegung	con un profondo e intenso sentimento intimo
munter, aber immer gemächlich	allegro ma sempre comodo
musizieren	suonare insieme
nach und nach belebter	poco a poco più animato
nach und nach immer schneller	poco a poco sempre più veloce
nicht unbedingt nötig	non è assolutamente necessario
noch ruhiger als am Anfang	ancora più calmo dell'inizio
ohne im Geringsten hervorzutreten	senza mettersi assolutamente in evidenza
ohne Rücksicht	senza riguardo
ohne Unterbrechung weiter	continuare senza interruzioni
reuig andächtig	pentendosi piosamente
schattenhaft	ombreggiato (ombroso)
schnarren	come una raganella
schreitend	avanzando solennemente
schrittmäßig	passo a passo
sehr innig zu spielen	da eseguire intimamente
sehr stürmisch und stets drängend	molto impetuoso e sempre accelerando
schmerzlich leidenschaftlich, doch nicht schneller	dolorosamente appassionato ma non più presto
so schnell wie möglich	il più presto possibile
stets streng im Zeitmaß	senza alcuna licenza
stets zunehmen und vorangehen	sempre andando e crescendo
Traumeswirren	sogni confusi
übernehmen	assumere / adossarsi
umstimmen	cambiare l'accordatura
unbeholfen / täppisch / anmutlos	goffo / sgraziato
unmerklich / in unmerkbarer Weise	impercettibilmente
Urlicht	luce divina
von hier bis zum Schluss allmählich langsamer werden	da adesso fino alla fine rallentare progressivamente

to be performed with melancholy and sorrow	interpréter avec mélancolie et douleur
with reasonable use of the pedal	avec un usage raisonnable de la pédale
with deep and intense intimate expression	avec beaucoup d'émotion intérieure
lively, but always comfortable	gai, mais toujours à l'aise
to play together	faire de la musique d'ensemble
little by little more animated	peu à peu plus animé
gradually getting faster	accélerer de plus en plus
not absolutely necessary	n'est pas absolument nécessaire
even calmer than at the beginning	encore plus calme qu'au début
without coming forward at all	surtout ne pas se mettre en valeur
without consideration	sans égard
to continue without interruption	continuer sans interruption
repentant devoted	en se repentant pieusement
shadowy	ombragé
like a rattle	comme une crécelle
going forward solemnly	en avançant solennellement
step by step	pas-à-pas
to be performed in a very intimate way	à exécuter d'une façon très intime
very impetuous and always speeding up	très fougueux et en accélerant continuellement
painfully passionate, but not faster	douloureusement passionné, mais jamais plus vite
as fast as possible	le plus rapidement possible
always strictly a tempo	toujours strictement en mesure
always moving on and increasing	en augmentant et en avançant de façon continue
confused dreams	rêve confus (Cortot: hallucinations)
to take on / to take over	assumer / se charger de
to change the tuning	changer l'accordage
clumsy / awkward	maladroit / disgracieux
imperceptible	imperceptiblement
divine light	lumière divine
from here to the end, getting gradually slower	dès maintenant jusqu'à la fin ralentir peu à peu

vorwärtstreiben / vorwärtsdrängen	spingere (procedere)
weit ausspannen	ampliando molto
wie ein Gespräch	come una conversazione
wie ein Kondukt	come un convoglio funebre
wie eine Vogelstimme	come il canto di un uccello
wie im Vorspiel	come nel preludio
wie überhörend	come se non si sentisse
wieder das alte Zeitmaß, aber stets vorwärtsgehen	nuovamente il tempo precedente ma sempre andando speditamente
ziemlich lebhaft, immer noch beschleunigen	vivo assai, continuando sempre ad accelerare
zurücktreten	passare in secondo piano

pushing	pousser (avancer)
extending widely	en amplifiant beaucoup
like a conversation	comme une conversation
like a funeral procession	comme un convoi funèbre
like a bird's song	comme le chant d'un oiseau
as in the prelude	comme dans le prélude
as if one does not hear	comme si on n'entendait pas
again in the former tempo, but always pushing	à nouveau le tempo précédant, mais en avançant sans arrêt
quite lively, still accelerating	assez vif, toujours en accélérant
to pass in the second ground	passer au deuxième plan

English and American specialist terms	Terminologia inglese ed americana
all along	tutto il tempo
along	lungo
as fast as possible	il più presto possibile
a shade slower	una sfumatura più lento
as if coming from a distance	come da lontano
at a brisk pace	tempo animato
awkwardly	maldestramente
back to first speed / back to pattern	tornando al tempo
back to refrain	tornando al ritornello
becoming ferocious	diventando selvaggio
boisterously	tempestoso
bouncy	rimbalzante
brassy	come degli ottoni
brightly	brillantemente
bring out the melody	far risaltare la melodia
bubbly	spumante
bumpily	sobbalzando
buzz along	sempre ronzando
casually	casualmente
choppily	mutevole
chug along	sciolto / rilassato
clap hands	battere le mani
clashing	rumoroso
crisp	vivo / frizzante
cussedly	ostinato
dazzling	abbagliante / radioso
delicately	delicatamente
devised	improvvisato / escogitato
doggedly	ostinato
dragging	trascinato
driving tempo	andando
drowsily	sonnolento
dryly	seccamente
early	presto
eloquently	eloquentemente
evenly	in modo uguale
explosive	esplosivo

Englische und amerikanische Fachausdrücke	Terminologie anglaise et américaine
die ganze Zeit	tout le temps
entlang	le long
so schnell wie möglich	aussi vite que possible
eine Nuance langsamer	une nuance plus lent
wie aus weiter Ferne	comme au lointain
in forscher Gangart	d'un mouvement animé
ungeschickt / unbeholfen	maladroitement
zurück zum Anfangstempo	en retournant au mouvement
zurück zum Refrain	revenez au refrain
wild werdend	en devenant sauvage
stürmisch	tempétueux
hüpfend	bondissant
wie Blechinstrumente	comme des cuivres
glanzvoll / strahlend	brillamment
Melodie hervorheben	faire ressortir la mélodie
sprudelnd	pétillant
holprig	en sautant
dahinsummend	en bourdonnant sans arrêt
gelegentlich	par hasard
wechselhaft	changeant
lässig gehend	relaxé
in die Hände klatschen	battre des mains
lärmend	bruyant
frisch	pétillant
stur	obstiné
delikat / zart	délicatement
glänzend / blendend	radieux
improvisiert	improvisé
hartnäckig	obstiné
schleppend	traînant
vorantreibendes Tempo	en allant
verschlafen / schläfrig	d'un air endormi
trocken	sèchement
frühzeitig / baldig	tôt
redegewandt	éloquement
gleichmäßig	de façon égale
explosiv	explosif

fade out	svanire
fading	perdendosi
fair	bello
fairly	abbastanza
final ending	parte finale
flexibly	flessibile
frenchy	alla francese
gaily	gaiamente
gaily moving	movendo allegramente
gay but strict	gioioso ma preciso
gentle	garbato
gently flowing	dolcemente scorrevole
gliding	scorrevole
gossipy	pettegolo
gradually picking up speed	accelerando poco a poco
groovy	vitale
hammer it out	molto chiaro e martellato
handclapping	battendo le mani
happily	felicemente
heavily	pesantemente
"homespun style"	stile "casalingo"
hungrily	affamato
in a grand manner	con grandezza
in an easy going manner	in maniera comoda
in a pensive mood	pensieroso
in a song-like manner	come una canzone
in a steady pace	d'un passo uguale
in a straightforward manner	avanzando in modo deciso
jogging along	correndo leggermente
jokingly	scherzando
jolly	ameno
jumping	saltando
just a little faster	solo un poco più presto
just a little slower	solo un poco più lento
keep moving	sempre mosso
langorously	languidamente
lazily	pigramente
left hand loud	la mano sinistra forte

ausklingen / ausblenden	expirer
ausklingend	en se perdant
schön / hell	beau
ziemlich	assez
Schlussteil *m*	partie finale
flexibel	flexible
kokett	à la française
fröhlich / frech	gaîment
fröhlich bewegend	joyeusement animé
fröhlich, aber exakt	joyeux mais exact
sanft	affable
sanft dahinfließend	en s'écoulant doucement
gleitend	alerte
geschwätzig	bavard
allmählich schneller werdend	en accélerant peu à peu
fit / vital	en pleine forme
sehr scharf hervorheben	très clair et martelé
in die Hände klatschen	en battant des mains
glücklich	heureux
schwer	lourdement
„hausgemacht" / schlicht	style "maison"
hungrig	affamé
elegant / großzügig	avec beaucoup d'envergure (ou: de style)
auf unbeschwerte Art	de façon decontractée
in einer nachdenklichen Stimmung	d'humeur pensive
wie ein Lied	comme une chanson
mit gleichmäßigem Schritt	d'une allure égale
entschieden vorwärtsgehen	en avançant d'une façon déçidée
locker dahinlaufend	en courant légèrement
spaßend / scherzend	en plaisantant
vergnügt	jovial
springend	en sautant
nur ein wenig schneller	seulement un peu plus vite
nur ein wenig langsamer	seulement un peu plus lent
immer weiter bewegen	toujours en mouvement
schmachtend	langoureusement
träge	paresseusement
linke Hand laut	la main gauche appuyée

leisurely	comodamente
let it ring	lasciare risuonare
like a hymn	come un inno
like a prayer	come una preghiera
lilting	cantando melodiosamente
lively jumping	saltando gioiosamente
lumbering	pesantemente
meditatively	meditativo
menacingly	minacciosamente
mighty	potente
moderately fast	moderatamente rapido
moody	lunatico
mournfully	tristemente
moving along	sempre movendo
no speed limit	senza limite di velocità
notice the expression	osservate i segni dinamici
optional ending	fine facoltativa
pattern (rhythm)	modello (ritmo)
patterned	misurato
perky	vispo / gaio
picking up	riprendendo
plodding	faticosamente
pound it out	fare risaltare
quick four	tempo veloce a quattro
quietly moving	andando tranquillamente
quite	piuttosto
real	vero
reflective	riflessivo
restrained waltz tempo	ritmo di valzer ritenuto
reverently	riverente
rhythmically	ritmicamente
right hand soft	la mano destra leggera
rippling	mormorando / gorgogliando
rolling along	ondulando tutto il tempo
rolling motion	movimento ondulante
seadreamy	sognante / “sogno marittimo”

mit Muße / entspannt	decontracté
lass es klingen	laisser résonner
wie eine Hymne	comme un hymne
wie ein Gebet	comme une prière
trällernd / beschwingt singend	en chantant mélodieusement / fredonnant
lebhaft hüpfend	en sautant joyeusement
schwerfällig	pesant
besinnlich / nachdenklich	méditatif
drohend	de façon menaçante
mächtig	puissant
mäßig schnell	modérément rapide
launenhaft	lunatique
trauervoll	tristement
durchgehend bewegt	en mouvement continu
ohne Tempobeschränkung	sans limitation de vitesse
beachte die Ausdrucksvermerke	observez les nuances
möglicher (freigestellter) Schluss	fin facultative
Muster (Rhythmus)	modèle (rythme)
gegliedert / gemessen	mesuré
keck / flott	pimpant / hardi
wieder aufnehmend	en reprenant
mühsam	lourdement / traînant
hervorhebend / heftig anschlagend	mettre en évidence
schneller Vierertakt	mouvement rapide à quatre temps
ruhig gehend	en allant tranquillement
ziemlich	plutôt
wirklich / echt	vrai
nachdenklich	réfléchi
zurückhaltendes Walzertempo	rythme de valse retenu
ehrfurchtsvoll	révérent
rhythmisch	rythmiquement
rechte Hand leise	la main droite légère
murmelnd	en murmurant / gargouillant
dahinströmend	en ondulant tout le long
rollende Bewegung	mouvement ondulant
träumerisch / „wie ein Meerestraum“	rêveur / “rêve maritime”

shuffling	strascicando
skip	salto / balzo
slinky	furtivamente
slow doo-wop tempo	tempo lento di "scat"
slowly but moving	lentamente però andando
snappish	beffardo
solidly	solidamente
somewhat	alquanto
somewhat hurrying	un poco affrettando
sophisticated	sofisticato
spooky	spiritato
sprightly	brioso
stamp out	estinguendo
stately tempo	maestoso
steadily	fermamente
steady walking	camminando regolarmente
stealthy	furtivo
steaming	a tutto vapore
strained	teso
strict	preciso
stroll along	passeggiando
strong and forceful	forte e potente
strut	pavoneggiandosi
strutting tempo	con andatura solenne
subtle	sottile / astuto
swaying	oscillando
swishing	sibilando
take time	prendete tempo
tempo "disturb the neighbours"	tempo "disturba i vicini"
the top voice	la voce superiore
to interlude	all'interludio
very rhythmically	ben ritmato
waddling	ondeggiando / scodinzolando
weeping willow	salice piangente
well contrasted	ben contrastato
whistfully	meditabondo
with a back beat	accento sul tempo debole
with a clear tone	con un suono chiaro
with a fling	rilassato
with a full rich tone	con una sonorità ricca e piena

schleppend / schlurfend	traînant
Sprung	saut / bond
verstohlen	furtivement
langsames „scat"-Tempo	tempo lent de "scat"
langsam, aber mit Bewegung	lentement mais avec allant
schnippisch	narquois
fest / solide	solidement
ein wenig	quelque peu
etwas eilend	légèrement pressant
spitzfindig / raffiniert	sophistiqué
spukhaft / gespenstisch	hanté
spritzig	vif
verlöschend	en éteignant
imposant	majestueux
stetig	fermement
gleichmäßig gehend	en marchant régulièrement
verstohlen	furtif
mit Volldampf	à toute vapeur
angespannt	tendu
strikt	rigoureux
dahinschlendern	en se promenant
stark und kräftig	fort et puissant
einherstolzierend	en se pavanant
feierlich	d'allure solennel
subtil	subtil
schwankend	en oscillant
schwirrend	en sibilant
sich Zeit lassen	prenez votre temps
Tempo „störe die Nachbarn"	tempo "dérange les voisins"
die obere Stimme	la voix supérieure
zum Zwischenspiel gelangen	à l'interlude
sehr rhythmisch	très rythmique
watschelnd	en dandinant
Trauerweide	saule pleureur
mit deutlichem Gegensatz	bien contrasté
nachdenklich	d'un air songeur
Betonung auf der schwachen Taktzeit	les accents sur les temps faibles
mit einem klaren Ton	avec un ton clair
lässig hingeworfen	décontracté
mit einem vollen, reichen Ton	avec une sonorité riche et pleine

with a gentle motion	tranquillamente mosso
with a Glenn Miller flavour	con un profumo di Glenn Miller
with a lilt	allegramente ritmato
with ambition	con ambizione
with an easy flow	scorrendo tranquillamente
with a steady insistence	con grande insistenza
with a singing tone	con un suono cantabile
with a springing touch	con un tocco saltellante
with a steady pulse	con un impulso ritmico regolare
with a warm expression	con un'espressione intensa
with bad humor	di cattivo umore
with dash	con slancio
with deep feeling	con profonda espressione
with drive	con impulso
with dry humour	con un'umore secco
with feeling	con sentimento
with firm step	d'un passo deciso
with full tone	con un suono pieno
with good humour	di buon umore
with great expression	con grande espressione
with great warmth	con grande calore
with imagination	con immaginazione
with inflections of plainsong	con delle inflessioni di canto gregoriano
with much precision	molto preciso
with pity	con pietà
with quiet dignity	con una tranquilla dignità
with regained strength	con recuperata forza
with simple tenderness	con semplice tenerezza
with sincere sympathy	con sincera simpatia
with spiritual feeling	con sentimento spirituale
with sport	giocoso
with steady heavy motion	pesante e regolare
with sure rhythm	con un ritmo sicuro

mit sanfter Bewegung	avec un mouvement calme
mit einem Hauch von Glenn Miller	avec un parfum de Glenn Miller
mit einem flotten Rhythmus	rythmé allégrement
ehrgeizig	avec ambition
ruhig dahinfließend	en s'écoulant tranquillement
mit gleichbleibendem Nachdruck	avec une grande insistance
mit singendem Klang	d'un ton chantant
mit hüpfendem Anschlag	avec un toucher sautillant
mit gleichmäßigem Puls	avec une pulsation réguliére
mit warmem Ausdruck	avec une intense expression
mit schlechter Laune	de mauvaise humeur
mit Schwung	avec élan
sehr gefühlvoll	avec une profonde expression
mit Schwung / intensiv rhythmisch	avec de l'entrain
mit trockenem Humor	avec un humour sec
mit Gefühl	avec sentiment
mit festem Schritt	d'un pas décidé
mit vollem Klang	avec un son plein
mit guter Laune	de bonne humeur
sehr ausdrucksvoll	avec une grande expression
mit viel Wärme	avec beaucoup de chaleur
mit Phantasie	avec imagination
mit gregorianischen Schattierungen	avec des nuances de plain-chant
sehr genau	avec beaucoup de précision
mitleidig	avec pitié
mit stiller Würde	avec une tranquille dignité
mit neuer Kraft	avec une vigueur retrouvée
mit schlichter Zärtlichkeit	avec simple tendresse
mit herzlicher Sympathie	avec sincère sympathie
mit andächtigem Gefühl	avec un sentiment spirituel
mit Spaß / mit Vergnügen	avec enjouement
mit stetiger, heftiger Bewegung	pesant et régulier
mit sicherem Rhythmus	avec un rythme sur

Jazz, Rock, Pop	Jazz, Rock, Pop
all-star band	complesso jazz / formato da musicisti noti
background	sottofondo
backline	gli strumenti e gli accessori sulla scena
band	complesso jazz o rock
bandleader	il capo del complesso
barrelhouse piano style	pianoforte con suono metallico
beat (1960)	"colpo"; stile musicale
Bebop (1940)	uno stile di jazz
big band	grande complesso
blues ending	finale di Blues
Blues (1912)	una delle forme principali del jazz (schema di 12 battute)
Boogie-Woogie (1928)	stile pianistico (schema di 12 battute)
bounce	ritmo rimbalzante
break	interruzione e pausa
bridge	ponte
call and response	principio: appello e risposta
chorus	ritornello (schema di 32 battute)
combo	piccolo complesso
comeback	il ritorno
commercial	commerciale
Cool Jazz (1948)	jazz "freddo"
country blues (1850)	blues autentico
country music	musica campestre
creative music (1970)	sostituisce la parola jazz
crooner	cantante con voce sentimentale
cue	gesto o segno per attacca
dirty tones	suoni "sporchi"/ strascicati
disco music (1975)	musica in voga nelle discoteche
Dixieland (1920)	jazz suonato dai bianchi
double time / duple time	tempo doppio
drive	impulso
featuring	nel ruolo principale

Jazz, Rock, Pop	**Jazz, Rock, Pop**
Jazzensemble aus berühmten Musikern	formation de jazz avec des musiciens connus
Hintergrund	musique de fond
gesamtes Instrumentarium und Zubehör auf der Bühne	les instruments et les accessoires sur la scène
Musikgruppe Jazz oder Rock	formation de jazz ou de rock
Leiter einer Musikgruppe	chef de l'ensemble
Klavierstil mit klirrendem Klang	piano avec un son métallique
„Schlag"; Musikrichtung	"coup"; style de musique
ein Jazzstil	un style de jazz
große Musikgruppe	grande formation
Blues-Schlusswendung	final de Blues
eine der Hauptformen des Jazz (Grundschema: 12 Takte)	une des principales formes du jazz (schéma de 12 mesures)
ein pianistischer Stil (Grundschema: 12 Takte)	style pianistique (schéma de 12 mesures)
hüpfender Rhythmus	rythme rebondissant
Unterbrechung und Pause	interruption et pause
Überleitung	pont / passage
Ruf-Antwort-Prinzip	principe: appel-réponse
Grundmelodie; Refrain (Grundschema: 32 Takte)	refrain (schéma de 32 mesures)
kleine Musikgruppe	petit ensemble
Wiederkehr	le retour
kommerziell	commercial
„kühler" Jazz	jazz "froid"
authentischer Blues	blues authentique
ländliche Musik	musique champêtre
ersetzt das Wort Jazz	remplace le mot jazz
Sänger mit sanfter Stimme / Schnulzensänger	chanteur avec voix sentimentale
Hinweis für Einsatz	geste ou signe pour attaque
„dreckige" Töne, schleifend	sons "sales", traînants
Diskomusik	musique en vogue dans les discothèques
Jazz, von Weißen gespielt	jazz joué par les blancs
Verdopplung des Tempos	tempo double
Schwung / Antrieb	impulsion
in der Hauptrolle	dans le rôle principal

feeling	sentimento
Folk-Rock (1965)	fusione dei due generi
Free Jazz (1960)	jazz “libero”
Funk (1950/1970)	stile di jazz, in seguito di Pop
Fusion (1970)	fusione di generi musicali o di culture differenti
gimmick	un trucco
Gospelsong (1930)	canto religioso dei neri
growl	cantare e soffiare al tempo stesso
Hard Rock (1970)	rock “duro”
head arrangement	improvvisazione “concordata”
headline	la melodia o il testo che rimane nella memoria
Heavy Metal (1970)	hard rock
Hillbilly (1900)	musica campestre eseguita dai bianchi negli S.U.
hit	un grande successo
hit-parade	la parata dei successi
hit song	canzonetta a successo
Honky Tonk music (1900)	musica eseguita nelle bettole
hot (1925)	uno dei primi jazz
hot jazz (1925)	jazz “caldo” tradizionale
house rent party / skiffle	festa privata con musica
Intro	2, 4 o 8 battute d’introduzione
Jam Session	concerto spontaneo, improvvisato
Jazz (1880)	forma musicale afroamericana
Jubilee	musica afroamericana religiosa
juke box / music box	juke-box
jungle style (1920)	stile “giungla”
latin american music	musica sudamericana
lead	melodia principale
light show	l’illuminazione dello spettacolo
live	dal vivo
locked hands style / block chords	melodia suonata parallelamente con le due mani

Gefühl	sentiment
Fusion der zwei Stile	fusion des deux genres
„freier“ Jazz	jazz “libre”
ein Jazzstil, später Popstil	un style de jazz, ensuite de Pop
in der Popmusik Verschmelzung verschiedener Kulturen	fusion de cultures ou genres différents de musique
ein Kniff	un truc
religiöser Gesang der Schwarzen	chant religieux des noirs
Singen und Blasen gleichzeitig	chanter et souffler en même temps
„harter“ Rock	rock “dur”
vereinbarte Improvisation	improvisation “décidée”
der „Aufhänger“, Musik und Text	la mélodie ou le texte qui restent dans la mémoire
harter Rock	hard rock
ländliche Volksmusik der Weißen in den USA	musique champêtre produite par des blancs aux E.U.
großer Erfolg	un grand succès, un tube
Schlagerparade	la parade des succès
erfolgreicher Schlager	chanson à succès
Country-Musik in Western-Bars	musique exécutée dans une gargote
einer der frühesten Jazzstile	un des premiers jazz
„heißer“ Jazz, traditionell	jazz “chaud” traditionnel
Privatfest mit Musik	fête privée avec de la musique
2, 4 oder 8 Takte Einleitung (Kurzform für Introduktion)	2, 4 ou 8 mesures d’introduction
zwanglose Zusammenkunft von Jazzmusikern zu gemeinsamem Spielen	concert spontané, bœuf
afroamerikanische Musikform	forme musicale afroaméricaine
afroamerikanische geistliche Musik	musique afroaméricaine religieuse
Musikbox / Musikautomat	jukebox
„Urwald“-Stil, Dschungelstil	style “jungle”
lateinamerikanische Musik	musique sudaméricaine
führende Melodie	mélodie principale
Konzertlichtgestaltung	l’éclairage du spectacle
Direktübertragung	sur le vif
auf dem Klavier Melodie mit beiden Händen parallel spielen	mélodie jouée parallèlement avec les deux mains au piano

English and American specialist terms	Terminologia inglese ed americana
loft jazz / midwest jazz	jazz non commerciale, praticato negli scantinati
long playing / LP	microsolco
Mainstream (1940)	jazz moderato
marching band / street band	antiche bande americane
medium	tempo moderato
musical	commedia musicale
music hall	varietà
Negro Spiritual	musica religiosa dei neri americani
New Orleans / Old Time Jazz (1900)	prima forma del jazz
New Wave (1975)	altra forma di Rock
off beat	l'accento sui tempi deboli / contrattempo
off pitch / off key	fuori dal tono giusto
on beat	l'accento in battere
paradiddle	figura ritmica per il batterista
play party	serata danzante con canti ma senza strumenti
Pop Music (1960)	sintesi tra la canzone e il Rock
power	potenza
Progressive Jazz (1945)	sviluppo del "Big band"
Punk Rock	musica di stile provocativo
Ragtime (1870)	stile pianistico
Rap	ritmi parlati
Reggae (1965)	forma musicale giamaicana
revival	ripresa, rinascita
rhythm section	sezione ritmica
Rhythm and Blues (1940)	uno stile di jazz
riff	brevi motivi ripetuti
rim shot	tecnica particolare di percussione
Rock (1965)	continuazione del Rock'n'Roll e del beat
Rockabilly (1950)	origine del Rock'n'Roll
scat	canto sillabato

nicht vermarktete Musik, in Kellern gespielt	jazz non commercial, pratiqué dans les cantines
Langspielplatte	microsillon
gemäßigter Jazz	jazz modéré
frühere USA-Marschmusik	anciennes fanfares américaines
mittleres Tempo	tempo modéré
Musical / musikalische Komödie	comédie musicale
Varieté	variété / café-concert
geistliche Musik der Afroamerikaner	musique religieuse des noirs
erste Form des schwarzen Jazz	première forme de jazz
eine Form von Rock	autre forme de Rock
Betonung auf dem schwachen Schlag	l'accent sur les temps faibles
weg von der exakten Tonhöhe	à côté du ton exact
Betonung auf dem starken Schlag	l'accent sur les temps forts
ein rhythmisches Element für den Schlagzeuger	un élément rythmique pour le batteur
Tanzabend mit Gesang, aber ohne Instrumente	soirée dansante avec des chants, mais sans instruments
Synthese zwischen Schlager und Rock	synthèse entre la chanson et le rock
Kraft, Stärke	puissance
eine Weiterentwicklung der „Big Band"	un développement du "Big Band"
Punk, provokativer Musikstil	musique provocative, choquante
ein Klavierstil	style pianistique
gesprochener Rhythmus	rythmes parlés
Musikform aus Jamaika	forme musicale de la Jamaique
Wiederaufleben	reprise, renaissance
Rhythmusgruppe	section rythmique
ein Jazzstil	un style de jazz
kleine wiederholte Figuren	brefs motifs répétés
Trommelschlag besonderer Art (auf den Rand)	technique particulière de percussion
Fortsetzung von Rock'n'Roll und Beat	continuation du Rock'n'Roll et de la musique beat
frühe Spielart des Rock'n'Roll	origine du Rock'n'Roll
Silbengesang	syllabes chantées

section	sezione
shout (1930)	stile vocale "urlato"
shuffle	motivo ritmico
ska (1950)	forma ritmica
smear	tipo di portamento
Soft Rock (1970)	rock morbido
Soul (1950)	"anima", musica pop afroamericana
sound	sonorità
square dance	ballo popolare in uso negli S.U.
standard	pezzo di repertorio
steel band	piccoli complessi diffusi a Trinidad, composti di strumenti a percussione ricavati da basi di bidoni
stomp	forma ritmica
straight	esecuzione fedele all'originale
sweet music	musica dolce
Swing (1930)	stile di jazz
syncopated music	musica sincopata
tag / ending	coda; alcune battute aggiunte
talkbox	scatola parlante
tap-dance / step dance	tip-tap
Third Stream (1950)	sintesi tra il jazz e la musica contemporanea
timing	senso del tempo
two beat	accenti uguali su uno e tre
uptempo	tempo molto veloce
verse	strofa
walking bass	un motivo "camminante" al basso
West Coast Jazz (1950)	jazz "bianco" in California
work songs	canti degli schiavi al lavoro

(Instrumenten-)Gruppe	section
„schreiender“ Vokalstil	style vocal “hurlé”
eine Rhythmusfigur	un motif rythmique
eine rhythmische Form	une forme rythmique
Verschleifen der Töne	genre de “portamento”
„sanfter“ Rock	rock doux
„Seele“, afroamerikanische Popmusik	“âme”, musique pop des noirs
Klang	sonorité
berühmter Volkstanz aus den USA	danse populaire répandue aux E.U.
bekanntes, älteres Stück	morceau de répertoire
ein Schlagzeugensemble karibischen Ursprungs, auf leeren Benzin- oder Ölfässern spielend	un ensemble de percussionistes des Caraïbes (Trinidad) jouant sur des instruments fabriqués à partir de fonds de barils de pétrole
eine rhythmische Form	une forme rythmique
originalgetreu musizieren	exécution fidèle à l'original
sanfte Musik	musique douce
ein Jazzstil	un style de jazz
synkopierte Musik	musique syncopée
Schlusswendung	mesures finales ajoutées
Sprechkasten (E-Gitarre)	boîte parlante (guitare éléctronique)
Steptanz	claquettes
Synthese von Jazz und Neuer Musik	synthèse entre le jazz et la musique contemporaine
„Timing“ / richtiges Zeitgefühl	sens du temps
gleich starke Betonung auf eins und drei	accents égaux sur un et trois
sehr rasches Tempo	mouvement très rapide
Strophe	strophe / couplet
laufende Bassfigur	motif “allant” à la basse
„weißer“ Jazz in Kalifornien	jazz “blanc” en Californie
Arbeitslieder der Sklaven	chant des esclaves au travail

Danze
(Le seguenti danze portano lo stesso nome in tutte le lingue)

Dances
(The following dances bear the same term in all languages)

Baion
Bamba
Batucada
Beguine
Big apple
Black bottom
Boogie-Woogie
Bossa nova
Boston
Bounce
Break dance
Cakewalk
Calipso
Carioca
Cha-cha-cha
Charleston
Conga
Dirty dance
English waltz
Foxtrott
Guaracha
Highlife
Hully Gully
Hustle
Java
Jitterbug
Jive
Joropo
Kasatschok
Lambada

Tänze	**Danses**
(Die folgenden Tänze tragen in allen Sprachen den gleichen Namen)	(Les danses suivants portent le même nom dans toutes les langues)
Lambeth walk	Raspa
Letkiss	Rock'n'Roll
Lindy-Hop	Rumba
Machiche	Salsa
Madison	Samba
Mambo	Shake
Merengue	Shimmy
Milonga	Sirtaki
Musette	Slowfox
Onestep	Slop
Pachanga	Surf
Pasodoble	Tango
Quickstep	Twist
Ramble	Twostep
Ranchera	Valse hésitation

100 composizioni celebri / 100 famous works

Questa lista è stata redatta all'unico scopo di soddisfare la curiosità del lettore desideroso di conoscere la traduzione di un titolo particolare nelle varie lingue. Quindi non rappresenta una graduatoria sul valore musicale dei brani inseriti.

This list has been prepared with the purpose of satisfying the curiosity of the reader who wishes to understand the title of a particular piece in various languages. The list does not reflect any specific artistic criteria.

Italiano	English
Bach, J.S.	
Il clavicembalo ben temperato	The Welltempered Clavier
L'arte della fuga	The Art of Fugue
L'oratorio di Natale	Christmas Oratorio
L'offerta musicale	The Musical Offering
Bartók, Béla	
Il mandarino meraviglioso	The Miraculous Mandarin
Beethoven, L. van	
La consacrazione della casa	The Consecration of the House
Le creature di Prometeo	The Creatures of Prometheus
Sonata al chiaro di luna	Moonlight Sonata
Bellini, Vincenzo	
La sonnambula	The Sleepwalker
Berlioz, Hector	
La dannazione di Faust	Faust's Damnation
Bizet, Georges	
I pescatori di perle	The Pearl Fishers
Boieldieu, François	
La dama bianca	The White Lady
Borodin, Aleksandr	
Nelle steppe dell'Asia centrale	In the Steppes of Central Asia
Boulez, Pierre	
Il martello senza padrone	The Hammer without Master

100 berühmte Kompositionen

100 œuvres célèbres

Diese Liste wurde allein mit dem Ziel zusammengestellt, die Wissbegier des Lesers, der die Übersetzung eines Titels in den verschiedenen Sprachen erfahren möchte, zu befriedigen. Eine künstlerische Bewertung der aufgeführten Kompositionen ist damit nicht intendiert.

Cette liste a été rédigée dans l'unique but de satisfaire la curiosité du lecteur désireux de connaître la traduction d'un titre dans les differentes langues. Ainsi la liste ne reflète aucun critère artistique sur la valeur des titres insérés.

Bach, J.S.	
Das Wohltemperierte Klavier	Le clavecin bien tempéré
Die Kunst der Fuge	L'art de la fugue
Das Weihnachtsoratorium	L'oratorio de Noël
Das Musikalische Opfer	L'offrande musicale
Bartók, Béla	
Der wunderbare Mandarin	Le mandarin merveilleux
Beethoven, L. van	
Die Weihe des Hauses	La consécration de la maison
Die Geschöpfe des Prometheus	Les créatures de Prométhée
Mondscheinsonate	Sonate au clair de lune
Bellini, Vincenzo	
Die Nachtwandlerin	La somnambule
Berlioz, Hector	
Faust's Verdammnis	La damnation de Faust
Bizet, Georges	
Die Perlenfischer	Les pêcheurs de perles
Boieldieu, François	
Die weiße Dame	La dame blanche
Borodin, Aleksandr	
Eine Steppenskizze aus Mittelasien	Dans le steppes de l'Asie centrale
Boulez, Pierre	
Der Hammer ohne Meister	Le marteau sans maître

100 composizioni celebri	100 famous works
Cimarosa, Domenico	
Il matrimonio segreto	The Clandestine Marriage
Débussy, Claude	
Il mare	The Sea
L'angolo dei bambini	Children's Corner
La scatola dei balocchi	The Toy's Box
Preludio al pomeriggio di un fauno	Prelude to the Afternoon of a Faun
De Falla, Manuel	
Il cappello a tre punte	The Three-cornered Hat
La danza del fuoco	The Fire Dance
L'amore stregone	Love the Wizard
La vita breve	Life is Short
Notti nei giardini di Spagna	Nights in the Gardens of Spain
Donizetti, Gaetano	
La figlia del reggimento	The Daughter of the Regiment
L'elisir d'amore	The Love Potion
Dukas, Paul	
L'apprendista stregone	The Sorcerer's Apprentice
Dvořák, Antonín	
Sinfonia dal nuovo mondo	New World Symphony
Händel, G.F.	
Il fabbro armonioso	The Harmonious Blacksmith
Haydn, Joseph	
La creazione	The Creation
Le stagioni	The Seasons
Khatschaturjan, Aram	
La danza delle spade	Sabre Dance
Lehár, Franz	
Il paese del sorriso	The Land of Smiles
La vedova allegra	The Merry Widow

Cimarosa, Domenico	
Die heimliche Ehe	Le mariage secret
Débussy, Claude	
Das Meer	La mer
Die Ecke der Kinder	Le coin des enfants
Die Spielzeugkiste	La boite à joujoux
Präludium zum Nachmittag eines Fauns	Prélude à l'après-midi d'un faune
De Falla, Manuel	
Der Dreispitz	Le tricorne
Feuertanz	La danse du feu
Liebeszauber	L'amour sorcier
Ein kurzes Leben	La vie brève
Nächte in spanischen Gärten	Nuits dans les jardins d'Espagne
Donizetti, Gaetano	
Die Regimentstochter	La fille du régiment
Der Liebestrank	L'élixir d'amour
Dukas, Paul	
Der Zauberlehrling	L'apprenti sorcier
Dvořák, Antonín	
Symphonie aus der Neuen Welt	Symphonie du nouveau monde
Händel, G.F.	
Grobschmied-Variationen	Le forgeron harmonieux
Haydn, Joseph	
Die Schöpfung	La création
Die Jahreszeiten	Les saisons
Khatschaturjan, Aram	
Säbeltanz	La danse du sabre
Lehár, Franz	
Das Land des Lächelns	Le pays du sourire
Die lustige Witwe	La veuve joyeuse

Liszt, Franz	
Anni di pellegrinaggio	Years of Pilgrinage
Mahler, Gustav	
Il canto della terra	The Song of the Earth
Mendelssohn Bartholdy, Felix	
Il sogno di una notte di mezza estate	Midsummer Night's Dream
La filatrice	Spinning Song
Mare tranquillo e viaggio felice	Calm Sea and Prosperous Voyage
Monteverdi, Claudio	
L'incoronazione di Poppea	The Coronation of Poppea
Mozart, W.A.	
Cosi fan tutte	All Women do it
Il flauto magico	The Magic Flute
Il ratto dal serraglio	The Elopement from the Harem
La finta giardiniera	The Pretended Garden-Girl
La marcia turca	The Turkish March
Le nozze di Figaro	The Marriage of Figaro
Mussorgsky, Modest	
Quadri di un esposizione	Pictures at an Exhibition
Una notte sul monte calvo	Night on the Bare Mountain
Nicolai, Otto	
Le allegre comari di Windsor	The Merry Wives of Windsor
Offenbach, Jacques	
I conti di Hoffmann	The Tales of Hoffmann
Orfeo all'inferno	Orpheus in the Underworld
Pergolesi, Giovanni Battista	
La serva padrona	The Maid as Mistress

Liszt, Franz	
Pilgerjahre	Années de pèlerinage
Mahler, Gustav	
Das Lied von der Erde	Le chant de la terre
Mendelssohn Bartholdy, Felix	
Der Sommernachtstraum	Le Songe d'une nuit d'été
Das Spinnerlied	La fileuse
Meeresstille und glückliche Fahrt	Mer tranquille et voyage heureux
Monteverdi, Claudio	
Die Krönung der Poppea	Le couronnement de Poppée
Mozart, W.A.	
So machen es alle (Frauen)	Comme elles sont toutes
Die Zauberflöte	La flûte enchantée
Die Entführung aus dem Serail	L'enlèvement au serail
Die Gärtnerin aus Liebe	La prétendue jardinière
Türkischer Marsch	La marche turque
Figaros Hochzeit	Les noces de Figaro
Mussorgsky, Modest	
Bilder einer Ausstellung	Tableaux d'une exposition
Eine Nacht auf dem kahlen Berge	Une nuit sur le mont-chauve
Nicolai, Otto	
Die lustigen Weiber von Windsor	Les joyeuses commères de Windsor
Offenbach, Jacques	
Hoffmanns Erzählungen	Les contes d'Hoffmann
Orpheus in der Unterwelt	Orphée aux enfers
Pergolesi, Giovanni Battista	
Die Magd als Herrin	La servante maîtresse

Prokofjew, Sergej	
L'amore delle tre melarance	The Love for Three Oranges
Pierino ed il lupo	Peter and the Wolf
Puccini, Giacomo	
Il tabarro	The Cloak
Ravel, Maurice	
L'ora spagnola	The Spanish Hour
Respighi, Ottorino	
Le fontane di Roma	The Fountains of Rome
Rimskij-Korsakow, Nikolaj	
Il gallo d'oro	The Golden Cockerel
Il volo del calabrone	Flight of the Bumble Bee
La grande Pasqua russa	The Russian Easter
Rossini, Gioachino	
Il barbiere di Siviglia	The Barber of Seville
La Cenerentola	Cinderella
La gazza ladra	The Thievish Magpie
Schönberg, Arnold	
La mano felice	The Lucky Hand
Schubert, Franz	
Il viaggio d'inverno	The Winter Journey
La bella mugnaia	The Fair Maid of the Mill
La morte e la fanciulla	Death and the Maiden
La trota	The Trout
L'incompiuta	The Unfinished (Symphony)
Schumann, Robert	
Amor di poeta	Poet's Love
Amore e vita di donna	Woman's Love and Live
Scene infantili	Scenes from Childhood
Sinding, Christian A.	
Mormorio di primavera	Rustle of Spring

Prokofjew, Sergej	
Die Liebe zu den drei Orangen	L'amour des trois oranges
Peter und der Wolf	Pierre et le loup
Puccini, Giacomo	
Der Mantel	La houppelande
Ravel, Maurice	
Die spanische Stunde	L'heure espagnole
Respighi, Ottorino	
Römische Brunnen	Les fontaines de Rome
Rimskij-Korsakow, Nikolaj	
Der goldene Hahn	Le coq d'or
Der Hummelflug	Le vol du bourdon
Russische Ostern	La grande Pâques russe
Rossini, Gioachino	
Der Barbier von Sevilla	Le barbier de Séville
Aschenbrödel	Cendrillon
Die diebische Elster	La pie voleuse
Schönberg, Arnold	
Die glückliche Hand	La main heureuse
Schubert, Franz	
Die Winterreise	Le voyage d'hiver
Die schöne Müllerin	La belle meunière
Der Tod und das Mädchen	La mort et la jeune fille
Die Forelle	La truite
Die Unvollendete (Symphonie)	La symphonie inachevée
Schumann, Robert	
Dichterliebe	Amour de poète
Frauenliebe und -leben	Amour et vie de femme
Kinderszenen	Scènes d'enfants
Sinding, Christian A.	
Frühlingsrauschen	Le gazouillement du printemps

100 composizioni celebri	100 famous works
Smetana, Bedřich	
La mia patria	My Country
La sposa venduta	The Bardered Bride
Strauß, Johann (Sohn)	
Il bel Danubio blu	The Beautiful Blue Danube
Il pipistrello	The Bat
Strauss, Richard	
Il cavaliere della rosa	The Rose Cavalier
La donna senz'ombra	The Woman without a Shadow
Morte e trasfigurazione	Death and Transfiguration
Una vita d'eroe	A Hero's Life
Strawinsky, Igor	
Il bacio della fata	The Fairy's Kiss
La carriera di un libertino	The Rake's Progress
La sagra della primavera	Rite of Spring
La storia del soldato	The Soldier's Tale
L'uccello di fuoco	The Firebird
L'usignolo	The Nightingale
Tschaikowsky, Peter I.	
Il lago dei cigni	Swan Lake
La bella addormentata nel bosco	The Sleeping Beauty
Lo schiaccianoci	The Nutcracker
Romeo e Giulietta	Romeo and Juliet
Verdi, Giuseppe	
Il trovatore	The Troubadour
I vespri siciliani	The Sicilian Vespers
La forza del destino	The Force of Destiny
Un ballo in maschera	A Masked Ball
Vivaldi, Antonio	
Le quattro stagioni	The Four Seasons

Smetana, Bedřích

Mein Vaterland	Ma patrie
Die verkaufte Braut	La fiancée vendue

Strauß, Johann (Sohn)

An der schönen blauen Donau	Le beau Danube bleu
Die Fledermaus	La chauve-souris

Strauss, Richard

Der Rosenkavalier	Le chevalier à la rose
Die Frau ohne Schatten	La femme sans ombre
Tod und Verklärung	Mort et transfiguration
Ein Heldenleben	Une vie de héros

Strawinsky, Igor

Der Kuss der Fee	Le baiser de la fée
Die Karriere eines Wüstlings	La carrière d'un libertin
Das Frühlingsopfer	Le sacre du printemps
Die Geschichte vom Soldaten	L'histoire du soldat
Der Feuervogel	L'oiseau de feu
Die Nachtigall	Le rossignol

Tschaikowsky, Peter I.

Schwanensee	Le lac des cygnes
Dornröschen	La belle au bois dormant
Der Nussknacker	Casse-noisette
Romeo und Julia	Roméo et Juliette

Verdi, Giuseppe

Der Troubadour	Le trouvère
Die Sizilianische Vesper	Les vêpres siciliennes
Die Macht des Schicksals	La force du destin
Ein Maskenball	Le bal masqué

Vivaldi, Antonio

Die vier Jahreszeiten	Les quatre saisons

Wagner. Richard	
I maestri cantori di Norimberga	The Mastersingers of Nuremberg
Il vascello fantasma	The Flying Dutchman
L'anello del Nibelungo	The Nibelung's Ring
Weber, Karl Maria v.	
Il franco cacciatore	The Freeshooter
L'invito al valzer	Invitation to the Dance
Weill, Kurt	
L'opera da tre soldi	The Threepenny Opera

I nomi di persone come Carmen, Tosca, Lohengrin etc. sono invariabili.

Names of persons like Carmen, Tosca, Lohengrin etc. are invariable.

Wagner. Richard	
Die Meistersinger von Nürnberg	Les Maîtres chanteurs de Nuremberg
Der fliegende Holländer	Le vaisseau fantôme
Der Ring des Nibelungen	L'anneau du Nibelung
Weber, Karl Maria v.	
Der Freischütz	Le franc-tireur
Aufforderung zum Tanz	L'invitation à la valse
Weill, Kurt	
Die Dreigroschenoper	L'opéra de quat'sous

Personennamen wie Carmen, Tosca, Lohengrin usw. bleiben unverändert.

Les noms de personnes comme Carmen, Tosca, Lohengrin etc. sont invariables.

Opera	**Opera**
Parole spesso utilizzate – scelta	**Frequently used words – choice**
abbracciare	to hug
abito *m* / vestito *m* / costume *m*	suit / dress / costume
accanito / impietoso / senza pietà / spietato	ruthless / pitiless / merciless
accasciato / spossato / sfinito / esausto /stremato	worn out / crushed / exhausted / dejected
affranto	broken-hearted
affrontare / sfidare	to face / to brave / to challenge
aiuto!	help!
albero *m*	tree
amico *m* / compagno *m*	friend / fellow / comrade
ammazzare / uccidere	to kill
anello *m*	ring
anno *m*	year
arma *f*	weapon
asino *m*	donkey
assassino *m*	killer / murderer
autunno *m*	autumn / fall (Am.)
avaro / taccagno	avaricious / stingy
avvicinarsi	to approach / to get near
azzurro / celeste	sky-blue
babbo *m* / padre *m*	father
bacio *m*	kiss
balia *f*	nurse / nanny
bambola *f*	doll
bandiera *f* / stendardo *m*	flag / banner
barba *f*	beard
barca *f* / nave *f* / battello *m*	rowing boat / boat
benedire	to bless
bere / tracannare	to drink
bestia *f* / animale *m*	beast / animal
bianco	white
bicchiere *m* / calice *m* / coppa *f*	glass / goblet
blu	(dark) blue
bottiglia *f*	bottle

Oper / Opéra

Häufig gebrauchte Wörter – Auswahl	**Mots fréquemment utilisés – choix**
umarmen	embrasser
Anzug *m* / Kleid *n* / Tracht *f*	habit *m* / robe *f* / costume *m*
verbissen / unbarmherzig / ohne Mitleid / erbarmungslos	acharné / sans pitié / impitoyable
entkräftet / erschöpft / entmutigt	épuisé / abattu
niedergeschlagen	accablé / brisé
entgegentreten / herausfordern	affronter / faire face / défier
Hilfe!	à l'aide! / au secours!
Baum *m*	arbre *m*
Freund *m* / Gefährte *m* / Kamerad *m*	ami *m* / compagnon *m* / camarade *m*
töten / umbringen	tuer
Ring *m*	bague *f* / anneau *m*
Jahr *n*	an *m* / année *f*
Waffe *f*	arme *f*
Esel *m*	âne *m*
Mörder *m*	assassin *m* / meurtrier *m*
Herbst *m*	automne *m*
geizig / habgierig	avare
sich nähern	s'approcher
hellblau / himmelblau	azur / bleu ciel
Vater *m*	père *m*
Kuss *m*	baiser *m*
Amme *f*	nourrice *f*
Puppe *f*	poupée *f*
Fahne *f* / Flagge *f* / Banner *n*	drapeau *m* / étendard *m*
Bart *m*	barbe *f*
Kahn *m* / Boot *n* / Schiff *m*	barque *f* / bateau *m*
segnen	bénir
trinken	boire
Tier *n*	bête *f* / animal *m*
weiß	blanc
Glas *m* / Kelch *m*	verre *m* / calice *m* / coupe *f*
blau	bleu
Flasche *f*	bouteille *f*

Italiano	English
brancolare / annaspare	to grope / to reel
brigante *m* / bandito *m* / masnadiere *m*	bandit / highwayman
bruciare	to burn
brutto	ugly
buffone *m* / pagliaccio *m*	buffoon / clown
bugia *f* / bugiardo *m*	lie / liar
calunnia *f*	slander / libel
camera *f* / stanza *f*	room
canaglia *f* / furfante *m* / mascalzone *m*	rogue / scoundrel / villain
candela *f* / cero *m*	candle
casa *f* / palazzo *m*	house / palace
catena *f*	chain
cattivo / malvagio	bad / wicked / mean
cavallo *m* / cavalcare	horse / to ride
chiesa *f* / duomo *m*	church / cathedral
cieco	blind
cigno *m*	swan
cipiglio (con) / accigliato	scowling / frowning
combattimento *m* / battaglia *f*	fight / battle
comprare	to buy
con te	with you
condannare	to sentence
conte *m* / duca *m*	count / earl / duke
contrabbandiere *m*	smuggler
coppia *f*	couple
corona *f*	crown / coronet
corte *f*	court
crepuscolo *m*	twilight / dusk
crimine *m* / delitto *m*	crime / offense (Am.)
croce *f*	cross
culla *f*	cradle
dea *f*	goddess
depresso / scoraggiato	depressed / discouraged
detto …	called …
diavolo *m* / demonio *m*	devil / demon
difendere	to defend

Deutsch	Français
tappen / haspeln / taumeln	avancer à tâtons / tâtonner / tituber
Räuber *m* / Bandit *m*	brigand *m* / bandit *m*
brennen	brûler
hässlich	laid
Narr *m* / Possenreißer *m*	bouffon *m* / pitre *m*
Lüge *f* / Lügner *m*	mensonge *m* / menteur *m*
Verleumdung *f*	calomnie *f*
Zimmer *n*	chambre *f*
Schurke *m* / Gauner *m*	canaille *f* / vaurien *m* / fripouille *f*
Kerze *f*	bougie *f* / cierge *m*
Haus *n* / Palast *m*	maison *f* / palais *m*
Kette *f*	chaîne *f*
böse / schlecht / gemein	mauvais / méchant
Pferd *n* / reiten	cheval *m* / chevaucher / monter à cheval
Kirche *f* / Dom *m*	église *f* / cathédrale *f*
blind	aveugle
Schwan *m*	cygne *m*
mit finsterer Miene / stirnrunzelnd	d'un air sombre / renfrogné
Kampf *m* / Gefecht *n* / Schlacht *f*	combat *m* / lutte *f* / bataille *f*
kaufen	acheter
mit dir	avec toi
verurteilen	condamner
Graf *m* / Herzog *m*	comte *m* / duc *m*
Schmuggler *m*	contrebandier *m*
Paar *n*	couple *m*
Krone *f* / Kranz *m*	couronne *f*
Hof *m*	cour *f*
Dämmerung *f*	crépuscule *m*
Verbrechen *n* / Vergehen *n*	crime *m* / délit *m*
Kreuz *n*	croix *f*
Wiege *f*	berceau *m*
Göttin *f*	déesse *f*
niedergeschlagen / mutlos	déprimé / découragé
genannt …	dit …
Teufel *m* / Dämon *m*	diable *m* / démon *m*
verteidigen	défendre

Dio	God
disarmato	disarmed / unarmed
domestica *f* / serva *f*	maid / servant
donna *f*	woman
dormire	to sleep
dubbio / sospetto / ambiguo	doubtful / suspicious
eroe *m*	hero
esecrabile / odioso / spregevole / scellerato	hateful / contemptible / loathsome / despicable
estate *f*	summer
età *f*	age
evadere / fuggire / scappare	to escape / to flee / to run away
evviva	hurrah
fanfarone *m* / gradasso *m*	braggart / boaster
fannullone *m* / bighellone *m*	idler / loafer
fata *f*	fairy
fedele / leale	faithful / loyal
ferito	wounded / injured
figlio *m* / figlia *f*	son / daughter
finestra *f*	window
fingere / far finta	to pretend / to feign
fiore *m*	flower
folla *f* / massa *f*	crowd / throng
folletto *m* / spiritello *m*	sprite / elf / goblin
fontana *f* / fonte *f*	fountain / spring
forca *f* / patibolo *m*	gibbet / gallows
foresta *f* / bosco *m*	forest / wood
fortuna *f* / sfortuna *f*	luck / bad luck
frate *m* / monaco *m*	friar / monk
fratello *m* / sorella *f*	brother / sister
freccia *f*	arrow
frusta *f*	whip / lash
fucile *m*	rifle / gun
fulmine *m* / lampo *m*	lightning / thunderbolt
geloso	jealous
giallo	yellow
gioiello *m*	jewel
giorno *m*	day
giovane	young
giurare	to swear

Gott	Dieu
entwaffnet / unbewaffnet	désarmé / sans armes
Magd *f* / Dienerin *f*	domestique *m* / servante *f*
Frau *f*	femme *f*
schlafen	dormir
zweifelhaft / verdächtig	douteux / suspect / ambigu
Held *m*	héros *m*
fluchwürdig / hassenswert / verachtenswert	exécrable / odieux / méprisable
Sommer *m*	été *m*
Alter *n*	âge *m*
entkommen / fliehen / weglaufen	s'évader / échapper / s'enfuir
hoch lebe …	hourra / vive …
Angeber *m* / Prahler *m*	fanfaron *m*
Faulenzer *m* / Faulpelz *m*	fainéant *m* / paresseux *m*
Fee *f*	fée *f*
treu / lauter / loyal	fidèle / loyal
verwundet / verletzt	blessé
Sohn *m* / Tochter *f*	fils *m* / fille *f*
Fenster *n*	fenêtre *f*
vortäuschen / heucheln	feindre / faire semblant
Blume *f*	fleur *f*
Menge *f* / Masse *f*	foule *f* / masse *f*
Kobold *m*	lutin *m* / esprit *m*
Brunnen *m* / Quelle *f*	fontaine *f* / source *f*
Galgen *m*	gibet *m* / potence *f*
Wald *m*	forêt *f* / bois *m*
Glück *n* / Unglück *n*	chance *f* / malchance *f*
Mönch *m*	moine *m*
Bruder *m* / Schwester *f*	frère *m* / sœur *f*
Pfeil *m*	flèche *f*
Peitsche *f*	fouet *m*
Gewehr *n*	fusil *m*
Blitz *m*	foudre *f* / éclair *m*
eifersüchtig	jaloux
gelb	jaune
Schmuckstück *n* / Juwel *n*	bijou *m* / joyau *m*
Tag *m*	jour *m*
jung	jeune
schwören	jurer

giustizia *f*	justice
gloria *f*	glory
grotta *f* / caverna *f* / antro *m*	cave / cavern
guarito / sano	recovered / healthy
guerra *f*	war
ignobile / infame	ignoble / infamous
innamorato	in love
incontrare	to meet
infedele	unfaithful
ingannare / truffare / imbrogliare	to deceive / to swindle / to cheat
ingiusto	unjust / unfair
insulto *m* / ingiuria *f* / oltraggio *m*	insult / abuse / offence
intorno / attorno	around
intrigare / cospirare / complottare	to intrigue / to conspire / to plot
inverno *m*	winter
istigare / aizzare / fomentare	to instigate / to stir up
lacrima *f*	tear
ladro *m*	thief
lavare	to wash
letto *m*	bed
libertà *f*	freedom / liberty
litigare / bisticciare	to quarrel / to squabble
luna *f*	moon
lutto *m*	mourning
maledetto / dannato	cursed / damned
mamma *f* / madre *f*	mum / mother
mangiare	to eat
mare *m*	sea
marito *m* / sposo *m*	husband / bridegroom
mattina *f*	morning
medico *m* / dottore *m*	doctor
mellifluo / melenso / sdolcinato	mawkish / honeyed
mezzanotte *f*	midnight
mezzogiorno *m*	midday / noon
moglie *f* / sposa *f*	wife / bride
montagna *f* / monte *m*	mountain
navigare	to sail

Gerechtigkeit *f*	justice *f*
Ruhm *n*	gloire *f*
Grotte *f* / Höhle *f*	grotte *f* / caverne *f*
genesen / gesund	guéri / sain
Krieg *m*	guerre *f*
unehrenhaft / niederträchtig / schändlich	ignoble / infâme
verliebt	amoureux
treffen / begegnen	rencontrer
untreu	infidèle
betrügen / schwindeln / täuschen	tromper / escroquer
ungerecht	injuste
Beschimpfung *f* / Schmähung *f* / Beleidigung *f*	insulte *f* / injure *f* / outrage *m*
umher / herum	autour
intrigieren / verschwören / anzetteln	intriguer / conspirer / comploter
Winter *m*	hiver *m*
anstiften / hetzen / schüren	inciter / pousser à / ourdir
Träne *f*	larme *f*
Dieb *m*	voleur *m*
waschen	laver
Bett *m*	lit *m*
Freiheit *f*	liberté *f*
streiten / zanken	se disputer / se quereller
Mond *m*	lune *f*
Trauer *f*	deuil *m*
verflucht / verdammt	maudit / damné
Mama *f* / Mutter *f*	maman *f* / mère *f*
essen	manger
Meer *n*	mer *f*
Ehemann *m* / Bräutigam *m*	mari *m* / époux *m*
Morgen *m* / Vormittag *m*	matin *m*
Arzt *m*	médecin *m* / docteur *m*
süßlich / schnulzig	mielleux / doucereux
Mitternacht *f*	minuit *m*
Mittag *m*	midi *m*
Ehefrau *f* / Braut *f*	femme *f* / épouse *f* / mariée *f*
Berg *m*	montagne *f*
zur See fahren	naviguer

nebbia *f*	mist
nel frattempo	in the meantime
nemico *m*	enemy / foe
nero	black
neve *f*	snow
notte *f*	night
nozze *f.pl.* / matrimonio *m*	wedding / marriage
nuvola *f* / nube *f*	cloud
odiare / detestare	to hate / to detest
offrire	to offer
onesto / disonesto	honest / dishonest
onore *m*	honour
ora *f*	hour
osare	to dare
padrone *m* / capo *m*	master / boss / leader
pagare	to pay
pallido / cereo	pale / wan / waxed
pane *m*	bread
patria *f*	native country / fatherland
pazzo / demente / matto	crazy / mad / insane
penna *f* / piuma *f*	pen / feather
per fortuna	fortunately
per sempre / eternamente	for ever
perdere / vinto *m* / perdente *m*	to lose / loser
perdonare	to forgive
pericolo *m*	danger
piazza *f*	square
pietra *f* / sasso *m*	stone
pioggia *f*	rain
pomeriggio *m*	afternoon
porta *f*	door
potere *m*	power
povero / meschino	poor / miserable
prete *m*	priest
prigione *f* / carcere *m*	prison / jail
primavera *f*	spring
proibito / vietato	forbidden
pugnale *m* / coltello *m*	dagger / knife
purtroppo	unfortunately
ragazzo *m* / ragazza *f*	boy / girl

Nebel *m*	brouillard *m*
inzwischen	entre-temps
Feind *m*	ennemi *m*
schwarz	noir
Schnee *m*	neige *f*
Nacht *f*	nuit *f*
Hochzeit *f* / Trauung *f* / Ehe *f*	noces *f.pl.* / mariage *m*
Wolke *f*	nuage *m*
hassen / verabscheuen	haïr / détester
anbieten	offrir
ehrlich / unehrlich	honnête / malhonnête
Ehre *f*	honneur *m*
Stunde *f*	heure *f*
wagen	oser
Chef *m* / Anführer *m*	patron *m* / chef *m*
zahlen / bezahlen	payer
blass / kreidebleich	pâle / cireux
Brot *n*	pain *m*
Vaterland *n*	patrie *f*
verrückt / wahnsinnig / schwachsinnig	fou / insensé / dément
Füllfeder *f* / Feder *f*	plume *f*
zum Glück	heureusement
für immer / für ewig	pour toujours
verlieren / Verlierer *m*	perdre / perdant *m*
verzeihen	pardonner
Gefahr *f*	danger *m*
Platz *m*	place *f*
Stein *m*	pierre *f* / caillou *m*
Regen *m*	pluie *f*
Nachmittag *m*	après-midi *m*
Tür *f*	porte *f*
Macht *f*	pouvoir *m*
arm / armselig	pauvre / misérable
Priester *m* / Pfarrer *m*	prêtre *m*
Gefängnis *n* / Kerker *m*	prison *f*
Frühling *m*	printemps *m*
verboten	interdit / défendu
Dolch *m* / Messer *n*	poignard *m* / couteau *m*
leider	malheureusement
Junge *m* / Mädchen *n*	garçon *m* / fille *f*

rancore *m* / astio *m*	rancour / grudge
rapire	to kidnap
re *m* / regina *f*	king / queen
ricatto *m*	blackmail
rivolta *f*	revolt
rosso	red
schiavo *m*	slave
sconfitta *f*	defeat
sconvolto	dismayed / upset
segreto / celato	secret / clandestine
sera *f* / serata *f*	evening
soldato *m*	soldier
sole *m*	sun
sparare	to shoot
spia *f*	spy
sporco / sudicio	dirty / filthy
sposarsi	to get married / to marry
stupido / scemo / cretino / idiota	stupid / silly / fool / idiot
svenire	to faint
tappeto *m*	carpet
tavola *f*	table
terra *f*	earth
ti amo	I love you
tomba *f* / sepolcro *m*	grave / tomb / sepulchre
traditore *m*	traitor
tranello *m* / insidia *f* / agguato *m* / imboscata *f*	trap / snare / ambush
trono *m*	throne
ubriaco / ebbro	drunk / inebriated
uccello *m*	bird
umiliare / mortificare	to humble
uomo *m*	man
vano / inutile	vain / useless
vantarsi	to boast
vecchio / anziano	old / elderly
veleno *m*	poison
vendere	to sell
verde	green
vergogna *f*	shame
verità *f*	truth

Groll *m*	rancœur *f*
entführen	enlever
König *m* / Königin *f*	roi *m* / reine *f*
Erpressung *f*	chantage *m*
Aufstand *m*	révolte *f*
rot	rouge
Sklave *m*	esclave *m*
Niederlage *f*	défaite *f*
verstört / erschüttert / bestürzt	bouleversé
geheim / heimlich	secret / clandestin
Abend *m*	soir *m* / soirée *f*
Soldat *m*	soldat *m*
Sonne *f*	soleil *m*
schießen	tirer / faire feu
Spion *m*	espion *m*
schmutzig / dreckig	sale
heiraten	épouser / se marier
dumm / blöd / Dummkopf *m* / Idiot *m*	stupide / bête / crétin *m* / idiot *m*
in Ohnmacht fallen	s'évanouir
Teppich *m*	tapis *m*
Tisch *m*	table *f*
Erde *f*	terre *f*
ich liebe dich	je t'aime
Grab *n* / Gruft *f*	tombe *f* / tombeau *m*
Verräter *m*	traître *m*
Falle *f* / Hinterhalt *m*	piège *m* / embuscade *f*
Thron *m*	trône *m*
betrunken / berauscht	ivre / saoûl
Vogel *m*	oiseau *m*
demütigen / erniedrigen	humilier / abaisser
Mann *m*	homme *m*
vergeblich / unnötig	vain / inutile
prahlen	se vanter
alt / betagt	vieux / âgé
Gift *m*	poison *m*
verkaufen	vendre
grün	vert
Scham *f* / Schande *f*	honte *f*
Wahrheit *f*	vérité *f*

vero	true
viaggio *m*	journey
vigliacco / vile	cowardly / craven
villaggio *m* / paese *m* / città *f*	village / country / town
vinto	defeated
vita *f*	life
vittoria *f*	victory
voltarsi / girarsi	to turn / to pivot
zerbinotto *m* / farfallone *m* / bellimbusto *m*	fop / coxcomb / dandy

wahr	vrai
Reise *f*	voyage *m*
feige	lâche
Dorf *n* / Land *n* / Stadt *f*	village *m* / pays *m* / ville *f*
besiegt	vaincu
Leben *n*	vie *f*
Sieg *m*	victoire *f*
sich umdrehen / sich umwenden	se retourner / se tourner
Luftikus *m* / Stutzer *m* / Geck *m*	bellâtre *m* / gandin *m*

Indice alfabetico

Index

Register

Index